Piers Plowman

William Langland

WILL'S VISION OF
PIERS PLOWMAN

An Alliterative Verse Translation by
E. TALBOT DONALDSON

edited, introduced, and annotated by
ELIZABETH D. KIRK AND
JUDITH H. ANDERSON

W • W • NORTON & COMPANY •
New York • London

Copyright © 1990 by W. W. Norton & Company, Inc.
All rights reserved.
Printed in the United States of America.

The text of this book is composed in Baskerville, with
display type set in Bernhard Modern. Composition by JGH Composition.
Manufacturing by The Murray Printing Company.

First Edition

Library of Congress Cataloging-in-Publication Data

Langland, William, 1330?-1400?
    [Piers the Plowman]
    Will's vision of Piers Plowman / by William Langland ; an
alliterative verse translation by E. Talbot Donaldson ; edited,
introduced, and annotated by Elizabeth D. Kirk and Judith H.
Anderson. -- 1st ed.
        p.   cm.
    I. Donaldson, E. Talbot (Ethelbert Talbot), 1910-1987.   II. Kirk,
Elizabeth D.   III. Anderson, Judith H.   IV. Title.
    PR2013.D6   1989
821'.1--dc19   89-3251

ISBN 0-393-96011-0 {PBK}
ISBN 0-393-02772-4 {CLOTH}

W. W. Norton & Company, Inc., 500 Fifth Avenue, New York, N.Y. 10110
W. W. Norton & Company Ltd., 10 Coptic Street, London WC1A 1PU

Contents

Introduction

The Poem

Talbot Donaldson wrote in his first book on *Piers Plowman* that Langland "in his emphasis on the individual . . . was in advance of his own church and of his own nation — and, indeed, of himself." Paradoxically, as Donaldson also recognized, Langland was "a political and religious moderate," whose cast of mind was "conservative and traditionalist."[1] The poem that resulted from this curious paradox presents one of the great enigmas of all English poetry, as well as one of the major works of the Middle Ages. The poem is one of the most complexly introspective portrayals ever produced of how the mind works when it is attempting to solve the fundamental economic, religious, and political questions facing human societies. The poem is comic. It is social. It is satirical. But it is also a profound exploration of the processes of human thought, which drove one frustrated and fascinated student to calling it "a poem that hurts your mind," because it makes the reader think more probingly about the assumptions of its society and of the reader's own society than most texts require. The same distinctive linking of qualities that should be contradictory makes the poem a mystery in other aspects as well. Its literary form is archaic and yet innovative. Written to reinforce traditional ideas, it was read, even by some of its contemporaries and by many others since, as revolutionary. Even more bewilderingly, it exists in three strangely similar yet equally strangely divergent versions (known as the A-, B-, and C-texts), and for years scholars were concerned primarily with whether one poet or three wrote them. We know almost nothing of the writer to whom they are traditionally attributed.

The name of William Langland is associated with the poem from an early period. One manuscript has a fifteenth-century annotation that connects him with the Malvern Hills area of the West Midlands of England. He is said to be the son of a Stacy (that is, Eustace) de Rokayle, a member of the gentry class, who held lands at Shipton-under-Wychwood. (At this date, the fact that he did not bear his father's name need not mean he was illegitimate, though

---

1. E. Talbot Donaldson, *Piers Plowman: The C-text and Its Poet* (New Haven: Yale University Press, 1949), pp. 110–11.

it may.) The poem also connects its Dreamer-narrator with the Malvern Hills. Puns on the Dreamer-narrator's name of "Will" — at one point he calls himself "Long Will," who has "lived long in the land" (XV.152) — appear to confirm the name. The C-text introduces an account that may be autobiographical, though one can never assume that what is said about a narrator is put in for any reason other than to serve a literary function. The picture it presents is certainly plausible and compatible with the poem. Will describes himself as having received clerical training but as not being a priest. He lived and wrote partly in a seedy part of London where he lived with his wife and daughter and partly in the houses of people who gave him room and board, but not money, while he said prayers for them. (A translation of this passage is printed in the Appendix, pages 243–47.) Will pictures Reason and Conscience challenging him to defend his way of life as an eccentric wanderer and poet, constantly mulling over questions to which his society already had clear and accessible answers, and quite unable to point to any productive work he had accomplished.

Yet another of the poem's riddles lies in its three versions, which differ too much to fit modern ideas of how a single writer works but do not fit any better with notions, either medieval or modern, of how a poet rewriting someone else's poem treats a text. The now generally accepted view is that the same man kept revising the same poem over a lifetime as his ideas evolved, reworking it far more radically than any other writer we know of who continued to work on the same book for so long. But this knowledge does not offer the reader much help, since we still have no clearer model to which we can relate Langland than before. Why he did what he did remains as fascinating and difficult to explain as ever.

The A-text is agreed to be the earliest, and is almost unanimously considered unfinished.[2] The B-text revises A and adds enough new material to make the whole poem about three times as long and to put A's vision of contemporary society into a vast historical, biblical, and liturgical perspective. This version is the one translated here. It is the best known, partly because it was the first to be printed, as early as 1550, and partly because it has generally been preferred, at least on aesthetic grounds, since the nineteenth century. The C-text is a major revision of B except for the final few sections; whether the C-reviser was satisfied with them or whether his work was interrupted (by death, for example) we do not know. Even the dates of the versions are debated, but it is clear that the B-text was finished after the coronation of the boy-king

---

2. It breaks off somewhere in its *Passus* XI or XII and has a brief ending that everyone agrees is by another writer, though there is less consensus on just where the new material starts.

Richard II in 1377 and early enough to become well known by 1381. The number of surviving manuscripts — some fifty-three of all three versions and mixtures of versions — indicates that it must have been as well known, in one form or another, as the *Canterbury Tales*. The manuscripts, however, are in a far more chaotic condition than those of the *Canterbury Tales* and have presented one of the greatest challenges to its editors of any medieval text.

The poem's literary form affords another paradox. At first sight it seems extremely conventional and traditional compared to Chaucer. It is a dream vision, a form usually associated with courtly literature and generally about love, but here we have no love poem, or, if we do, it is a poem about divine love. It is also a personification allegory, in which ideas and forces like Anger or Hunger or Reason are presented as characters in a story who interact and debate both with each other and with the narrator. Yet it is not the sort of allegory we find in the fifteenth-century play *Everyman*, where personifications seem intended to reduce moral and religious ideas that would otherwise be abstract or difficult to something simple and plain. Quite the contrary: it uses allegory to make the reader think harder and face more problems.

The combination of a dream vision with allegory was not a new idea. The mixture had become a dominant, perhaps even *the* dominant, medieval narrative form, a development that is quite natural, since dreams have always seemed to people to be natural allegories of a sort. Both were long established and conservative forms. Neither of them is used today, at least in anything like its medieval form. Both were casualties of the social and literary changes in the seventeenth and eighteenth centuries, the period in which the novel was becoming the dominant narrative form for writers who wanted to portray their society and probe its assumptions and implications. As a result we have forgotten how to read dream allegories and must rediscover their structures if we are to recapture the pleasures they offer.

Langland's verse form is also highly conservative. He wrote in the so-called "alliterative long line," a direct descendant of the alliterative poetry of Anglo-Saxon England. This form was still being used by poets in the North and West and was brought to its fullest development in the jeweled craftsmanship of Langland's contemporary, the poet of *Pearl* and *Sir Gawain and the Green Knight*, but it became a lost tradition after the fifteenth century when it was superseded by the iambic pentameter line introduced by Chaucer. Such verse does not normally rhyme. Nor does it have a standard number of syllables and a regularly repeated alternation between stressed and unstressed syllables, of the kind we are used to in most

English poetry. Instead, each line contains at least four major stressed syllables, with varying numbers of unstressed syllables distributed among them; the stressed words are bound together by a pattern in which at least the first three of them begin with the same sound.[3] The Dreamer-narrator's first picture of the dream world (Pro. 14–19) in Middle English, which is translated on page 1, offers a good example:

> Ac as *I* be*hee*ld into the *E*est, an *hei*gh to the sonne,
> I seigh a *t*our on a *t*oft *t*rieliche ymaked,
> A *d*eep *d*ale bynethe, a *d*ongeon therInne
> With *d*epe *d*iches and *d*erke and *d*redfulle of sighte.
> A *f*air *f*eeld *f*ul of *f*olk *f*ond I ther bitwene
> Of alle *m*anere of *m*en, the *m*eene and the riche,
> *W*erchynge and *w*andrynge as the *w*orld asketh.

The alliterative style makes Langland's verse seem archaic and unfamiliar. At the same time, he pressed the traditional forms he chose to use to their limits and developed them in such striking ways that the result is the very opposite of traditional. His fascination with the color and detail of daily life led him to develop profoundly innovative ways of portraying social reality. His allegorical people mix with wittily and accurately observed "real" people who might feel quite at home in an Elizabethan play full of "humor" or "type" characters. In no other poem would Gluttony sit at the same table with Robin the rope-maker and Clarice the prostitute, as he does in this one. Both kinds of figures are given dialogue that often seems like realistic fiction to a modern audience nurtured on the novel. Langland writes penetrating, savage, and vital satire, and some passages of truly epic grandeur. He gives a vivid reality to the most elevated and serious subjects by mixing high and low diction in the same sentence, as when he talks of needing a "lump" of divine love or refers to both the Virgin Mary and Dame Mercy as "wenches." He takes advantage of the slippery transitions possible in Middle English syntax, though frowned on in modern English — at least when written down, because we all use them in conversation — to juxtapose strikingly different aspects of a subject, throwing their relatedness into relief and enacting the very processes of thought he is describing.

But Langland did far more than make allegory livelier and more graphic. He made personification a way of exploring what language itself does. By giving us a word and a concept for something, lan-

---

3. In this system, the letters *v* and *f* count as the same letter, but the sounds *s* and *sh*, or *ch* and *k*, do not. Any vowel or diphthong alliterates with any other, or with a word that begins with the letter *h*, especially in words in which, as in many modern British dialects, the *h* is lightly stressed or even not pronounced at all.

guage gives us access to that thing. Language gives us a kind of control over our experience that lets us probe it and think about it, but we pay a heavy price. Systems of words, as philosophers of language in Langland's time were explicitly discussing, limit our access to reality because they predefine the world for us; inevitably they partly screen us from our own experience by the veil of language through which we perceive it. Langland turns the personification allegory into a panoramic projection of this state of affairs. He expands the "society" of words and concepts, within which we necessarily have to carry on our exterior and interior lives, into a larger-than-life drama of interacting characters.

In short, *Piers Plowman* is in many ways more representative of its time than is Chaucer's poetry, so much so that it seems much stranger to us at first. It is hard to think of any other work that so strikingly opens a window on the Middle Ages and offers such a record of what it felt like to live and work and think within the constraints, channels, and possibilities of the period. Yet in some ways the very opposite is true: *Piers Plowman* tests the limits of medieval models of language and story and struggles to define the very nature of the search for knowledge more radically than the *Canterbury Tales* themselves. It is religiously and politically conservative and is determined to see its most deeply felt concerns for reform as returns to a trusted and authoritative past. The more scholars learn about the Middle Ages, the more they find that aspects of Langland's thought that were once taken for personal eccentricities actually reflect well-established tradition. Yet much of what seemed familiar and obvious to readers who rediscovered the poem in the nineteenth century must have seemed anything but obvious in Langland's own time. Its readers, then as now, have never been able to agree on whether—or when—to call the poem reactionary or revolutionary or mainstream, so inextricably are these elements entwined in its thought.

Even in its own day, it became for some readers a rallying point for radical social criticism and even action. The leaders of the Peasants' Revolt of 1381 were so sure that the poem and its wage-earning-laborer hero, Piers Plowman, expressed their hopes and dreams that they used phrases from the B-text of the poem in the letters they wrote to coordinate their plans. The author of one contemporary history actually lists Piers Plowman among the conspirators as if he were a historical person.[4] Apparently this use of his text horrified the poet so much that he decided to rewrite it in unmistakably conservative terms (whether that's how the C-version

4. M. V. Clark and V. H. Galbraith, "The Deposition of Richard II," *Bulletin of the John Rylands Library*, 14 (1930), p. 164.

actually turned out is more debatable). In the Renaissance, *Piers Plowman* was read as a prophecy of the Reformation and, in the nineteenth century, some believed it advocated reformed government and parliamentary democracy in the sense in which these terms were defining themselves in the England of that day. Different historical periods and different readers vary in how much they think *Piers Plowman* is about money and class, labor and government, and how much it is about the history of humanity from the Fall to the end of time. Certainly what makes Langland so distinctive a poet is bound up with his inability to think about either dimension of experience except through the medium of the other.

Behind these contradictory characteristics lies the will of one of the most profoundly original—if often infuriating—minds in history, no matter how conservative he was bent on being. His cast of thought is one that refuses to approach a problem from one point of view without putting that perspective to the test against the most cogent alternatives known to him. He had good reason to call the parts of his poem the "steps" of a journey (*passus* is Latin for "step"); we must all scramble after him along a road that skirts no obstacles and cuts no corners. Hence—to change the metaphor—the extraordinarily spiraling mode of the poem, in which the same issues return again and again, to be retested in the poem's widening perspective.

A poet asking fundamental questions about religion and society in the post-consensus world of the twentieth century must begin by telling the audience what the traditions to be examined say and by putting the case for a religious perspective since it cannot be taken for granted. Before the task can even begin, the poet has to make the unfamiliar familiar. Langland's problem was the reverse. The poet of *Piers Plowman* was writing for a society where a complete overlap between religious thought and social observation existed. Society and the Church were co-extensive, and the distinction we make between religious and secular spheres of experience did not exist. Yet Langland lived at a time when social, political, and economic changes that appear to us, by hindsight, as marking the beginning of the "modern" world were overtaking his society. That society was unprepared to understand what was happening. Most people were still trying to deal with these changes by envisaging them through models of the world and of the universe they inherited from a less complicated age.

To take one concrete example: the early Middle Ages had been primarily a barter economy, where money was not the central way in which society regulated the exchange of one person's work for another's. As a result, money was not considered an entity in its own right—something that makes new things happen, something that brings possibilities into being that were not there before, as the formation of capital does. The later Middle Ages were beginning to become a capitalist society and, as such, faced a new challenge to think about the ethics of money and the economy. Yet people were still trying to deal with the dangers and opportunities of trade without questioning the inherited idea that the nature of money as such is intrinsically irrelevant to determining what makes a society or an economy just. As a result, it was overwhelmingly difficult to deal with such issues as whether it is legitimate to gain interest on one's money while someone else is using it, or whether it is acceptable for a merchant to make money on goods that he has not made or altered but merely bought and sold. Langland's debate between Lady Meed—either "reward" or "the profit motive"—and Conscience, in Passūs III and IV, engages the issues underlying such problems. The fact that he wrote the debate at all is as remarkable and interesting as the conclusions he comes to.

It is impossible to do more than mention a few of the other things that were going on in this turbulent century. England was still a three-language nation, with Latin the language of learning and French that of chivalric culture, but English was coming into its own as a language used in government and education, and in serious writing. Government was becoming more of a centralized bureaucracy and less the personal household of the head of a feudal state and was increasingly conducted by middle-class civil servants, in addition to barons and lords. Parliament was playing a greater role, and the House of Commons was beginning to become more important. Three times during the century a king was forced to back down by the resistance of the nation; twice he was deposed and subsequently murdered in prison. The Peasants' Revolt was only the most dramatic sign of the unrest being felt all over Europe. The Black Death (bubonic plague) and its aftermath, following the famines of the 1320's, killed at least a third of the nation, and the resulting labor shortages and relocation of the population hastened many political and economic developments that were already under way. War with France was endemic. Lay literacy was spreading and with it concern for the state of the Church on the part of clergy and laity alike. It was a great age of mysticism, which produced major writers, like Walter Hilton and the author of *The Cloud of Unknowing*, some of them women, like Julian of Norwich and Margery Kempe; it was also an age of religious hysteria and paranoia, of pilgrimage and relic-seeking often carried to the point of superstition, and of emphasis on suffering and guilt. This was the age of the Great Schism in the Church, when there were two, and eventually three, rival popes excommunicating each other. The negative aspects of the state of religion that were criticized later by Protestants were already being voiced from within the Church itself by at least some of its most committed members. Some others went even further: the followers of John Wycliffe were translating the Bible into English and starting a movement that contributed to the coming of the Reformation in England. In the increasing backlash resulting from so much criticism within and without, the Church became much more rigid in attempting to impose conformity of belief and behavior. Philosophers like William of Ockham, no longer satisfied with the great syntheses constructed by the scholastics of the thirteenth century like St. Thomas Aquinas, were sharply separating the realms of reason and revelation, stressing the arbitrariness and unknowability of God, and bringing a skeptical eye to the nature of language and logic.

In such turbulence, the majority ignore the root causes, having far more immediate worries, and most of those who think about them at all attribute their difficulties to the special sinfulness of the present generation, believing that if society could only return to the simpler patterns and purer idealism and morality of the past, the problems would take care of themselves. Much medieval literature and thought, and especially much medieval preaching, carried the simple and graphic message "Repent enough — and God will get us out of this nightmare." William Langland, however, had a mind that could not help thinking directly about these questions, no matter how much the paradigm of nostalgia and repentance appealed to a side of him. For him, the problem of the religious poet was not primarily to inform, though he does inform. Rather, it was to force an audience inoculated by familiarity, one that, in a sense, already knew the answers, to think about these matters as if they were new. This meant he had to make the familiar unfamiliar, the taken-for-granted no less puzzling, fascinating, and infuriating than a foreign culture would be to a visiting anthropologist.

What makes the poem so challenging is not just the amount of detailed knowledge about law-courts and beer-sale, farms and cathedrals, prayers and crimes, the poet could take for granted his audience knew about (whereas we need footnotes) but also the fact that its very strategy is to destabilize its reader's preconceptions. *Piers Plowman* casts basic problems into forms that make it literally impossible to go on thinking about them in familiar ways. Langland has, in a sense, to deprive readers of the answers they already have long enough for them to rediscover the impact of the questions. Only by reinventing the questions can the meaning of the answers be recaptured or further answers found. The most important thing to keep remembering during the journey through *Piers Plowman* is that the reader who feels puzzled is reading right, not wrong. The text was created to make readers respond this way, by creating enough dislocations and omissions that they have to live their way through the process of detecting the connections between things in ways they never have before.

The Translation

The translator of *Piers Plowman*, even more than translators of other works, is faced with the temptation to make the poem simpler and clearer than it actually is. To some extent this is inevitable. A translator cannot translate without making up his mind one way or another about certain things that are open to debate, and Donaldson's Chaucer students will never forget his setting them translation exercises, accompanied by scathing remarks about the futility of putting Middle English that doesn't make sense into modern English that doesn't make sense either. But a translator who lets his translation turn into a reinterpretation, a glorified gloss, has sacrificed something central to the character of Langland's poem. Furthermore, the impact of Langland's style depends on his abrupt juxtaposition of words from widely divergent levels of diction and on the graphic sharpness of his often sardonic wording. He is concrete where the translator wants to be abstract and particular in the very midst of discussing the general. His syntax is sometimes contorted, not simply in ways that are natural in Middle English (in which case it should be translated into equally natural-sounding modern English) but also in ways that create special effects or juxtapositions. A translation constantly threatens to become blander, more uniform, less complex and compelling than its original. Donaldson's particular concern as a translator was to avoid these dangers as fully as possible. He did not want to tame the poem.

A second and related concern of his was to observe as closely as possible the actual constraints of Langland's alliterative meter. He found during the ten years he worked on the translation that, whereas one would suppose these two goals to be in tension with each other, in practice the more strictly he kept to the poem's formal demands, the better he could resist the temptation to rewrite, tidy, and rationalize it. Perhaps keeping faith with Langland's form gives a kind of distance that is good protection against trying to make the poem too much one's own, the poem Langland might have written if he had been somebody else.

The translation is entirely Donaldson's, and the editors have regarded the translation itself as outside their charge, except for the correction of an insignificant number of actual typographical errors or omissions in his finished manuscript. It should also be noted that he was translating his and George Kane's own edition of the poem, including line numbering, and that the translation will differ accordingly from translations of other editions; where he diverged from Kane-Donaldson, we have noted this fact. The notes, however, are our own, and he must not be held responsible for them, except where he had already annotated passages that appear in *The Norton Anthology of English Literature*, fifth edition (1986); these we have incorporated, altering only as necessary for consistency throughout the longer text. In writing the introduction, we have consulted the introductions Donaldson wrote for the *Norton Anthology* and for the entry on William Langland in *The Dictionary of the Middle Ages*, vol. VII (1986), but we have not used them directly.

Donaldson did, however, discuss with us the basic policy to be followed in preparing the annotation. An edition whose primary function is to widen the readership of *Piers Plowman* beyond the group who already study it requires the minimum annotation possible. We have attempted to avoid any notes that take sides in controversies over the character of the poem, explain future passages before the poet does, or point with admiration at features of the poem. It was our intention to annotate only where the reader's attention has already been broken by the absence of some crucial piece of information. We have interpreted the notion of "crucial" quite strictly and omitted much, particularly about contemporary events, that is of great interest. We hope that the translation will send those interested in the poem to the notes of the existing editions in Middle English, which are invaluable even if one is not using the text of the poem they provide.

The amount of annotation is, however, inevitably large. In an attempt to lessen it, we have placed recurrent words or words requiring lengthy explanation in a Gloss, whose principles are explained in the introductory section entitled "Using This Edition." These words are identified by an asterisk. In order to suggest qualities of the original poem, the edition does not follow modern conventions of paragraphing. For the convenience of the modern reader, however, the editors have employed a minimal amount of paragraphing in accordance with Donaldson's example in the *Norton Anthology*.

Synopsis of the Dreams

Piers Plowman consists of a number of parts—eight dreams, two of which contain a "dream within a dream"—which build cumulatively.

The dreams begin with a vision of contemporary England in all its variety, energy, and corruption, and then move on to a reconstruction of biblical history, ending with a portrayal of the Apocalyptic events just before the end of time, events that Langland found predictable from what he could see happening in the world about him as well as from reading the last book of the Bible.

The resulting structure turns on contrasting pairs of characters. Of these, the most important are the Dreamer-narrator, Will, and the titular hero, Piers Plowman. Piers, when we first meet him, looks like an honest farmer who, alone in the world of the poem, has heard of "Saint Truth" and can tell people how to find him. But Piers develops as the poem advances — and perhaps is already symbolic of more complex roles. By the end of the poem, he has come to represent the human nature in which Christ confronted the Devil in his death on the Cross and St. Peter founding the Church that was to perpetuate Christ's authority after his departure. Where the Dreamer is tentative, Piers is authoritative. Where the Dreamer sees confusion, Piers is in touch with truth. Where the Dreamer questions, Piers acts. The Dreamer is caught in historical time, but Piers transcends time. From a figure of labor and action in the world of economics and class, Langland fashions a figure of the "new man" Christ made possible when he entered human history and transformed it. Yet the poem shows how the advent of this new possibility is accompanied by the threat of greater corruption and degeneration than ever — unless, that is, the world awakens.

Dream I (Prologue and *Passūs* I–IV). The Dreamer sees the panorama of the world spread out before him between two towers, is taught the basic history and values needed to deal with it by Lady Holy Church, who also explains the two towers, and witnesses an attempt to marry Lady Meed (Reward) to False and the ensuing trial before the King, who proposes to marry her to Conscience instead. His proposal precipitates a debate between Lady Meed and Conscience, eventually adjudicated by Reason.

Dream II (*Passūs* V–VII). Reason calls for the repentance of society, and the Seven Deadly Sins respond with accounts of their misspent lives. The society decides to look for St. Truth, but no one knows where to find him except an unlearned plowman named Piers. Piers organizes the folk to help him plow his half-acre before he will be free to lead them. The attempt eventually breaks down, however, even though Piers summons Hunger to help him motivate the people to work. Truth sends Piers a pardon but, in one of the most controversial scenes in the poem, when Piers is told by a priest that the pardon only tells him to do well, he tears it up and decides to change his life. The puzzled Dreamer wakens and resolves to rely on Do-Well. (Dreams I and II make up what is often called the *Vision*, one of the two main parts into which the poem is often divided, the second and longer being called the *Lives of Do-Well, Do-Better, and Do-Best.*)

Dream III (*Passūs* VIII–XII). The Dreamer begins a search for Do-Well that turns into a discussion of Do-Well, Do-Better, and Do-Best, first with a pair of friars he meets in the waking world and then with Thought, Wit and his wife Study, and Clergy and his wife Scripture. This process is ultimately so frustrating to the Dreamer that he gives it up entirely to follow Fortune. (His doing so corresponds to the point where the A-version stops.) The period of the Dreamer's rebellion comes to an end when Lewte (Justice) persuades him to start writing again. He then hears Scripture preach and speaks with the Emperor Trajan, Nature, Reason, and Imaginative, who explain much that has been bothering him, especially about the fate of the righteous heathen and about the proper role of learning.

Dream IV (*Passūs* XIII–XIV). The Dreamer and Conscience are invited to dine with Clergy and Scripture, in whose company they meet Patience and a hypocritical Friar and hear of new teachings from the long-vanished Piers Plowman. Conscience and the Dreamer leave Clergy to keep things running as best he can until they return, and go off with Patience; they meet Hawkin the Active Man. (Dreams III and IV make up what is often called the *Life of Do-Well.*)

Dream V (*Passūs* XV–XVII). The Dreamer meets Anima, "Soul," and then Piers Plowman, who shows him his farm in the human heart, where the Tree of Charity grows, and introduces a survey of biblical history in which the Dreamer meets Abraham-Faith, Moses-Hope, and the Good Samaritan (Charity and Christ).

Dream VI (*Passus* XVIII). The Dreamer witnesses Christ's Crucifixion and his Harrowing of Hell. (Dreams V and VI have been considered the *Life of Do-Better.*)

Dream VII (*Passus* XIX). After the Dreamer attends Easter Mass with his family, he witnesses the Descent of the Holy Ghost and the beginnings of the Christian Church, which Piers cultivates. Piers builds a barn called Unity, and when the community is attacked by Pride and his followers, Conscience gathers the group in the barn and leads the defense.

Dream VIII (*Passus* XX). The waking Dreamer meets Need, then sleeps and sees the ultimate attack on Unity by Antichrist. After speaking with Nature and suffering the effects of old age, he enters Unity, only to find it overrun by the enemy with the help of Friar

Flatterer: then, hoping for grace, Conscience sets off alone in the ongoing search for Piers Plowman. (Dreams VII and VIII make up what has been considered the *Life of Do-Best*.)

Reading Suggestions

The suggestions that follow are based on a list compiled by Talbot Donaldson, to which the editors have added recent studies by Bowers and Alford.

Editions of the B-text in Middle English include the following: George Kane and E. Talbot Donaldson, *Piers Plowman* (1975), authoritative edition; A. V. C. Schmidt, *The Vision of Piers Plowman: A Critical Edition of the B-Text* (1978), helpful annotation; J. A. W. Bennett, *Piers Plowman: The Prologue and Passus I–VII* (1972), extensively annotated; W. W. Skeat, *The Vision of William Concerning Piers the Plowman in Three Parallel Texts Together with Richard the Redeless* (1886), the A-, B-, and C-texts, along with extensive annotation.

The following studies treat the B-text unless their titles specify otherwise. David Aers, *Piers Plowman and Christian Allegory* (1975); John A. Alford, ed., *A Companion to Piers Plowman* (1988); Ruth M. Ames, *The Fulfillment of the Scriptures: Abraham, Moses, and Piers* (1970); Judith H. Anderson, *The Growth of a Personal Voice: Piers Plowman and The Faerie Queene* (1976); Robert J. Blanch, ed., *Style and Symbolism in Piers Plowman* (1969); Morton W. Bloomfield, *Piers Plowman as a Fourteenth-Century Apocalypse* (1962); John Bowers, *The Crisis of Will in Piers Plowman* (1986); Mary Carruthers, *The Search for St. Truth: A Study of Meaning in Piers Plowman* (1973); Nevill K. Coghill, *Langland: Piers Plowman* (1964); E. Talbot Donaldson, *Piers Plowman: The C-Text and Its Poet* (1949); T. P. Dunning, *Piers Plowman: An Interpretation of the A-Text*, rev. ed., T. P. Dolan, ed. (1980); Robert Worth Frank, Jr., *Piers Plowman and the Scheme of Salvation: An Interpretation of Dowel, Dobet, and Dobest* (1957); Greta Hort, *Piers Plowman and Contemporary Religious Thought* (1938); S. S. Hussey, ed., *Piers Plowman: Critical Approaches* (1969); George Kane, *Piers Plowman: The Evidence for Authorship* (1965); Elizabeth D. Kirk, *The Dream Thought of Piers Plowman* (1972); Jeanne Krochalis and Edward Peters, eds. and trans., *The World of Piers Plowman* (1975); John Lawlor, *Piers Plowman: An Essay in Criticism* (1962); Daniel K. Murtaugh, *Piers Plowman and the Image of God* (1978); Charles Muscatine, *Poetry and Crisis in the Age of Chaucer* (1972); Dorothy L. Owen, *Piers Plowman: A Comparison with Some Earlier and Contemporary French Allegories* (1912); D. W. Robertson, Jr., and Bernard F. Huppé, *Piers Plowman and Scriptural Tradition* (1951); Elizabeth Salter, *Piers Plowman: An Introduction* (1962); Ben H. Smith, Jr., *Traditional*

Imagery of Charity in Piers Plowman (1966); Edward Vasta, ed., *Inter-pretations of Piers Plowman* (1968).

For additional suggestions, see the study by A. J. Colaianne, *Piers Plowman: An Annotated Bibliography of Editions and Criticism, 1550–1977* (1978).

Acknowledgments

Before all else, the editors wish to acknowledge their debt to the tradition of scholarship on *Piers Plowman* and especially to the editions of the B-text by W. W. Skeat, J. A. W. Bennett, and A. V. C. Schmidt and to the edition of the C-text by Derek Pearsall.[1] These are invaluable to any reader of the poem, and we have necessarily depended on the range of their collective commentary at every perplexing turn, like the proverbial dwarfs on the shoulders of giants. Indeed, we hope that one of the functions of our notes will be to send the reader on to these authorities for further information. Two articles, from which we have similarly benefited, are John Alford's "Some Unidentified Quotations in *Piers Plowman*" and Anne Middleton's "Two Infinites: Grammatical Metaphor in *Piers Plowman*."[2] Greta Hort's work on religious thought and Ben H. Smith's on charity in *Piers Plowman* have also proved useful.[3] The importance of a number of other critics to our work is indicated in the Reading Suggestions.

Talbot Donaldson himself expressed very special thanks to George Kane for reading carefully through the translation and offering provocative comments on it; yet he marveled that two friends could work so harmoniously for over twenty years on an edition of the B-text and yet could continue to hold such divergent interpretations of the poem. Needless to say, Kane is responsible neither for Donaldson's final decisions nor for the views or errors of the editors.

We wish also to thank Mary Carruthers for reviewing the translation and making helpful suggestions about what passages needed annotation in an edition of this kind, and we are aware of Donaldson's appreciation of her interest in the translation during its earlier phases. When our first draft was complete, Randy Bass gave us the perspective of a non-medievalist devotee of *Piers Plowman* on the notes. Elizabeth Kirk also wishes to thank her students at Brown University who used portions of that draft in a course and offered their comments. Alfred David's characteristic insight and encourage-

1. Bibliographical information for the B-text editions (in order of acknowledgment) is as follows: London: Oxford, 1886; Oxford: Clarendon, 1972; London: J. M. Dent, 1978; full titles for these editions are given in the Reading Suggestions. The title of Pearsall's edition is *Piers Plowman* (Berkeley: University of California Press, 1978). Like the editions of the B-text cited, it is generously annotated.

2. *Modern Philology*, 72 (1975), pp. 390–99; *ELH*, 39 (1972), pp. 169–88.

3. *Piers Plowman and Contemporary Religious Thought* (New York: Macmillan, 1938); *Traditional Imagery of Charity in Piers Plowman* (The Hague: Mouton, 1966).

ment proved invaluable as we made the final revisions. Rick Smith helped us read proofs. Throughout, Tamara Goeglein assisted us in verifying the accuracy of our manuscript and offered judicious suggestions about annotation. Her impressively painstaking work eliminated numerous errors and was conducive to the development of humility in the editors. We are additionally grateful to her for reminding us that even in the mazes of *Piers Plowman* common sense and enthusiasm are not incompatible.

We note gratefully the warm interest in the project shown from the start by John Benedict, editor and vice-president at W. W. Norton, and the carefulness of Norton's copy editor, Otto Sonntag. We gratefully acknowledge as well a grant from Indiana University to assist us in checking the manuscript. Derek Brewer, on behalf of Boydell & Brewer Ltd., kindly gave us permission to reprint Donaldson's translation of the autobiographical passage in the C-text, originally published in *Medieval English Religious and Ethical Literature: Essays in Honour of G. H. Russell*, edited by Gregory Krantzmann and James Simpson. Finally, we would acknowledge the pleasure we have had in preparing this text for publication. "Pleasure" is the word that Talbot himself would have used to describe his work, for over a decade, to translate this complex, occasionally frustrating, and thoroughly fascinating poem into a form that would truly render it accessible to a wider audience. Talbot's own scholarly career began with *Piers Plowman*; there is a certain rightness in this ending.

Using This Edition

The Gloss

Words appear in the Gloss at the back of the book if they fall into one of the following categories: (1) important concepts or names of allegorical figures that need more explanation than can readily be confined to a note; (2) modern cognates of Middle English words that have lost some pertinent meaning or connotation of the word they translate or have acquired further, potentially misleading ones; (3) names of places and people or terms for officials, institutions, and the like that recur frequently.

In every case these words are footnoted on their first occurrence in the text (or on the first occasion when a meaning not self-evident to the modern reader is involved). Where the Gloss entry is fuller than the footnote gloss, the footnote adds "(Gloss)" or, if substantially fuller, "see Gloss." On subsequent occurrences in a new *Passus* or after a substantial interval, the word is followed by an asterisk if the Gloss is relevant.

Foreign Words and Biblical References

Much annotation in the edition concerns the Latin words and lines, and the occasional French, that Langland scatters through his English. Where such words are sifted into an English sentence, the translation leaves them in their original language and translates them in a footnote. Where the whole line is in Latin, it is translated and italicized in the text itself, and the translator has deliberately used a more archaic and formal kind of language, suggestive of the King James Bible or of the liturgy, to mark the contrast with Langland's own style. As in the Kane-Donaldson edition, where the Latin line is an integral part of Langland's statement, it is given its own line number; where it is a parenthetical citation of authority, it is indented and given no number of its own and is referred to by the number of the line before, followed by the letter *a*.

Langland generally quoted from memory or used manuscripts now considered faulty, and as a result his passages often vary somewhat from modern editions of the Bible or of the other works on which he draws. He sometimes attributes a verse to one source when it is actually from another, as commonly happens in a manuscript culture where few people own their own copies of books, so that to "know" a text means to remember it. Biblical references in the notes are to the Vulgate, the Latin Bible current in Langland's time, and they follow its numbering rather than that of the King James Bible, since it is closer to Langland's citations and since many of them are to the Apocrypha or deuterocanonical books, biblical works not included in Protestant Bibles. Donaldson's text and the notes always translate what Langland has, rather than what he should have, written, however: thus Langland's line is translated where it differs from the official Vulgate text. Biblical verses in the text are expanded in the notes only if their gist is unlikely to be clear from Langland's citation.

Books of the Latin Vulgate

Old Testament

(Note: the footnotes contain the more familiar names and forms of names of books in the Protestant Bible, Apocrypha, or deutero-canonical books: for example, "Chronicles," "Song of Solomon," "1 Samuel," and "Tobit," rather than "Paralipomenon," "Canticle of Canticles," "1 Kings," and "Tobias," respectively. To facilitate cross-reference, both are given below; the more familiar form comes first, preceded by its abbreviation.)

Gen.	Genesis
Exod.	Exodus
Lev.	Leviticus
Num.	Numbers
Deut.	Deuteronomy
Josh.	Joshua
Judg.	Judges
Ruth	Ruth
1 Sam.	1 Samuel; also 1 Kings
2 Sam.	2 Samuel; also 2 Kings
1 Kings	1 Kings; also 3 Kings
2 Kings	2 Kings; also 4 Kings
1 Chron.	1 Chronicles; Vulgate: 1 Paralipomenon
2 Chron.	2 Chronicles; Vulgate: 2 Paralipomenon
Ezra	Ezra; also 1 Esdras
Neh.	Nehemiah; also 2 Esdras
Tobit	Tobit; Vulgate: Tobias
Judith	Judith
Esther	Esther
Job	Job
Ps.	Psalms

Prov.	Proverbs
Eccl.	Ecclesiastes
Song. Sol.	Song of Solomon; Vulgate: Canticle of Canticles; also popularly, Song of Songs
Wisd.	Wisdom; also Wisdom of Solomon
Ecclus.	Ecclesiasticus; also Sirach
Isa.	Isaiah; Vulgate: Isaias
Jer.	Jeremiah; Vulgate: Jeremias
Lam.	Lamentations
Baruch	Baruch
Ezek.	Ezekiel; Vulgate: Ezechiel
Dan.	Daniel
Hos.	Hosea; Vulgate: Osee
Joel	Joel
Amos	Amos
Obad.	Obadiah; Vulgate: Abdias
Jonah	Jonah; Vulgate: Jonas
Micah	Micah; Vulgate: Micheas
Nahum	Nahum
Hab.	Habakkuk; Vulgate: Habacuc
Zeph.	Zephaniah; Vulgate: Sophonias
Haggai	Haggai; Vulgate: Aggeus
Zech.	Zechariah; Vulgate: Zacharias
Mal.	Malachi; Vulgate: Malachias
1 Macc.	1 Maccabees; Vulgate: 1 Machabees
2 Macc.	2 Maccabees; Vulgate: 2 Machabees

New Testament

Matt.	Matthew	1 Tim.	1 Timothy
Mark	Mark	2 Tim.	2 Timothy
Luke	Luke	Tit.	Titus
John	John	Phil.	Philemon
Acts	Acts	Heb.	Hebrews
Rom.	Romans	Jam.	James
1 Cor.	1 Corinthians	1 Pet.	1 Peter
2 Cor.	2 Corinthians	2 Pet.	2 Peter
Gal.	Galatians	1 John	1 John
Eph.	Ephesians	2 John	2 John
Phil.	Philippians	3 John	3 John
Col.	Colossians	Jude	Jude
1 Thess.	1 Thessalonians	Rev.	Revelation; Vulgate: Apocalypse
2 Thess.	2 Thessalonians		

The Text of
PIERS PLOWMAN

Prologue

In a summer season when the sun was mild
I clad myself in clothes as I'd become a sheep;
In the habit of a hermit unholy of works[1]
Walked wide in this world, watching for wonders.
And on a May morning, on Malvern Hills,[2]   5
There befell me as by magic a marvelous thing:
I was weary of wandering and went to rest
At the bottom of a broad bank by a brook's side,
And as I lay lazily looking in the water
I slipped into a slumber, it sounded so pleasant.   10
There came to me reclining there a most curious dream
That I was in a wilderness, nowhere that I knew;
But as I looked into the east, up high toward the sun,
I saw a tower on a hill-top, trimly built,
A deep dale beneath, a dungeon tower in it,   15
With ditches deep and dark and dreadful to look at.
A fair field full of folk I found between them,
Of human beings of all sorts, the high and the low,
Working and wandering as the world requires.
    Some applied themselves to plowing, played very rarely,   20
Sowing seeds and setting plants worked very hard;
Won what wasters gluttonously consume.
And some pursued pride, put on proud clothing,
Came all got up in garments garish to see.
To prayers and penance many put themselves,   25
All for love of our Lord lived hard lives,

---

1. For Langland's opinion of hermits, see lines 28–30 below.
2. These hills in the west of England overlook a broad plain that seems to encompass the core of the country as one looks east toward London; this region is probably also the poet's original home.

Hoping thereafter to have Heaven's bliss—
Such as hermits and anchorites[3] that hold to their cells,
Don't care to go cavorting about the countryside,
With some lush livelihood delighting their bodies.   30
And some made themselves merchants—they managed better,
As it seems to our sight that such men prosper.
And some make mirth as minstrels can
And get gold for their music, guiltless, I think.
But jokers and word jugglers, Judas' children,[4]   35
Invent fantasies to tell about and make fools of themselves,
And have whatever wits they need to work if they wanted.
What Paul preaches of them I don't dare repeat here:
Qui loquitur turpiloquium[5] is Lucifer's henchman.
Beadsmen[6] and beggars bustled about   40
Till both their bellies and their bags were crammed to the
        brim;
Staged flytings[7] for their food, fought over beer.
In gluttony, God knows, they go to bed.
And rise up with ribaldry, those Robert's boys.[8]
Sleep and sloth[9] pursue them always.   45

   Pilgrims and palmers[1] made pacts with each other
To seek out Saint James[2] and saints at Rome.
They went on their way with many wise stories,
And had leave to lie all their lives after.
I saw some that said they'd sought after saints: 50
In every tale they told their tongues were tuned to lie
More than to tell the truth—such talk was theirs.
A heap of hermits with hooked staffs
Went off to Walsingham,[3] with their wenches behind them.
Great long lubbers that don't like to work   55
Dressed up in cleric's dress to look different from other men
And behaved as they were hermits, to have an easy life.

---

3. Both are vowed to a religious life of solitude, hermits in the wilderness, anchorites in popu-
lated areas, walled up in a tiny dwelling. (Gloss: the function of the Gloss at the end of this
volume is explained in the Introduction, under "Using This Edition.")
4. Minstrels who entertain with jokes and fantastic stories are regarded as descendants of Christ's
betrayer, Judas.
5. "Who speaks filthy language": not Paul, though cf. Eph. 5.3–4.
6. Prayer-sayers (also referred to as prayer-bidders and street-beadsmen), i.e., people who
offered to say the prayers, sometimes counted on the beads of the rosary, for the souls of those
who gave them alms.
7. Contests in which the participants took turns insulting each other, preferably in verse.
8. I.e., robbers.
9. Not just laziness but irresponsibility more generally; see Gloss.
1. Virtually professional pilgrims who took advantage of the hospitality offered them to go on
traveling year after year. Strictly speaking, "palmers" were pilgrims who had been to Jerusalem
or who had made lifelong commitments to pilgrimage (Gloss).
2. I.e., his shrine at Compostela, in Galicia, in Spain (Gloss).
3. English town, site of a famous shrine to the Virgin Mary (Gloss).

I found friars there — all four of the orders[4] —
Preaching to the people for their own paunches' welfare,
Making glosses[5] of the Gospel that would look good for
    themselves;   60
Coveting copes,[6] they construed it as they pleased.
Many of these Masters may clothe themselves richly,
For their money and their merchandise[7] march hand in
    hand.
Since Charity[8] has proved a peddler and principally shrives
    lords,
Many marvels have been manifest within a few years.   65
Unless Holy Church and friars' orders hold together better,
The worst misfortune in the world will be welling up soon.
   A pardoner[9] preached there as if he had priest's rights,
Brought out a bull[1] with bishop's seals,
And said he himself could absolve them all   70
Of failure to fast, of vows they'd broken.
Unlearned men believed him and liked his words,
Came crowding up on knees to kiss his bulls.
He banged them with his brevet[2] and bleared their eyes,
And raked in with his parchment-roll rings and brooches.   75
Thus you give your gold for gluttons' well-being,
And squander it on scoundrels schooled in lechery.
If the bishop were blessed and worth both his ears,
His seal should not be sent out to deceive the people.
— It's nothing to the bishop that the blackguard preaches,   80
And the parish priest and the pardoner split the money
That the poor people of the parish would have but for them.
   Parsons and parish priests complained to the bishop
That their parishes were poor since the pestilence-time,[3]
Asked for license and leave to live in London,   85
And sing Masses there for simony,[4] for silver is sweet.

---

4. In Langland's day there were four orders of friars in England: Franciscans, Dominicans, Carmelites, and Augustinians.
5. Interpretations.
6. Monks', friars', and hermits' capes. "Masters" (next line): masters of divinity.
7. The "merchandise" sold by the friars for money is shrift, that is, confession and remission of sins, which by canon law cannot be sold.
8. The ideal of the friars, as stated by St. Francis, was simply love, i.e., charity.
9. An official empowered to pass on from the pope temporal indulgence for the sins of people who contributed to charitable enterprises — a function frequently abused; see Gloss.
1. Papal license to act as a pardoner, endorsed by the local bishop (Gloss).
2. Pardoner's license.
3. Since 1349, England had suffered a number of epidemics of the plague, the "Black Death," which had caused famine and depopulated the countryside.
4. Buying and selling the functions, spiritual powers, or offices of the Church for money. Wealthy persons, especially in London, set up foundations to pay priests to sing Masses for their souls and those of their relatives (Gloss).

Bishops and Bachelors, both Masters and Doctors,[5]
Who have cures under Christ and their crowns shaven
As a sign that they should shrive their parishioners,
Preach and pray for them, and provide for the poor,   90
Take lodging in London in Lent and other seasons.
Some serve the king and oversee his treasury,
In the Exchequer and in Chancery[6] press charges for debts
Involving wards' estates and city-wards,[7] waifs and strays.
And some like servants serve lords and ladies   95
And in the stead of stewards[8] sit and make judgments.
Their Masses and their matins and many of their Hours[9]
Are done undevoutly: there's dread that in the end
Christ in his consistory[1] will condemn full many.

  I pondered on the power that Peter had in keeping   100
To bind and unbind as the Book tells,[2]
How he left it with love as our Lord commanded
Among four virtues, most virtuous of all,
That are called "cardinals"—and closing gates[3]
Of the kingdom of Christ, who may close and lock them,   105
Or else open them up and show Heaven's bliss.
But as for the cardinals at court that thus acquired their
          name
And presumed they had the power to appoint a pope
Who should have the power that Peter had—well I'll not
          impugn them,
For the election belongs to love and to learning: 110
Therefore I can and cannot speak of court further.

    Then there came a king, knighthood accompanied him,

---

5. Doctor most commonly, as here, means Doctor of Divinity, but can also mean medical doctor in some contexts. "Bachelors": i.e., bachelors of divinity; elsewhere, may also mean a novice knight; see Gloss.

6. The Exchequer was a royal commission that received revenue and audited accounts; Chancery dealt with petitions addressed to the king. Both typically had bishops or other clerics among their officers, if not at their heads.

7. The king was guardian of an underage heir ("ward") to the holdings of one of his major noblemen and could claim dues from the subdivisions of a city ("city-wards"), lost property, and strayed cattle (or, according to another interpretation, the property of deceased aliens with no legitimate heirs).

8. The manager of a large household or estate.

9. Clerics organized their day around seven canonical "hours," or periods of liturgical prayer called offices, of which matins was the first (Gloss).

1. Literally, a bishop's court or the senate of cardinals convened by the pope to deliberate on church affairs.

2. Matt. 16.18–20 recounts Christ's giving Peter and the succeeding popes this authority to make pronouncements on earth that will also be binding in Heaven.

3. The four cardinal virtues are prudence, temperance, justice, and fortitude and are distinguished from the three "theological" virtues of faith, hope, and charity; Langland plays below on the fact that "cardinal," from Latin cardo, "hinge" (hence "gates") is also the term for the superior group of ecclesiastics who, from 1179, had acquired the power to elect the pope.

Might of the community[4] made him a ruler.
And then came Kind Wit, and he created clerks[5]
To counsel the king and keep the commons safe.   115
The king in concert with knighthood and with clergy as well
Contrived that the commons should provide their commons[6]
    for them.
The commons with Kind Wit contrived various crafts,
And for profit of all the people appointed plowmen
To till and to toil as true life requires.   120
The king and the commons and Kind Wit the third
Defined law and lewte[7] — for every kind of life, known
    limits.
Then a lunatic looked up — a lean one at that —
And counseled the king with clerkly words, kneeling before
    him:
"Christ keep you, sir King, and the kingdom you rule   125
And grant you to lead your land so that Lewte loves you,
And for your righteous ruling be rewarded in Heaven."
And after in the air on high an angel of Heaven
Came low to speak in Latin, for illiterate men lacked
The jargon or the judgment to justify themselves,   130
But can only suffer and serve; therefore said the angel:
" *I'm a king. I'm a prince!' — Neither perhaps when you've gone
    hence.*
*You, King, who're here to save   the special laws that King Christ
    gave.*
To do this better you will find   it's well to be less just than kind.
By you law's naked truth   wants to be clothed in ruth.[8]   135
Such seeds as you sow,   such a crop will grow.
If you strip law bare,   bare law will be your share.
If you sow pity,   you'll be sitting pretty."[9]
Then a Goliard[1] grew angry, a glutton of words,
And to the angel on high answered after: 140

---

4. The important Middle English word *commune, communes* has three meanings Langland plays on in this passage: (1) the community taken as a whole; (2) the common people; (3) the food that supports the community; see Gloss. "Might": in Middle English, "might" simply means the strength necessary to do a particular thing, not necessarily overwhelming force.
5. Clerics, intellectuals; see Gloss. "Kind Wit": natural acumen, good sense, experiential knowledge; see Gloss.
6. The first occurrence of *commons* in this line means "common people"; the second, "food."
7. Justice, as distinct from the law as such; see Gloss.
8. Pity.
9. The bad Latin verses seem to have been current in Langland's time. Many such jingles have distinctive internal rhyme; when this is so, they have been printed with a space between the half-lines.
1. A wandering student or cleric; goliards wrote songs and poetry, often satirical or ribald and attacking the clerical establishment. By relating the word to "glutton," Langland plays on its derivation from Old French *gole*, "throat."

"Since the name of king, rex, comes from regere, 'to rule,'
Unless he law directs, he's a wright without a tool."[2]
Then all the commons commenced to cry in Latin verse
To the king's council—let who will construe it:
"What the king ordains   is to us the law's chains."[3]   145
  With that there ran a rabble of rats together,
And little mice along with them, no less than a thousand,
Came to a council for their common profit;
For a cat of court came when he pleased
And leapt lightly over them and when he liked seized them,   150
And played with them perilously, and pushed them about.[4]
"For dread of various deeds we hardly dare move,
And if we grumble at his games he will grieve us all,
Scratch us or claw us or catch us in his clutches.
So that we'll loathe life before he lets us go.   155
If by any wit we might withstand his will
We could be lofty as lords and live at our ease."
A rat of renown, most ready of tongue,
Said as a sovereign salve for them all:
"I've seen creatures," he said, "in the city of London   160
Bear chains full bright about their necks,
And collars of fine craftsmanship;[5] they come and go without
          leashes
Both in warren and in wasteland, wherever they please;
And at other times they are in other places, as I hear tell.
If there were a bell to clink on their collars, by Christ, I
          think   165
We could tell where they went and keep well out of their
          way.
And right so," said the rat, "reason tells me
To buy a bell of brass or of bright silver
And clip it on a collar for our common profit
And hang it over the cat's head; then we'd be able to hear   170
Whether he's riding or resting or roving out to play.
And if he desires sport we can step out
And appear in his presence while he's pleased to play.
And if he's angry we'll take heed and stay out of his way."
This whole convention of vermin was convinced by this
          advice,   175
But when the bell was brought and bound to the collar

---

2. The Latin couplet is contemporary. "Wright": workman, maker.
3. A metrical version of a Roman legal maxim.
4. Langland gives an original twist to the familiar fable about "belling the cat."
5. The rat conflates the gold chains of office worn by city magnates with the collars of dogs.

There was no rat in the rabble, for all the realm of France,
That dared bind the bell about the cat's neck
Or hang it over his head to win all England;
But they held themselves faint-hearted and their whole plan
    foolish, 180
And allowed all their labor lost, and all their long scheming.
A mouse that knew much good, as it seemed to me then,
Strode forth sternly and stood before them all,
And to the rats arrayed there recited these words:
"Though we killed the cat, yet there would come another 185
To scratch us and all our kind though we crept under
    benches.
Therefore I counsel all the commons to let the cat alone,
And let's never be so bold as to show the bell to him.
While he's catching conies[6] he doesn't crave our flesh,
But feeds himself on rich food—let's not defame him. 190
For a little loss is better than a long sorrow:
We'd all be muddling through a maze though we'd removed
    one foe.
For I heard my sire say, seven years ago,
Where the cat is a kitten, the court is wholly wretched.
That's how Holy Writ reads, whoever wants to look: 195
Woe to the land where the king is a child![7]
For no creature may rest quiet because of rats at night,
And many a man's malt we mice would destroy,
And also you rabble of rats would ruin men's clothing
If it weren't for the court-cat that can outleap you. 200
For if you rats held the reins, you couldn't rule yourselves.
I speak for myself," said the mouse, "I foresee such trouble
    later,
That by my counsel neither cat nor kitten shall be grieved—
And let's have no carping of this collar, that cost me
    nothing.
And though it had cost me money, I'd not admit it had— 205
But suffer as himself wishes to slay what he pleases,
Coupled and uncoupled let them catch what they will.
Therefore I warn every wise creature to stick to what's his
    own."
—What this dream may mean, you men that are merry,
You divine, for I don't dare, by dear God in Heaven. 210
   Yet scores of men stood there in silken coifs
Who seemed to be law-sergeants[8] that served at the bar,

6. Rabbits.
7. Eccl. 10.16.
8. Important lawyers; "coifs": a silk scarf was a lawyer's badge of office.

Pleaded cases for pennies[9] and impounded the law,
And not for love of our Lord once unloosed their lips:
You might better measure mist on Malvern Hills   215
Than get a "mum" from their mouths till money's on the
    table.
Barons and burgesses[1] and bondmen also
I saw in this assemblage, as you shall hear later;
Bakers and brewers and butchers aplenty,
Weavers of wool and weavers of linen,   220
Tailors, tinkers, tax-collectors in markets,
Masons, miners, many other craftsmen.
Of all living laborers there leapt forth some,
Such as diggers of ditches that do their jobs badly,
And dawdle away the long day with *"Dieu save dame Emme."*[2] 225
Cooks and their kitchen-boys kept crying, "Hot pies, hot!
Good geese and pork! Let's go and dine!"
Tavern-keepers told them a tale of the same sort:
"White wine of Alsace and wine of Gascony,
Of the Rhine and of La Rochelle, to wash the roast down
    with."   230
All this I saw sleeping, and seven times more.

Passus† I

What this mountain means, and the murky dale,
And the field full of folk I shall clearly tell you.
A lady lovely of look, in linen clothes,
Came down from the castle and called me gently,
And said, "Son, are you asleep? Do you see these people,   5
How busy they're being about the maze?
The greatest part of the people that pass over this earth,
If they have well-being in this world, they want nothing
    more:
For any heaven other than here they have no thought."
I was afraid of her face, fair though she was,   10

---

9. Pennies were fairly valuable coins in medieval England (Gloss). "Impounded": detained in legal custody.
1. Town-dwellers who had full rights as the citizens of a municipality (Gloss). In contrast, barons were members of the higher aristocracy, and bondmen were peasants who held their land from a lord in return for customary services or rent.
2. "God save Dame Emma": presumably a popular song.
† *Passus*—Latin "step"—is the word the poet uses for the sections of his poem, which is conceived as a journey or pilgrimage.

And said, "Mercy, madam, what may this mean?"
"The tower on the hill-top," she said, "Truth[1] is within it,
And would have you behave as his words teach.
For he is father of faith, formed you all
Both with skin and with skull, and assigned you five senses   15
To worship him with while you are here.
And therefore he ordered the earth to help each one of you
With woolens, with linens, with livelihood at need,
In a moderate manner to make you at ease;
And of his kindness declared three things common to all: 20
None are necessary but these, and now I will name them
And rank them in their right order—you repeat them after.
The first is vesture to defend you from the cold;
The second is food at fit times to fend off hunger,
And drink when you're dry—but don't drink beyond reason   25
Or you will be the worse for it when you've work to do.
For Lot in his lifetime because he liked drink
Did with his daughters what the Devil found pleasing,
Took delight in drink as the Devil wished,
And lechery laid hold on him and he lay with them both,   30
Blamed it all on the wine's working, that wicked deed.
   Let us make him drunk with wine, and let us lie with him,
       that we may preserve seed of our father.[2]
By wine and by women there Lot was overcome
And there begot in gluttony graceless brats.
Therefore dread delicious drink and you'll do the better:
Moderation is medicine no matter how you yearn.   35
It's not all good for your ghost[3] that your gut wants
Nor of benefit to your body that's a blessing to your soul.
Don't believe your body for it does the bidding of a liar:
That is this wretched world that wants to betray you;
For the Fiend and your flesh both conform to it,   40
And that besmirches your soul: set this in your heart,
And so that you should yourself be wary I'm giving this
       advice."
   "Ah, madam, mercy," said I, "your words much please
       me.
But the money minted on earth that men are so greedy for,
Tell me to whom that treasure belongs?"   45
"Go to the Gospel," she said, "that God himself spoke

---

1. Langland plays on three meanings of the term "Truth": (1) fidelity, integrity—as in modern
"troth"; (2) reality, actuality, conformity with what is; (3) God, the ultimate truth; see Gloss.
2. Gen. 19.32.
3. Spirit.

When the people approached him with a penny* in the
　　temple
And asked whether they should worship[4] with it Caesar the
　　king.
And he asked them to whom the inscription referred
'And the image also that is on the coin?'　　　　　　　　　　50
'*Caesaris*,'[5] they said, 'we can all see it clearly.'
'*Reddite Caesari*,' said God, 'what *Caesari* belongs,[6]
And *quae sunt Dei Deo*, or else you do wrong.'
For rightfully Reason[7] should rule you all,
And Kind Wit* be keeper to take care of your wealth　　　55
And be guardian of your gold to give it out when you need it,
For economy[8] and he are of one accord."
　　Then I questioned her courteously, in the Creator's name,
"The dungeon in the dale that's dreadful to see,
What may it mean, madam, I beseech you?"　　　　　　　60
"That is the Castle of Care: whoever comes into it
Will be sorry he was ever born with body and soul.
The captain of the castle is called Wrong,
Father of falsehood, he founded it himself.
Adam and Eve he egged to evil,　　　　　　　　　　　65
Counseled Cain to kill his brother;
He made a joke out of Judas with Jewish silver,[9]
And afterwards on an elder tree hanged him high.
He's a molester of love, lies to every one;
Those who trust in his treasure are betrayed soonest."　　70
　　Then I wondered in my wits what woman it might be
Who could show from Holy Scripture such wise words,
And I conjured her in the high name, ere she went away,
To say who she really was that taught me so well.
"I am Holy Church," she said, "you ought to know me:　　75
I befriended you first and taught the faith to you.
You gave me gages[1] to be guided by my teaching
And to love me loyally while your life lasts."

4. "Worship" in Middle English often means religious celebration, but the worship of God is only one instance of showing the appropriate honor and respect to someone or something; the word can therefore be used about objects other than God.
5. Caesar's.
6. "Render unto Caesar"; "to Caesar." In the next line the Latin clause means "What are God's unto God." See Matt. 22.15–21.
7. Langland distinguishes the role of reason, as the distinctive human capacity to reach truth by discursive reasoning, from the functions of a number of other related mental processes and sources of truth (for example, from Kind Wit in the next line); see Gloss.
8. I.e., prudent management.
9. For the fall of Adam and Eve, see Gen. 3; for Cain's murder of Abel, see Gen. 4. In the next lines, for Judas' betrayal of Jesus, see Matt. 26.14–16; for his death (line 68), see Matt. 27.3–6.
1. I.e., pledges (at baptism).

Then kneeling on my knees I renewed my plea for grace,
Prayed piteously to her to pray for my sins,   80
And advise me how I might find natural faith[2] in Christ,
That I might obey the command of him who made me man.
"Teach me of no treasure, but tell me this one thing,
How I may save my soul, sacred as you are?"
"When all treasures are tried, Truth* is the best.   85
I call on *Deus caritas*[3] to declare the truth.
It's as glorious a love-gift as dear God himself.
For whoever is true of his tongue, tells nothing untrue,
Does his work with truth, wishes no man ill,
He is a god by the Gospel, on ground and aloft,   90
And also like our Lord by Saint Luke's words.[4]
Clerks who've been taught this text should tell it all about,
For Christians and non-Christians lay claim to it both.
To keep truth kings and knights are required by reason,*
And to ride out in realms about and beat down wrong-doers, 95
Take *transgressores*[5] and tie them up tight
Until Truth has determined their trespass in full.
For David in his days when he dubbed knights[6]
Made them swear on their swords to serve Truth forever.
That is plainly the profession that's appropriate for knights, 100
And not to fast one Friday in five score winters,
But to hold with him and with her who ask for truth,
And never leave them for love nor through a liking for
            presents,
And whoever passes that point is an apostate to his order.
    For Christ, King of Kings, created ten orders,[7]   105
Cherubim and seraphim, seven such and another.
Gave them might* in his majesty — the merrier they thought
        it —
And over his household he made them archangels,
Taught them through the Trinity how Truth may be known,
And to be obedient to his bidding — he bade nothing else.   110
Lucifer with his legions learned this in Heaven,
And he was the loveliest of light after our Lord

2. The Middle English phrase is "kynde knowynge": see Gloss under "kind."
3. "God [is] love": 1 John 4.8.
4. Not Luke, but see 1 John 4.16 and cf. Ps. 81.6. The phrase "a god by the Gospel" is
Langland's; what he means by it will be a recurrent theme.
5. Transgressors: the Latin word appears at Isa. 53.12.
6. Behind the idea that King David created knighthood probably lies his selection of officers
for his army (1 Chron. 12.18) translated into chivalric terms; like other heroes, he was typically
portrayed in the Middle Ages as a chivalric figure, just as God's creation of the angels, below,
is pictured in terms of a medieval aristocratic household.
7. I.e., ten orders of heavenly beings: seraphim, cherubim, thrones, dominions, virtues, powers,
principalities, archangels, angels, and the nameless order that fell with Lucifer.

Till he broke obedience—his bliss was lost to him
And he fell from that fellowship in a fiend's likeness
Into a deep dark hell, to dwell there forever,   115
And more thousands went out with him than any one could
      count,
Leaping out with Lucifer in loathly shapes,
Because they believed Lucifer who lied in this way:
I shall set my foot in the north and I shall be like the most high.[8]
And all that hoped it might be so, no Heaven could hold
      them,   120
But they fell out in fiend's likeness fully nine days together,
Till God of his goodness granted that Heaven settle,
Become stationary and stable, and stand in quiet.
When these wicked ones went out they fell in wondrous wise,
Some in air, some on earth, some deep in hell,   125
But Lucifer lies lowest of them all.
For pride that puffed him up his pain has no end.
And all that work with wrong will surely make their way
After their death-day to dwell with that wretch.
But those who wish to work well, as holy words direct,   130
And who end, as I said earlier, in Truth that is the best
May be certain that their souls will ascend to Heaven
Where Truth is in Trinity, bestowing thrones on all who
      come.
Therefore I say as I said before, by the sense of these texts
When all treasures are tried, Truth is the best.   135
Let unlearned men be taught this, for learned men know it,
That Truth is the trustiest treasure on earth."
   "Yet I've no natural knowledge,"[9] said I, "you must teach
     me more clearly
Through what force faith is formed in my body and where."
"You doting dolt," said she, "dull are your wits: 140
Too little Latin you learned, lad, in your youth.
    Alas, I repine   for a barren youth was mine.[1]
It's a natural knowledge that's nurtured in your heart
To love your Lord more dearly than you love yourself,
To do no deadly sin though you should die for it.
This I trust is truth: whoever can teach you better,   145
Look to it that you let him speak, and learn it after.
For thus his word witnesses: do your work accordingly.

---

8. Cf. Isa. 14.13–14, which has "throne" (*sedem*) where Langland has "foot" (*pedem*).
9. Instinctive or experiential knowledge; Langland's phrase, a recurrent and important one,
is "kynde knowynge"; see Gloss under "kind."
1. Proverbial.

For Truth tells us that love is the trustiest medicine in
    Heaven.
No sin may be seen on him by whom that spice is used.
And all the deeds he pleased to do were done with love.   150
And he[2] taught it to Moses as a matchless thing, and most
    like Heaven,
And also the plant of peace, most precious of virtues.
For Heaven might not hold it,[3] so heavy it seemed,
Till it had with earth alloyed itself.
And when it had of this earth taken flesh and blood,   155
Never was leaf upon linden lighter thereafter,
And portable and piercing as the point of a needle:
No armor might obstruct it, nor any high walls.
Therefore Love is leader of the Lord's people in Heaven,
And an intermediary as the mayor is between community
    and king.   160
Just so Love is a leader by whom the law's enforced
Upon man for his misdeeds—he measures the fine.
And to know this naturally, it's nourished by a power
That has its head in the heart, and its high source.
For a natural knowledge* in the heart is nourished by a
    power   165
That's let fall by the Father who formed us all,
Looked on us with love and let his son die
Meekly for our misdeeds, to amend us all.
Yet he[4] did not ask harm on those who hurt him so badly,
But with his mouth meekly made a prayer for mercy—   170
For pity for those people who so painfully killed him.
Here you may see examples in himself alone,
How he was mighty* and meek, and bade mercy be granted
To those who hanged him high and pierced his heart.
    Therefore I implore rich persons to have pity on the poor: 175
Though you're mighty men at law, be meek in your deeds,
For the same measure you mete out, amiss or otherwise,
You shall be weighed with it when you go hence.
> *With the same measure that ye mete it shall be measured to*
>   *you again.*[5]
For though you are true of your tongue and truly earn your
    profits

2. I.e., Truth.
3. I.e., love, which, as the passage goes on, becomes embodied in Christ.
4. I.e., Christ, not the Father as in the sentence before. In such slippery transitions from one subject to another, Langland takes advantage of the greater flexibility of Middle English syntax; and usually, as here, the transition reflects an important connection of ideas, in this case the relationship between God's action and Christ's.
5. Luke 6.38.

And are as chaste as a child crying at a church service,   180
Unless you really love and relieve the poor
And share in a goodly way such goods as God sends you,
You have no more merit in Mass nor in Hours*
Than Malkin for her maidenhead that no man desires.[6]
For James the gentle[7] enjoined in his books   185
That faith without works is worse than nothing,
And as dead as a doornail unless the deed goes with it.
    Faith without works is dead.[8]
Let chastity without charity be chained in hell!
It's as lifeless as a lamp that has no light in it.
Many chaplains are chaste, but their charity is missing.   190
None are harder of heart than they are when they're
    promoted—
Unkind to their kin and to all Christian people,
Chew up their charity and chide for more—
May such chastity without charity be chained in hell!
You curates who keep yourselves clean of your bodies,   195
You're encumbered with covetousness—you can't escape it,
So hard has Avarice hasped you together.
That's no truth of the Trinity but treachery of hell:
And a lesson to unlearned men to delay their alms-giving,
For in the Evangel we find these very words: 200
Date et dabitur vobis,[9] for I endow you all.
That is the love-latch that lets my grace out
To comfort the care-worn overcome with sin.
Love is Life's doctor,* and next[1] our Lord himself,
And also the strait[2] street that goes straight to Heaven.   205
Therefore I say as I said before, by the sense of these texts,
When all treasures are tried, Truth is the best.
Now that I've told you what Truth is—there's no treasure
    better—
I may delay no longer now: our Lord look after you."

---

6. Malkin: traditionally a name for a slut, here for a woman who would be a slut if she could but who is still a virgin only because she is too undesirable.
7. "Gentle" in Middle English kept the connection between gentle qualities and the ideals associated with the chivalric or "gentle" class (Gloss).
8. Jas. 2.26.
9. "Give and it shall be given unto you": Luke 6.38.
1. Next to.
2. I.e., narrow; see Matt. 7.13–14.

Passus II

Still kneeling on my knees I renewed my plea for grace
And said, "Mercy, madam, for Mary's love in heaven,
Who bore the blissful babe that bought[1] us on the Cross,
Teach me some talent to distinguish the false."
"Look on your left side, and lo, where he stands,   5
Both False and Favel[2] and lots of fellows of theirs."
I looked on my left side as the lady told me
And was aware of a woman wonderfully dressed.
Her gown was faced with fur, the finest on earth;
Crowned with a coronet — the king has none better.   10
Her fingers were filigreed fancifully with gold,
And rich rubies on them, as red as hot coals,
And diamonds most dear of cost, and two different kinds of
    sapphires,
Pearls and precious water-stones to repel poisons.[3]
Her robe was most rich, dyed with red-scarlet,[4]   15
With ribbons of red gold and with rich stones.
Her array ravished me — I'd seen such riches nowhere.
I wondered who she was and whose wife she might be.
  "Who is this woman," said I, "so worthily attired?"
"That is Meed[5] the maid who has harmed me very often   20
And maligned my lover — Lewte* is his name —
And has told lords who enforce laws lies about him.
In the Pope's palace she's as privileged as I am,
But Soothness[6] would not have it so, for she is a bastard,
And her father was false — he has a fickle tongue   25
And never told the truth since the time he came to earth.
And Meed has manners like his, as men say is natural:
    Like father, like son. A good tree brings forth good fruit.[7]
I ought to be higher than she: I came of better parentage.
My father is the great God, the giver of all graces,

---

1. Redeemed.
2. "Lying"; it is the name of characters representing deceit in Old French literature, but also occurs as an actual English proper name.
3. "Water-stones": water-sapphires, not the same as sapphire itself, but often used as a jewel. Medieval lapidaries attributed specific healing powers to many precious stones.
4. Scarlet was a fine, rich cloth, not necessarily always dyed red, so the phrase is not redundant; "red" in the next line is a traditional intensifier in the expression "red-gold," where it means "rich, bright," rather than the color red.
5. "Reward, recompense, the profit motive": the range of contradictory meanings, positive and negative, the term can involve (such as bribery, gift, just compensation, and heavenly salvation) emerges as the scene advances; how Meed should be defined will be a prime subject of *Passūs* ii–iv (Gloss).
6. Truth, truthfulness, fidelity.
7. The first phrase is proverbial; the second, from Matt. 7.17.

One God without beginning, and I'm his good daughter.   30
And he's granted me that I might marry Mercy as my own,
And any man who's merciful and loves me truly
Shall be my lord and I his love, aloft in Heaven;
And the man who takes Meed — I'll bet my head on it —
Shall lose for her love a lump of *caritatis*.[8]   35
What does David the King declare of men that crave meed
And of the others on earth who uphold truth,
And how you shall save yourselves? The Psalter[9] bears
          witness:
Lord, who shall dwell in thy tabernacle? etc.
And now this Meed is being married to a most accursed
          wretch,   40
To one False Fickle-Tongue — a fiend begot him.
Favel through his fair speech has these folk under
          enchantment,
And it's all by Liar's leadership that this lady is thus wedded.
Tomorrow will be made the maiden's bridal,
If you wish you may witness there who they all are   45
That belong to that lordship, the lesser and the greater.
Acquaint yourself with them if you can, and keep clear of
          them all,
And don't malign them but let them be until Lewte* becomes
          justice
And has power to punish them — then put forth your
          evidence.
Now I commend you to Christ," said she, "and to Christ's
          pure mother,   50
And don't let your conscience be overcome by coveting
          Meed."
     Thus that lady left me lying asleep,
And how Meed was married was shown me in a dream —
How all the rich retinue that rule with False
Were bidden to the bridal for both sides of the match,   55
Of all manner of men, the moneyless and the rich;
To marry off this maiden many men were assembled,
Including knights and clerks and other common people,
Such as assizers* and summoners,* sheriffs and their clerks,

---

8. "Of love"; Langland plays on the difference between two aspects of love: desire and "charity," disinterested love. "Lump": the word is the one Langland actually uses, which had in Middle English the same down-to-earth connotations as in modern English. To speak of measuring love by the lump is characteristic of Langland's shifting registers of language, which force, sometimes startlingly, a sharpened awareness of words and their meanings where familiarity has obscured them.
9. The Book of Psalms, or a separate volume containing them. They were collectively attributed to King David. The next line is from Ps. 14.1.

Beadles and bailiffs and brokers of merchandise,   60
Harbingers and hostelers and advocates of the Arches[1] —
I can't reckon the rabble that ran about Meed.
But Simony and Civil[2] and assizers of courts
Were most intimate with Meed of any men, I thought.
But Favel was the first that fetched her from her bedroom   65
And like a broker brought her to be joined to False.
  When Simony and Civil saw the couple's wish
They assented for silver to say as both wanted.
Then Liar leaped forth and said, "Lo, here's a charter
That Guile with his great oaths has given them jointly."   70
And he prayed Simony to inspect it and Civil to read it.
Simony and Civil both stand forth
And unfold the conveyance that False has made;
Then these characters commence to cry on high:
        Let men now living and those to come after know, etc.[3]
"Let all who are on earth hear and bear witness   75
That Meed is married more for her property
Than for any goodness or grace or any goodly parentage.
Falseness fancies her for he knows she's rich,
And Favel with his fickle speech enfeoffs[4] them by this
            charter
That they may be princes in pride and despise Poverty,   80
Backbite and boast and bear false witness,
Scorn and scold and speak slander,
Disobedient and bold break the Ten Commandments;
And the Earldom of Envy and Ire together,
With the Castelet[5] of Quarreling and uncurbed Gossip,   85
The County of Covetousness and the countryside about,
That is Usury and Avarice — all I grant them
In bargainings and brokerings with the Borough of Theft,
With all the Lordship of Lechery in length and in breadth,

---

1. All these are officials whose functions made them particularly open to bribery. Assizers were members of the assize or inquest that was the ancestor of the modern jury ("assizers of courts" in line 63); summoners were the officials who served summonses to the ecclesiastical courts; the sheriff was the king's chief administrator in each shire; beadles were manorial officials who summoned to court and collected fines; the bailiff was the chief representative of the lord of the manor; harbingers were responsible for requisitioning on the spot, on the king's behalf, materials and labor needed for such projects as building. "The Arches": the Archbishop of Canterbury's court in London, Bow Street.
2. I.e., civil (as opposed to criminal) law, especially noted for its bribery and corruption in the later Middle Ages (Gloss). "Simony": buying and selling the functions, spiritual powers, or offices of the Church (Gloss).
3. The formula for the beginning of a charter, or a "conveyance," a common legal document, often conveying rights or property.
4. I.e., he grants them territory as a feudal lord does, not as an outright gift but specifically to be held by them as his liegemen, in return for military and other service.
5. I.e., little castle.

As in works and in words and with watching of eyes,   90
And in wild wishes and fantasies and with idle thoughts,
When to do what their wills would they want[6] the strength."
Gluttony he gave them too and great oaths together,
And to drink all day at diverse taverns,
And to jabber there, and joke, and judge their fellow-
    Christians;   95
And to gobble food on fasting days before the fitting[7] time,
And then to sit supping till sleep assails them,
And grow portly as town-pigs, and repose in soft beds,
Till sloth and sleep sleek their sides;
And then they'll wake up with Wanhope,[8] with no wish to
    amend,   100
For he believes he's lost — this is their last fortune.
"And they to have and to hold and their heirs after them
A dwelling with the Devil, and be damned forever,
With all the appurtenances of Purgatory, into the pain of
    hell,
Yielding for this thing at some year's end   105
Their souls to Satan, to suffer pain with him,
And to live with him in woe while God is in Heaven."
To witness which thing Wrong was the first,
And Piers the pardoner of Pauline doctrine,[9]
Bart the beadle of Buckinghamshire,   110
Reynold the reeve[1] of Rutland district,
Mund the miller and many more besides.
"In the date of the Devil this deed is sealed
In sight of Sir Simony and with Civil's approval."
    Then Theology grew angry when he heard all this talk,   115
And said to Civil, "Now sorrow on your books,
To permit such a marriage to make Truth angry;
And before this wedding is performed, may it befall you foul!
Since Meed is *mulier*[2] — Amends is her parent —
God granted to give Meed to truth,   120
And you've bestowed her on a deceiver, now God send you
    sorrow!

6. Lack.
7. Fasts required abstinence from certain foods for specified periods of time. Some fasts ended
in midafternoon.
8. Despair, considered the ultimate development of sloth (Gloss).
9. A puzzling phrase, which may refer to the "crutched" or "Pauline" friars (but friars were
not usually pardoners) or possibly to the clerics so common around St. Paul's Cathedral in
London.
1. The superintendent of a large farming estate. "Bart": Langland has "Bette," which, since
it cannot be a woman's name, may be a form of "Batty," a nickname for Bartholomew.
2. Literally, "woman"; technically, a woman of legitimate birth.

The text does not tell you so,[3] Truth knows what's true,
For *dignus est operarius*[4] to have his hire.
And you've fastened her to False — fie on your law!
For you live wholly by lies and by lecherous acts.   125
Simony and yourself are sullying Holy Church;
The notaries[5] and you are noxious to the people.
You shall both make amends for it, by God that made me!
You know well, you wastrels, unless your wits are failing,
That False is unflaggingly fickle in his deeds,   130
And like a bastard born of Beëlzebub's kindred.
And Meed is *mulier*, a maiden of property:
She could kiss the king for cousin if she wished.
Work with wisdom and with your wit as well:
Lead her to London where law is determined —   135
If it's legally allowable for them to lie together.
And if the Justice judges it's right to join her with False,
Yet be wary of the wedding, for Truth is wise and discerning,
And Conscience[6] is of his council and knows all your
          characters,
And if he finds that you've offended and are one of False's
          followers,   140
It shall beset your soul most sourly in the end."
   Civil assents to this, but Simony was unwilling
Till he had silver for his seal and the stamps of the notaries.
Then Favel fetched forth florins[7] enough
And bade Guile, "Go give gold all about,   145
And don't neglect the notaries, see that they need nothing.
And fee False Witness with florins enough,
For he may overmaster Meed and make her obey me."
When this gold had been given, there was great thanking
To False and Favel for their fair gifts.   150
And they all came to comfort False from the care that
          afflicted him,
And said, "Be sure we shall never cease our efforts
Till Meed is your wedded wife through wit of us all,
For we've overmastered Meed with our merry speech
So that she grants to go with a good will   155

---

3. I.e., scripture does not support their plan.
4. "Worthy is the laborer": Luke 10.7.
5. Medieval notaries could, like modern ones, be officials charged with drawing up or attesting to important documents; a notary could also simply be an important person's clerk or secretary.
6. The term in Middle English included not only moral conscience, just as in modern English, but also awareness in a broader sense; the meaning of Conscience, like that of Meed, shifts and expands in his encounter with her and with Reason (Gloss).
7. Gold coins (Gloss).

To London to learn whether law would
Judge you jointly in joy forever."
Then False felt well pleased and Favel was glad,
And they sent to summon all men in shires about,
And bade them all be ready, beggars and others,   160
To go with them to Westminster[8] to witness this deed.
And then they had to have horses to haul them thither;
Then Favel fetched foals of the best;
Set Meed on a sheriff shod all new;
And False sat on an assizer* that softly trotted,   165
And Favel on Fair Speech, clad in feigning clothes.
Then notaries had no horses, and were annoyed also
Because Simony and Civil should walk on foot.
But then Simony swore and Civil as well
That summoners* should be saddled and serve them all: 170
"And let these provisors[9] be put into palfrey's harness;
Sir Simony himself shall sit on their backs.
Deans and subdeans,[1] you draw together,
Archdeacons and officials and all your registrars,[2]
Let them be saddled with silver to suffer our sins   175
Such as adultery and divorce and clandestine usury,
To bear bishops about, abroad on visitations.
Pauline's people,[3] for complaints in the consistory,*
Shall serve myself, Civil is my name.
And let the commissary[4] be cart-saddled and our cart pulled
          by him,   180
And he must fetch us victuals from *fornicatores*.[5]
And make a long cart of Liar, loaded with all the rest,
Such as twisters and tricksters that trot on their feet."
False and Favel fare forth together,
And Meed in the midst and her serving men behind.   185
I've no opportunity to tell of the tail of the procession,
Of many manner of men that move over this earth.

---

8. An area (now part of London) famous for its courts of justice.
9. Clerics nominated to their benefices directly by the pope (going over the head of the local and national hierarchy); petitions for such offices were regularly accompanied by bribes.
1. Like the secular officials above, these and the officers in the next line are clerics whose functions were thought to make them particularly open to bribery. "Dean": a cleric who was either the head of the body of priests attached to a cathedral or (if a rural dean) in charge of a group of parishes under a bishop. "Subdean": a parish priest chosen to assist the bishop in administering church discipline in a portion of the diocese.
2. Bishops' notaries. "Archdeacon": the bishop's second in command, in charge of part of the diocese. "Official": the presiding judge of an archbishop's, bishop's, or archdeacon's court.
3. A problem phrase; see II.109 above. "Visitations": bishop's official inspection tours of his diocese.
4. The bishop's official representative in part of his diocese, who can act for him in his absence and who presides over the bishop's court.
5. Fornicators.

But Guile was foregoer and guided them all.
  Soothness* saw them well and said but a little,
And pressed ahead on his palfrey and passed them all   190
And came to the King's court and told Conscience* about it,
And Conscience recounted it to the King afterward.
"By Christ!" said the King, "if I can catch
False or Favel or any of his fellows,
I'll be avenged on those villains that act so viciously,   195
And have them hanged by the neck, and all who support
      them.
Shall no bondsman be allowed to go bail for the least,
But whatever law will allot, let it fall on them all."
And he commanded a constable that came straightway
To "detain those tyrants, despite their treasure, I say;   200
Fetter Falseness fast no matter what he gives you,
And get Guile's head off at once—let him go no farther;
And bring Meed to me no matter what they do.
Simony and Civil, I send to warn them
That their actions will hurt Holy Church forever.   205
And if you lay hand on Liar, don't let him escape
Before he's put in the pillory, for any prayer he makes."
  Dread stood at the door and heard this declaration,
How the King commanded constables and sergeants
That Falseness and his fellowship should be fettered and
      bound.   210
Then Dread came away quickly and cautioned the False
And bade him flee for fear and his fellows too.
Then Falseness for fear fled to the friars;
And Guile in dread of death dashed away fast.
But merchants met with him and made him stay   215
And shut him up in their shop to show their wares,
Appareled him as an apprentice to wait on purchasers.
Lightly Liar leapt away then,
Lurking through lanes, belabored by many:
Nowhere was he welcome for his many tales,   220
Everywhere hunted out and ordered to pack,
Till pardoners* took pity and pulled him indoors;
Washed him and wiped him and wound him in cloths,
And sent him on Sundays with seals[6] to church,
Where he gave pardon for pennies* by the pound about.   225
Then doctors* were indignant and drafted letters to him

---

6. A pardoner needed the bishop's seal on the document that gave him license, in a particular diocese or district, to preach and collect money for indulgences.

That he should come and stay with them to examine urine.
Apothecaries wanted to employ him to appraise their wares,
For he was trained in their trade and could distinguish many
      gums.[7]
But minstrels and messengers met with him once   230
And had him with them half a year and eleven days.
Friars with fair speech fetched him thence;
To keep him safe from the curious they coped him as a friar[8]
But he has leave to leap out as often as he pleases,
And is welcome to come when he wants, and he stays with
      them often.   235
All fled for fear and flew into corners;
Except for Meed the maid none remained there.
But truly to tell she trembled for dread
And twisted about tearfully when she was taken into custody.

Passus III

Now Meed* the maid alone among them all
Is brought before the King by beadles and bailiffs.[1]
The King called a clerk—I can't recall his name—
To take Meed the maid and make her at home.
"I will sound her out myself and ask straightforwardly   5
What man of this world she would prefer.
And if she works with wit and follows my will
I will forgive her her guilt, so God help me."
Courteously the clerk then, as the King commanded,
With his arm around her waist led her away to a chamber;   10
But there was mirth and minstrelsy that Meed might be
      pleased.
Those who work at Westminster* worship her all.
Gently with joy the justices together
Bustle to the bedroom where the bride dwells,
Comforted her kindly with Clergy's* permission,   15
And said, "Don't mourn, Meed, or make any sorrow,
For we'll take care of the King and clear your way
To be wedded as you will, whatever you please,
For all Conscience's* calculations and craftiness, I'm sure."
Mildly Meed then made her thanks to them all   20

7. I.e., gums used as perfumes, spices, or medicines.
8. Clothed him in a friar's cape.
1. Chief representative of the lord of the manor. "Beadle": server of summonses to the manorial
court.

For their great goodness, and gave them each one
Cups of clean gold and copes sewn with silver,
Rings with rubies and riches aplenty,
The lowest lad of the household a Lamb of gold.[2]
Then they took their leave, these lords, of Lady Meed.   25
With that came clerks* to comfort her also,
And bade her be blithe: "For we'll be your men
And work your will while your life lasts."
She replied to this promise pleasantly, saying to them
That she would love them loyally and make lords of them,   30
And in the consistory* at court call out their names.
"No stupidity shall stop him, the scholar I love,
From being first advanced, for I am recognized
Where clever clerks like cripples bring up the rear."
Then there came a confessor coped as a friar;   35
To Meed the maid meekly he bowed
And said very softly, in shrift as it were,
"Though learned men and unlearned had both lain with you,
And though Falsehood had followed you all these fifteen
          winters,
I shall absolve you myself for a seam[3] of wheat,   40
And also be your go-between and bear your message well
To ecclesiasts and knights at court, to chop Conscience
          down."
Then Meed knelt to that man for the misdeeds she'd done
And shrove herself of her sins—shameless, I think;
Told him a tale and tipped him a noble[4]   45
To be her beadsman[5] and her go-between as well.
Then he absolved her swiftly and said thereafter,
"We've a window being worked on that will cost us a lot;
If you'd glaze that gable and engrave your name there,
Your soul should be certain to have Heaven."   50
    "If I were sure of that," said the woman, "I would spare
          nothing
To be your friend, friar, and fail you never—
As long as you love lords that practice lechery
And don't malign ladies that love it well too.
It's a frailty of the flesh—you find it in books—   55
And a natural enough urge, innate in our kind.

2. A French gold coin, so called because it bore—ironically in the context—the image of the
lamb of God. Here Meed's behavior fits her simplest definition as bribery, and the insistence
on her scarlet clothing (one of whose associations is with whores and with the Whore of Babylon
in the Book of Revelation) is a notable element in her developing meaning.
3. A pack-horse load.
4. A gold coin worth eighty pennies.
5. I.e., to say prayers for her.

If you can escape the scandal, the scar is soon healed:
It's the sin of the seven soonest remitted.
Have mercy," said Meed, "on men that practice it,
And I'll find funds for your church roof, provide you with a
    cloister,   60
Have your walls white-washed and your windows glazed,
And have painted and portrayed who paid for the work,
So that every soul shall see I'm a sister of your house."
   But God forbids such engraving to all good people—
Inscribing in stained glass the story of their beneficence,   65
Lest pride be portrayed there and pomp of this world.
For God can see your conscience and the kindness of your
    will
And the cost to you—and your covetousness, and whom the
    capital belonged to.
Therefore learn from me, you lords, to leave off such writing,
Inscriptions on stained glass of the story of your gifts,   70
Or to go calling for God's men when you give alms,
For fear you have your hire here and your Heaven as well.
    Let not the left hand know what the right hand is doing.[6]
"Let not your left hand, late or early,
Be aware what work you do with your right hand."
For thus God in the Gospel bids good men give their alms.— 75
   Mayors and mace-bearers[7] that are intermediaries between
The King and the commons* in keeping the laws,
Who should punish on pillories and pining-stools[8]
Brewers and bakers, butchers and cooks;
For these are the ones in the world who work most harm   80
To the poor people that purchase small portions;
Because they poison the people privily and often
They get rich through their retail-sales and buy rental
    property
With what the poor people should be putting in their bellies:
For if their earnings were honest, their houses were less high, 85
And they'd buy no borough-freeholds[9]—you can be sure of
    that.[1]

---

6. Matt. 6.3.
7. The mace, or staff of office, was carried before a public official and symbolized his power;
the mace was originally a weapon of war.
8. Chairs on which criminals or other kinds of offenders (usually women) were exposed to public
shame.
9. This kind of landownership was the securest and most lucrative way of owning rental property:
the owner owns the land and the tenements built on it outright, or at least has life-ownership
of them—unlike many owners of buildings in a town who had a mere lease on the land itself
and therefore had to pay rent to someone else for the land under their own buildings.
1. This sentence, which began at line 76, is neither a "complete sentence" by the standards
of modern grammar nor logically connected with the immediate dramatic situation between

But Meed the maid has made a plea to the mayor
To accept silver from all such sellers,
Or presents of unminted metal such as medals of silver,
Rings or other riches on behalf of retailers: 90
"For my love," said that lady, "love them each one
And suffer them to sell at prices somewhat unreasonable."
— Solomon the sage[2] had something to say
To amend mayors and men that administer the laws,
And took this as his text that I intend to repeat: 95
*Fire shall consume the tabernacles of those who willingly accept
     bribes, etc.*[3]
Among these lettered lords this Latin signifies
That fire shall fall on and conflagration consume
The house and home of any who desires
Presents to be proffered him as perquisites of his office. —   100
     The King came from council and called for Meed
And sent for her straightway; sergeants fetched her
And brought her to his bower with bliss and with joy.
Courteously the King commenced to speak;
To Meed the maid in this manner he spoke: 105
"Unwisely, woman, you have worked often.
But worse work you never did than when you took False.
But I forgive you that guilt and grant you my grace
From now to your death-day: do so no more.
I have a knight called Conscience, has come lately from
     abroad;   110
If he wants you for his wife, will you have him?"
"Yes, lord," said that lady, "Lord forbid else!
If I'm not wholly at your behest, have me hanged!"
     Then Conscience was called to come and appear
Before the King and his council, clerks and others.   115
Kneeling to the King, Conscience questioned him humbly
What his will was and what he should do.
"Will you have this woman if I will assent?
For she craves your company, to become your mate."
Said Conscience to the King, "Christ forbid it!   120
Before I wed such a wife, woe betide me!

Meed and the friar. Such passages recur in Langland, reflecting the associative energy of his
thought, sometimes overwhelming surface coherence. They are characteristic of the way his
poetry reproduces the urgency and spontaneous probing of a mind yoking many variables
together and pursuing them with the passion of conversation and argument, rather than of more
formal rhetoric.
2. Old Testament king, David's successor, supposed author of the "Wisdom Books" in the Bible;
see "Sapience" in Gloss.
3. Job 15.34.

She is frail and unfaithful, fickle of her speech;
She makes men misbehave many score times.
In trust of her treasure she troubles a great many.
Wives and widows she teaches wantonness,   125
Gives them lessons in lechery who love her gifts.
She felled your father through false promises,[4]
Poisoned popes, impaired Holy Church.[5]
There's not a better go-between, by him that made me,
Between Heaven and hell though one searched the whole
          earth.   130
Her tail is ticklish, her tongue is too ready,
She's as common as the cartway to comers and goers,
To monks, to messengers, to leper-men in hedges.
Assizers* and summoners,* such men prize her.
Sheriffs of shires would be shamed but for her.   135
She makes men lose their lives and their land both;
She permits prisoners to go free, pays for their release,
And gives the jailers gold and groats[6] together
To unfetter the False, to flee where he likes.
She takes the true man by the top and ties him up fast   140
And hangs him out of hatred who has harmed no one.
To be excommunicated in the consistory* she doesn't care a
          bean;
Because she gives copes to the commissary[7] and coats to his
          clerks
She is absolved as soon as she herself pleases.
She may almost as much do in a month only   145
As your secret seal in six score days.
She's privileged with the Pope—provisors* know it;
She and Sir Simony put the seals on the bulls.[8]
She blesses bishops she knows to be ignorant;

---

4. At the date when this passage was written, the King was Edward III, whose father, Edward II, was murdered in prison, after his wife and her lover led a revolt and forced him to resign the throne; however, no story ascribing his death to bribery survives. (Meed gives her version of her dealings with Edward and his father below.) Here, as often, Langland comments on specific historical events as well as on the more general referents for his allegorical analysis.
5. The phrase "poisoned popes" refers to the Emperor Constantine, who, when he converted to Christianity and made it the official religion of the Roman Empire, allegedly gave the pope temporal rulership and lands, thus, according to a later passage in the poem, "poisoning" the Church; see XV.557–61. (This gift, the "Donation of Constantine," was actually an eighth-century forgery.)
6. A silver coin worth four pennies, no small sum.
7. The bishop's official representative in part of his diocese, who can act for him in his absence and who presides over the bishop's court.
8. For an abbey to hold an election of an abbot, or for a bishop to appoint a cleric to hold a benefice, a letter of permission from the king under his personal seal was needed. But if an individual or a religious order wanted to circumvent this provision, a timely bribe to the papal court could cause the king's order to be preempted by a papal bull (Gloss) appointing the briber.

Prebendaries,[9] parsons, and priests she supports   150
To maintain mistresses and concubines all their mortal days,
And to bring forth bastards forbidden by law.
Where she stands well with the King, woe to the realm!
For she is favorable to False and befouls Truth often.
By Jesus, with her jewels she corrupts your justices   155
And tells lies against the law, and lays down obstacles
So that faith may not go freely forth, her florins* rain so
        thick.
She leads the law as she likes and arranges lovedays[1]
And makes men lose for love of her so that lawyers may
        profit —
A maze for a poor person though he pleads forever.   160
Law is so lordly and loath to make an end;
Without presents or silver pennies* he pleases very few.
Barons and burgesses* she brings into sorrow,
And all the commons into care that crave to live in truth.
Clergy and covetousness she couples together.   165
This is the life of that lady, now Lord give her sorrow!
And all that maintain her men, let mischance betide them!
For poor men have no power to plead though they smart,
Such a master Meed is among men of property."

    Then Meed mourned and lamented to the King,   170
To have a chance to challenge the charges Conscience made.
The King granted her grace with a good will.
"Excuse yourself if you can: I can say no more,
For Conscience accuses you to cut you off from court
        forever."
    "No, lord," said that lady, "believe him the less   175
Until you realize rightly where the wrong lies.
Where misery prevails most, Meed may help.
And you can be sure, Conscience, I didn't come here to
        quarrel,
Nor to disparage you personally in the pride of my heart.
And you're well aware, Conscience — unless you wish to lie —   180
That you've relied on my largesse lots of times,
And also grasped my gold and given it where you pleased.
It's a wonder to me why you're waxing angry now.
I'm still able — as I always was — to honor you with gifts
And to maintain your manhood more than you admit.   185

9. Priests holding a special stipend usually resulting from their having a function at a cathedral
above and beyond whatever ordinary parish position they also held.
1. Manor courts set aside certain days to try to reconcile adversaries in a negotiated settlement;
this laudable aim was too often achieved by bribery rather than by genuine resolution of the
conflict.

But you've defamed me foully before the King here,
For I never killed any king or counseled others to,
Or carried on as you declare—I call the King to witness.
In Normandy in my name he was not injured,
But you yourself for sure shamed him often,   190
Crept into a cabin for cold of your toes,
Worried that winter would last for ever,
And dreaded your death from a dark cloud,
And hurried homeward for hunger of your belly.[2]
Without pity, pillager, you plundered poor men   195
And bore their brass on your back to Calais to sell,[3]
While I stayed longer with my sire to save his life.
I made his fighting men merry and stopped their mourning;
I banged them on their backs and emboldened their hearts
And had them hopping for hope to have me at will.   200
If I'd been marshall of his men, by Mary of Heaven,
I'd have dared lay my life, and no less a pledge,
He'd have been lord of that land in length and in breadth,
And also king of that country to raise his kin's estate,
The least brat of his blood a baron's peer.   205
Cowardly, Conscience, you counseled him thence
To leave his lordship for a little silver
Which is the richest realm that the rain falls on.[4]
    It becomes a king who takes care of a realm
To give meed to men who meekly serve him,   210
To aliens,[5] to all men, to honor them with gifts.
Meed makes him beloved and his manhood esteemed.
Emperors and earls and all kinds of lords
With gifts get young men to gallop on their errands.
The Pope and his prelates expect to get presents,   215
And they give meed to men to maintain their laws.
Servants for their service—we see well the truth—
Take meed from their masters as they may agree.

---

2. A good example of a passage where Conscience is being conceived of as consciousness or awareness more generally than merely ethical conscience; Meed accuses him of being what makes the soldiers realize they are cold, hungry, and frightened.
3. The English army scavenged its way back to Calais to embark for home. Brass (i.e., copper pans) was probably typical of the little left in fought-over villages; Calais, a major commercial center, was in English hands and prosperous.
4. Edward III waged a disastrous campaign against France from October 1359 to May 1360, in which a winter of severe hardship, topped off by the "Black Monday" hailstorm of April 14, led Edward to sign a treaty giving up his claim to the French crown and most of his French territories except Aquitaine, receiving in return only the large ransom paid for King John of France (the "little silver" of line 207). The "dark cloud" in line 193 probably refers to the "Black Monday" storm.
5. Perhaps mercenary soldiers or perhaps other foreigners who are useful to him in dealing with foreign affairs or commercially in trade or banking.

Beggars for the prayers they bid[6] beg men for meed;
Minstrels for their mirth demand their meed.   220
The king has meed from his men to make peace in the land;
Tutors that teach clerks trust to receive meed;
Priests that preach to the people good behavior
Ask for meed and mass-pennies and their meals as well;
All kinds of craftsmen crave meed for their apprentices;[7]   225
Meed and merchandise must go together;
No life, as I believe, can last without meed."
   Said the King to Conscience, "By Christ, it strikes me
Meed has argued so ably, I think she has the upper hand."
   Kneeling to the King on knees, "No!" said Conscience.   230
"Meed must be counted of two kinds, sir King, by your
     leave:
The first God of his grace grants in his bliss
To those who work well while they are here.
The prophet preaches of this, and put it in the Psalter:*
    Lord, who shall abide in thy tabernacle?[8]
'Lord, who shall inhabit your home with your holy saints,   235
Or rest on your holy hills?' David asks this,
And David resolves it himself as the Psalter tells:
    He that enters without spot and works justice.[9]
'Those who enter of one color[1] and of one will
And have done their work with right and with reason,
And he who does not lead his life making loans for usury,   240
But who informs poor people and pursues truth.'
    He that puts not out his money to usury nor takes rewards
      against the innocent.[2]
And all that help the innocent and hold with the righteous,
Without meed give aid to them and help the truth,
Such manner of men, my lord, shall have this first meed
From God at their great need when they go hence.   245
   There is a meed immeasurable that men in power desire;[3]
To maintain misdoers they accept men's meed;
And the Psalter in a Psalm's end speaks of them:
In whose hands are iniquities; their right hand is full of bribes.[4]
And he that grasps their gifts, so God help me,   250
Shall bear a bitter cost for them, or the Book lies.

6. Pray.
7. I.e., the fee craftsmen charge for training apprentices.
8. Ps. 14.1.
9. Ps. 14.2.
1. I.e., without spot.
2. Ps. 14.5.
3. Conscience here begins to describe the second kind of meed.
4. Ps. 25.10.

Priests and parsons who want pampered lives,
Who take meed and money for Masses that they sing,
Will have reward in this world as Matthew has granted
    them:
    Verily, verily, they have received their reward.[5]
  What laborers and lowly folk unlearned get from their
    masters,   255
It is in no manner meed but a measurable hire.
There is no meed in merchandise, I may well assert it:
It is a plain permutation, one pennyworth for another.
  But have you never read *Regum*,[6] you wretched Meed,
Why that vengeance fell on Saul and on his children?   260
God sent to Saul by Samuel the prophet
To say that Agag of Amalek and all his people as well
Should die for a deed done by their forebears.
'Therefore,' said Samuel to Saul, 'God himself commands you
To be obedient to his bidding and fulfill his will.   265
Go to Amalek with your host and whatever you find there
    slay it.
Both men and beasts, burn them to death;
Widows and wives, women and children,
Furniture and farmsteads, whatever you find there
Burn it — don't bear it away, be it never so rich.   270
Despite meed or money make sure you demolish it.
Destroy it and spare it not, you will speed the better.'
But because he coveted their cattle and spared the King,
Forbore him and his beasts both, as the Bible witnesses,
Otherwise than he was warned by the prophet,   275
God said to Samuel that Saul must die
And all his seed for that sin shamefully end.
Such a mischance Meed made the King have
That God hated him always and all his heirs as well.
The *culorum*[7] of this case I don't care to show;   280
Lest I should have harm from it, I will make no end;
For so wags the world with those who wield power
That whoever furnishes them with facts is the first to be
    blamed.[8]
Because Kind Wit* taught me, I, Conscience, know this,
That Reason shall reign and rule all realms,   285
And just as Agag had shall happen to some.

5. Matt. 6.5.
6. "[The Book] of Kings": see 1 Sam. 15.
7. "Conclusion": from *saeculorum*, which, in the phrase in *saecula saeculorum*, "for ever and ever,"
concludes many prayers.
8. It is not clear whether Conscience will not finish the *story* (or if so how its ending could have
harmed him) or will not draw any *conclusions* from it (presumably because doing so would be
too direct a criticism of the King's own behavior, though it is not clear just how).

Samuel shall slay him and Saul shall be blamed
And David shall be diademed and dominate them all,
And one Christian king care for each one of us.
Meed shall no more be master on earth,   290
But Love and Lowliness and Lewte* together,
These shall be governors on this ground to guard true men,
And whoever trespasses against Truth and takes things
      against his will,
No living man but Lewte shall apply the law to him.
For such service shall no sergeant[9] wear a silk scarf   295
Nor face his cap with fur for defending clients.
Meed of misdoers makes many lords
And over lords' laws she leads the realm.
But Kind Love[1] shall come yet and Conscience with him
And make a laborer of Law; such love shall arise   300
And such a peace among the people and a perfect trust
That Jews shall judge in their wit—and be joyful at heart—
That Moses or Messiah has come to middle earth,
And have marvel in their minds that men are so true.
All that arm themselves with broad sword, with spear or
      dagger,   305
Axe or hatchet or any other weapon,
Shall be doomed to death unless they reduce it
To sickle or to scythe, to plowshare or to coulter.
     They shall beat their swords into plowshares, etc.[2]
Each man shall play with a plow, pickax or spade,
Spin or spread dung—or spoil himself in sloth.   310
Priests and parsons with *Placebo* shall hunt
And ding upon David[3] each day till evening.
On hunting or on hawking[4] if any of them go
The living he delights in he shall lose straightway.
Shall neither king nor knight, constable nor mayor,   315
Lay such care upon the commons as to make them come to
      court
And put them in a panel and have them plight their oaths.[5]

---

9. I.e., law-sergeant, barrister-at-law, an important lawyer.
1. Natural, innate, instinctive love; see Gloss under "Kind."
2. Isa. 2.4. "Coulter": part of a plow.
3. I.e., say their Psalter continuously (the Psalms being attributed to King David). "*Placebo*": "I will please [the Lord]": Ps. 114.9.
4. Hunting and hawking were forbidden to clerics, though widely indulged in all the same.
5. Serving on such panels was considered a great hardship, not simply because this function, like jury duty today, was time-consuming. Instead of assessing evidence, medieval "jurors" took oaths vouching for the credibility of one of the parties to the lawsuit. This would be a demanding enough responsibility at the best of times, but under the problematical conditions of medieval "justice" (of which Langland is so critical) jurors were often subjected to great pressures in the form of bribes, threats, or even blackmail. It is understandable that as late as the fifteenth century it was not uncommon for an individual facing legal proceedings to have more faith in trial by ordeal or combat than in a jury.

But by the facts evinced in evidence one verdict shall award
Mercy or no mercy, as Truth may agree.
King's court and common court, consistory* and chapter,[6]   320
All will be but one court and one man be justice:
That will be True Tongue, a tidy man who never troubled
    me.
There shall be no battles, and no man bear weapon,
And the smith that smithies[7] any shall be smitten to death
    with it.
    Nation shall not lift up sword against nation, etc.[8]
And before this fortune befalls men shall find the worst   325
By six suns and a ship and half a sheaf of arrows;
And the middle of a moon shall make the Jews convert,
And for that sight Saracens shall sing *Gloria in excelsis*,[9]
For to Makomet and Meed mishap shall come that time;
For *better is a good name than great riches.*"   330
    Meed at that moment grew as mad as the wind:
"I know no Latin?" said she. "Clerks know the truth.
See what Solomon says in his Sapience-Book:[1]
'They that give gifts, take heed, are granted the victory,
And much worship as well,' as holy words tell: 335
He will acquire honor who gives gifts, etc."[2]
"I can well believe, lady," said Conscience, "that your Latin
    is good,
But you are like a lady that read a lesson once,
It was *omnis probate*,[3] and that pleased her heart
Since the line was no longer at the leaf's end.   340
If she'd looked overleaf on the lefthand side,
She would have found fell words following thereafter:
Quod bonum est tenete[4] — a text that Truth made.
And that was your mistake, madam: you could find no
    more written
When you searched Sapience, sitting in your study.   345

6. "King's court" and "common court" were the courts for criminal and civil cases, respectively; "consistory" was the bishop's court; "chapter" was the deliberative and adjudicative meeting of the members of a monastery or convent, or of the canons (priests) attached to a cathedral.
7. Forges.
8. Isa. 2.4. The meaning of the images in the cryptic prophecy that follows has been much debated; the important point is its Apocalyptic character. Riddling prophecies are frequent at this period.
9. "Glory [to God] in the highest": Luke 2.14. "Makomet" (line 329) is Mohammed, the founder of Islam. The Latin in line 330 comes from Prov. 22.1.
1. Four biblical "Wisdom Books" are attributed to King Solomon. This one is the Book of Wisdom or the Wisdom of Solomon, which, along with Ecclesiasticus, is now considered canonical by Catholics but not by Protestants. The other two are Proverbs and Ecclesiastes.
2. Prov. 22.9.
3. "Prove [i.e., test] all things": 1 Thess. 5.21.
4. "Hold that which is good": 1 Thess. 5.21.

The text you have told us would be true for lords,
But you lacked a clever clerk that could have turned the
      page.
And if you search Sapience again, you shall find what
      follows,
A most troublesome text to those that take meed:
But he steals the spirit of those who accept.[5]   ·   350
And that is the tail of the text that you tried to quote,
That though we win worship and with meed have the victory,
The soul that accepts the gift by so much is enslaved."

Passus IV

"Stop it!" said the King. "I'll stand for this no longer.
You shall settle your dispute, I say, and serve me both.
Kiss her," said the King, "Conscience, I command you."
"No, by Christ," said Conscience, "you can banish me from
      court.
Unless Reason recommends it, I will rather die."   5
"And I command you," said the King to Conscience then,
"Ride off right now and bring Reason here.
Command him to come and consult on this affair.
For he shall rule my realm and direct me what's best
About Meed and other matters—what man shall wed her;   10
And account with you, Conscience, so Christ help me,
How you lead my liegemen, learned and unlearned."
"I am glad of that agreement," Conscience gave answer,
And went straight away to Reason and whispered in his ear,
Told him what the King intended and then took his leave.   15
"I'll get ready to ride," said Reason. "Rest for a while,"
And called Cato his servant,[1] courteous of speech,
And also Tom-True-Tongue-Tell-Me-No-Tales-
Nor-Lies-To-Laugh-At-For-I-Loved-Them-Never.[2]
"Set my saddle upon Suffer-Till-I-See-My-Time,   20
And get him well girded with girths of wit.
Hang the heavy bridle on him to hold his head low,
For he will whinny 'weehee' twice before we get there."

---

5. Prov. 22.9; see line 336 above.
1. Dionysius Cato, supposed author of the *Distichs of Cato*, an early fourth-century collection of maxims, one of the first books studied in medieval grammar schools; here the name suggests the relationship between Reason and elementary education.
2. Reason depends partly on the quality of the raw material available to him to work on, as well as (next line) on the patience to wait until a problem has reached the point where it can be solved by rational analysis.

Then Conscience on his colt canters forth fast
And Reason rides with him, reckoning together   25
What machinations Meed makes on this earth.
One Warren Wisdom and Witty[3] his fellow
Followed them fast, for they had business
In the Exchequer and in Chancery,[4] to be discharged of suits,
And they ride fast because Reason could direct them the best   30
How to save themselves from shame and harms.
But Conscience was well-acquainted with them—they loved
        covetousness—
And bade Reason ride fast and reckon with neither.
"There are wiles in their words and with Meed is their home.
Where wrath and wrangling are, there they rake in silver,   35
But where love and lewte* are they don't like to come.
        Grief and unhappiness in their ways, etc.[5]
They give no respect to good faith, God knows the truth.
        The fear of God is not before their eyes, etc.
For they'd do more for a dinner or a dozen capons
Than for the love of our Lord and all his beloved saints.
Therefore, Reason, let them ride, those rich men, by
        themselves,   40
For they have no care for Conscience or Christ, as I think."
Then Reason took the high road, riding fast
As Conscience counseled him till they came to the King.
Courteously the King then came to meet Reason
And between himself and his son set him on the bench,   45
And they exchanged wise words a long while together.

    Then came Peace into the parliament and presented a plea,
How regardless of his resistance Wrong had seized his wife,
And how he ravished Rose, Reginald's widow,
And Margaret of her maidenhead, no matter how she
        struggled.   50
"Both my fowls and my farrows fall prey to his followers.
I don't dare for fear of him fight or complain.
He borrowed Bayard[6] from me and never brought him back,
And I got no farthing[7] for him for any plea I made.
He encourages his company to kill my hired hands,   55
Preempts what I have to sell, harasses me in my bargaining,
Breaks down my barn doors, bears away my wheat

---

3. The morally ambiguous potential of these forms of intelligence may be clearer in the context of the Gloss entry "wit."
4. The government body that dealt with petitions addressed to the king.
5. Ps. 13.3; the Latin in line 37a is from the same verse.
6. A common and proverbial name for a horse.
7. A coin worth a quarter of a medieval penny.

And leaves only a talley in return for ten quarters of oats.[8]
And then he beats me to boot and lies by my maid.
Because of him I hardly have the heart to stir."   60
 The King knew he was telling truth, for Conscience told
  him so,
That Wrong was a wicked wretch who wrought much sorrow.
Therefore Wrong grew afraid and felt out Wisdom,
If he would make peace for him with his pennies — and he
  proffered him many
And said, "If I had the love of my lord the King, little
  would I care   65
Though Peace and his party pled at law forever."
Then Wisdom and Warren Witty both won money
Because Wrong had committed so criminal an act,
And they went to warn Wrong with this wise advice:
"Whoever works wilfully will often stir up anger;   70
I say it for myself, you'll see it's true,
Unless Meed makes amends, mischance will come upon you,
For both your life and your land lie in his grace."
Whereupon Wrong wooed Wisdom most eagerly
To make his peace with his pennies, paid out handy-dandy.[9]   75
Then Wisdom and Wit[1] went together
And led Meed along with them to get leniency for him.
Peace put forth his head with his pate all bloodied:
"Without guilt, God knows, I got this wound."
Conscience and the commons* could perceive the truth,   80
But Wisdom and Wit went about trying
To overcome the King with cash if they could.
The King swore by Christ and by his crown both
That Wrong should be punished properly in payment for
  his deeds,
And commanded a constable to cast him in irons: 85
"He shall not see his feet once in seven years!"
"Why, God knows," said Wisdom, "that wouldn't be wise.
If he may make amends, let Bail manumit[2] him
And put up pledges for his crimes and purchase recompense,
Amend that misdeed and be evermore the better."   90

8. "Ten quarters": eighty bushels. "Talley": a receipt in the form of a stick notched to indicate the amount owed; the stick was then split so each party had half. In practice, recipients of talleys, like Peace, too generally had the bitter experience of never seeing their money.
9. I.e., surreptitiously. "Handy-dandy": a game in which one player shakes something between his two hands and then suddenly closes them, leaving the other player to guess which hand the object is now in; similarly, Wrong passes Wisdom the money without anyone seeing what is in the hands.
1. Mental capacity, intellectual ability; see Gloss.
2. I.e., free.

Wit agreed with this and his words advised the same:
"Better that betterment blot out badness
Than for badness to be beaten and betterment no better."
Then Meed began to humble herself, and asked for mercy
And proffered Peace a present all of pure gold.   95
"Have this from me, man," said she, "to amend your hurt,
For I will warrant well and truly, Wrong will do so no more."
Then Peace piteously prayed to the King
For mercy on that man who misdid him so often.
"Because he's compensated me well, as Wisdom counseled
            him,   100
I forgive him his guilt with a good will.
So long as you assent, I can say no more.
Since Meed has made me amends, I may ask nothing
            further."
"No!" cried the King, "so Christ help me,
Wrong will not run off so before the record's all before me.   105
If he got off so easily, then all he'd do is laugh
And often be the bolder to beat my servants.
Unless Reason has ruth on him, he'll remain in the stocks
As long as I live, unless Lowliness³ go bail for him."
    Some people appealed to Reason then to have pity on
            that scoundrel   110
And to counsel the King and Conscience as well
That Meed might be his bailsman — thus they begged Reason.
"Don't speak to me," said Reason, "of showing any pity
Till lords and ladies all love truth
And scorn all scurrility, to speak it or hear it;   115
Till Parnel's⁴ proud finery is put away in her chest,
And the cherishing of children is chastised with rods,⁵
And scoundrels' sanctity is considered of no value;
Till clerkly covetousness is to clothe and feed the poor;
And religious roamers *Recordare*⁶ in their cloisters   120
As Saint Benedict* bade them, Bernard* and Francis;⁷
And till preachers' preaching is proved on themselves;
Till the King's counsel is the common profit;
Till bishops' bay horses become beggars' chambers,⁸

3. Humility (Gloss). "Ruth": pity.
4. I.e., Pernelle, a woman's name.
5. I.e., until children are not spoiled.
6. "Remember": the first word of the Offertory in the Mass. "Religious" (Gloss).
7. Founder of the Franciscan Order (1182-1226). St. Benedict (480?-543?): founder of the
Benedictine Order, whose Rule influenced most subsequent Western monastic orders. St.
Bernard of Clairvaux (1091-1153), founder of the Cistercian Order.
8. I.e., till bishops spend their money on housing beggars rather than on fine horses.

Their hawks and their hounds help to poor religious houses; 125
And till Saint James* is sought where I shall assign,
And no man go to Galicia⁹ unless he goes for ever.
And all Rome-runners for robbers abroad
Take no silver overseas that shows the King's sign,¹
Neither groats* nor gold engraved with the King's mark,   130
Upon forfeiture of those funds if he's found at Dover,
Unless it's a merchant or his man or a messenger with
        letters,
Provisor* or priest or penitent for his sins.
And yet," said Reason, "by the rood,² I shall render no
        mercy
While Meed maintains her mastery in the court of law.   135
But I can show examples as I see them here and there:
I say it for myself, if it so were
That I were king with crown, a kingdom's ruler,
No wrong in my realm that I recognized as such
Should go unpunished in my power, for peril of my soul,   140
Nor get my grace with gifts, so God help me,
Nor have mercy for any Meed unless meekness caused it,
For a man named *Nullum Malum* met with *Impunitum*
And bade *Nullum Bonum* be *Irremuneratum*.³
Let your confessor, sir King, construe you this in English,   145
And if you put it into practice, I'll pledge my ears
That Law will be a laborer and load dung onto fields,
And Love will lead your land as you like best."
    Clerks who were confessors conferred together
To construe this clause all for the King's profit,   150
But not for comfort of the commons or for the King's soul.
For I saw Meed in the meeting-hall wink at men of law
And laughing they leapt to her, and many left Reason.
Warren Wisdom winked at Meed
And said, "Madam, I am your man, whatever my mouth
        blabs;   155
I'm flustered by florins,"* said that fellow, "and my tongue
        falters often."
All righteous people recorded that Reason spoke the truth.
Kind Wit* accorded with this and commended his words,

9. Part of Spain, site of the famous pilgrimage center of St. James at Compostela.
1. "Rome-runners" is the subject of the verb "take," whose indirect object is "for robbers abroad."
The immense sums paid to the pope annually were a burning issue, which had been protested
in Parliament in 1376; they had been estimated as five times the royal revenue.
2. Cross, crucifix (Gloss).
3. Behind the chopped Latin is the widely quoted statement "The just judge is he . . . who
leaves no evil [*Nullum Malum*] unpunished [*Impunitum*] and no good [*Nullum Bonum*] unrewarded
[*Irremuneratum*]."

As did most of the people in the palace, and a good part of
     the great,
And agreed that Meekness was a master and Meed a cursed
     slut.   160
Love allowed her of little worth and Lewte yet less
And said it so loud that Soothness* heard it,
"Whoever wants her for wife for wealth of her goods,
If he doesn't come to be called a cuckold, cut off my nose."
Meed moped then and made heavy cheer   165
Because most of the commons in that court called her a
     whore.
But an assizer* and a summoner* pursued her fast,
And a sheriff's clerk cursed one and all:
"For I have often," he said, "helped you at the bar,[4]
And yet you never gave me a gift as good as a bean."   170
The King called Conscience and afterward Reason
And recorded that Reason had rightfully spoken,
And awesomely and angrily he cast his eye on Meed,
And his wrath was aroused with law, for Meed had almost
     ruined it,
And he said, "Through your law I believe I lose many
     reversions.[5]   175
Meed overmasters law and much obstructs the truth.
But Reason will reckon with you if I reign for any time,
And judge you justly, by this day, just as you deserve.
Meed shall not make bail for you, by Mary in Heaven!
I will have Lewte in law, and let be all your arguing!   180
By the judgment most people here have passed, let
     punishment fall on Wrong."
Said Conscience to the King, "Unless the commons* will
     assent,
It's very hard, by my head, actually to effect this,
And to arbitrate equitably for all your liegemen."
"By him that was crucified on the Cross, sir King," said
     Reason,   185
Unless I rule your realm thus, rip out my guts—
If you bid Obedience be of my party."
"And I assent," said the King, "by Saint Mary my lady!
Let my council come of clerks and earls.
But Reason, you shall not readily retire from here;   190

---

4. I.e., in court.
5. Disputed property that reverts to the king. When Meed bribes every representative of the
legal system to get indictments for treason, felony, or disputed inheritances dismissed, the Crown
loses reversions.

As long as I live, I'll not let you go."
"I'm ready," said Reason, "to remain with you always;
So long as Conscience belongs to your council, I care for
     nothing else."
"I agree gladly," said the King, "God forbid otherwise!
As long as I live let's live together."   195

Passus V

  Accompanied by his knights the King came to church
To hear matins and Mass, and went to meat[1] after.
Then my slumber ceased, and I was sorry when I woke
That I'd not slept more soundly and seen more.
But before I'd gone a furlong faintness overcame me   5
And I couldn't walk a foot further for lack of sleep.
I sat down softly and said my Creed,[2]
And I babbled on my beads and they brought me to sleep.
  Then I dreamed much more than I mentioned before,
For I saw the field full of folk that I told you of before,   10
And how Reason arrayed himself to preach the whole realm
     a sermon
And with a Cross before the king thus commenced his
     teaching.
He proved that these pestilences were caused purely by sin,
And the southwestern wind on Saturday at evening[3]
Occurred obviously because of pride, and for no cause else.   15
Peartrees and plumtrees were puffed to the ground
In meaning, you men, you must do better;
Beeches and broad oaks were blown to the earth
And turned their tails upward, betokening dread
That deadly sin before Doomsday should undo us all.   20
I might mumble of this matter for a long time
But I shall say as I saw, so God help me,
How standing in the people's sight Reason started his
     sermon.
He bade Waster get to work at what he knew best
And win back what he'd wasted with some kind of work.   25
And he prayed Parnel[4] to put away her robe's embroidery

---

1. Food, nourishment.
2. The basic formulation of Christian belief, which every Christian was supposed to know by heart. The liturgy provided several formulations for use at different times of the church year.
3. A storm on January 15, 1362, severe enough for mention in several chronicles. "Pestilences": since 1349, England had suffered a number of epidemics of the plague.
4. A woman's name.

And keep it in her closet in case she needed money.
He taught Tom Stowe to take two sticks
And fetch Felice home from where females are punished.[5]
He warned Wat his wife was to blame   30
That her head was worth a mark[6] and his hood not a groat.*
He bade Bart cut a bough or two
And beat Betty with it unless she got busy at her chores.
He charged chapmen[7] to chastise their children:
"Don't let your plentiful profits pamper them in youth,   35
And out of fear of the pestilence's power don't please them
          overmuch.
My sire said to me and so did my dame,
'The more you dote on your dear child, the more discipline
          he needs.'
And Solomon said the same in Sapience-Book:*
    He that spareth the rod hateth his son.[8]
'Whoever spares the switch spoils his children.' "   40
And then he prayed prelates and priests together,
"What you preach to the people, practice it yourselves,
And do it in deed, it shall do you good.
Live the lessons you teach us: we'll believe you the more."
And then he directed religious* to obey their rule strictly,   45
"Lest the king and his council curtail your rations
And be stewards in your stead till you learn to restrain
          yourselves."
And then he counseled the king to hold his commons in love:
"It's your treasure and treacle[9] at need if treason's not
          involved."
And then he prayed the Pope to have pity on Holy Church   50
And before he granted any forgiveness to govern himself.
"And you that look after the laws, let truth be your aim
More than gold or gifts if you will gratify God.
For whoever is contrary to truth, he tells in the Gospel,
Verily I say unto you, I know you not.[1]   55
And you that seek Saint James* and saints at Rome,
Seek Saint Truth, for he can save you all.

---

5. Women were punished for being shrewish wives, dishonest tradesmen, etc., by being plunged in water on a "ducking stool"; presumably Tom is to fetch his wife home and beat her (with the "two sticks") himself instead of relying on the community to discipline her. "Tom Stowe": the name, like those in the next few lines, is a generic one, comparable to the modern "John Smith."
6. Equivalent to 160 pennies, several weeks' wages.
7. Merchants, tradesmen.
8. Prov. 13.24.
9. A powerful medicine.
1. Matt. 25.12.

Qui cum Patre et Filio:[2] fair befall them
That are swayed by my sermon." And thus spoke Reason.
　　Then Repentance ran forth and repeated his theme　　　60
And made Will[3] weep water from his eyes.
　　Parnel Proud-Heart fell prone to the ground
And lay long before she looked up and cried, "Lord, mercy!"
And made her promise to him that created us all
That she would unsew her shirt and set a haircloth within　　65
To vanquish her flesh that was fiercely sinful.
"High heart shall never overcome me but I'll hold myself low
And suffer myself to be slandered—and I never did so
　　　　before.
But now I'll make myself meek and beg for mercy
From all of whom I've had envy in my heart."　　　　　70
　　Lecher said, "Alas!" and to our Lady cried
To stand between himself and God and beseech mercy for
　　　　his sins,
Provided he should on Saturdays seven years thereafter
Drink only with the duck and dine but once.
　　Envy with heavy heart asked for shrift　　　　　75
And grieving for his guilt began his confession.
He was pale as a sheep's pelt, appeared to have the palsy.
He was clothed in a coarse cloth—I couldn't describe it—
A tabard[4] and a tunic, a knife tied to his side.
Like those of a friar's frock were the foresleeves.　　　80
Like a leek that had lain long in the sun
So he looked with lean cheeks, louring foully.
His body was so blown up for anger that he bit his lips
And shook his fist fiercely, he wanted to avenge himself
With acts or with words when he saw his chance.　　　85
Every syllable he spat out was of a serpent's tongue;
From chiding and bringing charges was his chief livelihood,
With backbiting and bitter scorn and bearing false witness.
This was all his courtesy wherever he showed himself.
"I'd like to be shriven," said this scoundrel, "if shame would
　　　　let me.　　　　　　90
By God, I'd be gladder that Gib had bad luck
Than if I'd won this week a wey[5] of Essex cheese.

---

2. "Who with the Father and the Son [lives and reigns for ever and ever]": the traditional formula of praise to God with which the sermon concludes. This may suggest that "Saint Truth" is particularly associated with the Holy Spirit within the Trinity.
3. The human will; but "Will" is also, according to several later passages, the name of the Dreamer.
4. A loose, sleeveless jacket, worn over the tunic.
5. A very large measure.

I've a neighbor dwelling next door, I've done him harm often
And blamed him behind his back to blacken his name.
I've done my best to damage him day after day   95
And lied to lords about him to make him lose money,
And turned his friends into his foes with my false tongue.
His good luck and his glad lot grieve me greatly.
Between household and household I often start disputes
So that both life and limb are lost for my speech.   100
When I met the man in market that I most hated
I fondled him affectionately as if I were a friend of his:
He is stronger than I am—I don't dare harm him.
But if I had might and mastery I'd murder him once for all.
When I come to the kirk[6] and kneel before Christ's Cross   105
To pray for the people as the priest teaches,
For pilgrims, for palmers,* for all the people after,
Then crouching there I call on Christ to give him sorrow
That took away my tankard and my torn sheet.[7]
Away from the altar I turn my eyes   110
And notice how Heinie has a new coat;
Then I wish it were mine and all the web[8] it came from.
And when he loses I laugh—that lightens my heart,
And when he wins I weep and wail the time.
I condemn men when they do evil, yet I do much worse;   115
Whoever upbraids me for that, I hate him deadly after.
I wish that every one were my servant,
And if any man has more than I, that angers my heart.
So I live loveless like a loathsome dog
So that all my breast is blown up for bitterness of spirit.   120
For many years I might not eat as a man ought
For envy and ill will are hard to digest.
Is there any sugar or sweet thing to assuage my swelling
Or any *diapenidion*[9] that will drive it from my heart,
Or any shrift or shame, unless I have my stomach scraped?"   125
     "Yes, readily," said Repentance, directing him to live
          better;
"Sorrow for sins is salvation for souls."
"I am sorry," said Envy. "I'm seldom anything else,
And that makes me so miserable, since I may not avenge
          myself.

6. Church.
7. The loss of Envy's tankard and torn sheet, and his fury at it, are not explained in the text
or by modern scholars.
8. I.e., bolt of cloth.
9. "Sugar-stick," a medicine. Sugar, scarce and precious in the Middle Ages, was used to treat
illness.

I've been among burgesses* buying at London   130
And made Backbiting a broker to blame men's wares.
When he sold and I didn't, then I was ready
To lie and lour at my neighbor and belittle his merchandise.
I will amend this if I may, by might of God almighty."
    Now Wrath rouses himself, rubbing his white eyes,   135
Sniveling at his nose and his neck-flesh hanging.
"I am Ire," said he. "I have been a friar,
And the convent's gardener, making grafts on trees.
I grafted lies on limiters and on lectors[1] too
Till they put out leaves of lowly speech, pleasing to lords,   140
And then they blossomed abroad in bedrooms to hear shrifts.
And now a fruit has fallen from this that folk had much
      rather
Show their sins to them than be shriven by their parsons.
And now that parsons have perceived that friars get part of
      their revenue
These possessioners[2] preach disparagement of friars;   145
And friars find parsons deficient, as folk bear witness,
So that when friars preach to the people in places all about,
I, Wrath, run alongside them and read them my books.
Thus they speak of spirituality and each despises the other
Till they both become beggars and live by my spirituality,   150
Or else all become rich and ride; I, Wrath, rest never
But must follow these folk, for such is my grace.
I have an aunt who's a nun and an abbess at that.
She'd rather faint or fall dead than feel any pain.
I've been cook in her kitchen and the convent's servant   155
Many months with them and with monks as well.
I prepared stews for the prioress[3] and other poor ladies
And served them juicy suggestions—that Dame Joan was a
      bastard,
And Dame Clarice a knight's daughter, but her daddy was
      a cuckold,
And Dame Parnel a priest's wench—'She'll never be prioress   160

---

1. Friars who taught in universities. The next few lines detail their activities. "Limiters": friars licensed by a bishop to preach (and collect donations) in a given area.
2. Priests in possession of a parish whose inhabitants' donations supported them. (These donations were not optional but an annual tax of 10 percent—thus called "tithes," from Old English *teotha*, "tenth"—levied on the income of each parishioner from labor or business and, if he or she owned land, on the increase derived from the earth, such as crops, livestock born within the year, etc. The tithes were supposed to support the priest, maintain the church, and help the poor.) Parish clergy were consequently hostile to friars trying to horn in on either their functions or their income.
3. The second in command of a convent, or the mother superior of a smaller or secondary convent dependent on the first.

For she had a child in cherry-time: our whole chapter[4]
    knows it!'
With vicious verbiage I, Wrath, cooked their vegetables
Till 'You lie!' and 'You lie!' leapt out at once,
And each hit the other under the cheek.
Had they had knives, by Christ, they'd have killed each
    other.   165
(Saint Gregory[5] was a good pope and had good foresight
When he provided that the priesthood should be closed to
    prioresses.
They would have been *infamis*[6] then and there, they keep
    secrets so badly.)
I might live among monks, but mostly I shun it,
For there are many fierce fellows there to ferret out my
    deeds,   170
Both prior and sub-prior and our *pater abbas*[7]
And if I tell any tales they take counsel together
And make me fast Fridays on flat bread and water;
And I'm challenged like a child in the chapterhouse,
And lambasted on the bare arse and no breeches between.   175
Therefore it's no pleasure, I promise you, to live in those
    people's house.
I eat unwholesome fish there and the ale I drink is weak.
But once in a while when wine comes, when I drink in the
    evening,
I have a flux of a foul mouth for five days after;
All the nastiness I know about any of our brothers   180
I cough it up in our cloister so the whole convent knows it."
    "Now repent," said Repentance, "and don't reveal ever
Secrets you've discovered — neither by your speech nor look.
Don't drink with too much delight, nor too deeply either,
Lest your will and your wits be overwhelmed by wrath.   185
Esto sobrius," he said, and absolved me[8] after
And bade me will to weep, to amend my wickedness.
    Then came Covetousness; I can't describe him,

---

4. Governing body of a convent or monastery. "Cherry-time": i.e., in cherry season.
5. Not St. Gregory the Great* but Gregory IX, who, in the thirteenth century, had a collection of papal decrees made.
6. "Infamous." Presumably Wrath means they would be in violation of their priestly office by telling the secrets of the confessional.
7. "Father Abbot." The prior and sub-prior are the abbot's second and third in command, particularly responsible for order and discipline.
8. The first-person pronouns here and in the next line are clearly present in the manuscripts. One explanation of them is that they mark the greater participation of the Dreamer (Will) in this part of the scene — the part concerned with Wrath — or in the scene from here on. "*Esto sobrius*": "Be sober": 1 Pet. 5.8.

So hungrily and hollow Sir Harvey[9] looked.
He was beetle-browed and blubber-lipped with two bleary
        eyes;   190
And like a leather purse lolled his cheeks
Over his chops beneath his chin—they churned from age.
And like a bondsman's bacon his beard was shaved;[1]
With a hood on his head, a hat on top,
In a torn tabard of twelve winters' age.   195
Unless a louse could really leap, believe you me,
She wouldn't go walking on that weave, it was so threadbare.
"I've been covetous," said that caitiff, "I confess it here.
For some time I served Sim at the Nook,
And was pledged as his apprentice to promote his profits.   200
First I learned to lie a leaf or two:[2]
How to weigh wickedly was my first lesson,
To Wye and to Winchester I went to the fair
With many kinds of merchandise as my master bade me.
If the grace of guile hadn't gone among my wares   205
They'd have been unsold these seven years, so God help me.
Then I went to school with fabric-salesmen to study my
        primer,[3]
To stretch the selvage out to make it seem longer.
Among costly striped cloths I recorded a lesson:
Pierced them with a packneedle and pleated them together,   210
Pinned them in a press and put them on the rack
Till ten yards or twelve would extend to thirteen.[4]
My wife was a bread-winner; she made woolen cloth
And said to the spinster that she should spin it soft.
The pound that she paid by passed by a quarter   215
What my own scale showed when I weighed something
        honestly.[5]
I bought her barleymalt; she brewed it for sale.
Penny-ale and pudding-ale she poured together
For laborers and low folk—that lay off by itself.[6]

9. "Sir" implies rank or priesthood, but neither Covetousness' name nor his title has been explained by scholars.
1. The bondsman's cheaper bacon still had bristles on the rind.
2. I.e., a page at a time.
3. I.e., the "donet," the fourth-century grammar by Donatus, which was one of the first school-books a student encountered. Hence, metaphorically, the beginner's lesson in any craft or discipline.
4. Sir Harvey uses some kind of frame for stretching cloth illegally.
5. She cheats the spinner by weighing the wool with what is supposed to be a pound weight but is really one and a quarter. She wants softly twisted wool because it can be stretched afterwards to go further.
6. She sets off by itself a mixture of the better, thicker ("pudding") ale adulterated with the thinnest (penny a gallon) to pass off on the cheaper customers (at the price of the better, of course).

The best in my bedchamber was stored by the wall,   220
And whoever had a taste of it bought it thereafter,
A gallon for a groat,* God knows for no less,
When she served it out cup by cup—such craftiness she
    had.[7]
Rose the retailer was her right name:
She's lived the life of a huckster eleven years.   225
But now I swear, so may I thrive, I shall forgo sin
And never set my scales falsely or sell bad wares,
But make my way to Walsingham,* and my wife as well,
And call on the Cross of Bromholm to clear me of debt."[8]
   "Did you ever repent?" said Repentance, "or make
    restitution?"   230
"Yes, once I was at an inn," he answered, "with a heap of
    peddlers.
I rose when they were at rest and rifled their bags."
"That was no restitution," said Repentance, "but a robber's
    theft;
Actually you ought rather to have been hanged for that."
"I thought rifling was restitution, for I never learned to read, 235
And I know no French, in faith, but of the farthest end of
    Norfolk."[9]
"Did you ever practice usury," asked Repentance, "in all
    your lifetime?"
"No, I'm sure," he said, "except in my youth.
I learned a lesson among Lombards and Jews[1]
To put pennies on a scale and then pare the heaviest   240
And lend it for love of the cross and lose it for the pawn.[2]
Such mortgages I made him sign if he missed his day.

7. I.e., it is so much better than the common mix that everyone prefers it, and by doling it
out in separate cupfuls, probably with an inaccurate measure, she clears four pennies a gallon
for it.
8. The Priory of St. Andrew at Bromholm, near Walsingham, had what was believed to be
a miracle-working crucifix containing a fragment of the True Cross; Sir Harvey's prayer, which
echoes the petition for forgiveness in the Lord's Prayer ("Forgive us our debts as we forgive
our debtors"), has an ironically financial ring.
9. I.e., no French at all, far Norfolk being a remote region with a distinctive dialect. (Avarice
seems to think the all too unfamiliar word "restitution" is French.)
1. Though the medieval economy had come to depend heavily on financing through loans for
interest, usury (as opposed to compassionate, interest-free loans) was still strictly forbidden by
the Church. Consequently, business had made itself dependent on financiers from whom loans
(or loans thinly disguised as something else) could be obtained, especially from Jews and from
certain international bankers and merchants, primarily from Lombardy. The thriving business
these financiers conducted also made them (with typical social irrationality) hated scapegoats
and fueled the development of anti-Semitism in the later Middle Ages. Various ways to cir-
cumvent the prohibition against taking interest were devised. One, associated with the same
groups and mentioned in the next lines, was to clip some of the metal from coins and melt
it down; thus (line 247) Avarice lends coins that have all lost part of their edge.
2. Another way of getting around the ban on usury was to lend on security of a pawn (or a
manor, in line 243) worth considerably more than the loan and hope that the borrower would
default and lose the pawn. Sir Harvey makes the borrower sign a contract with no grace period
if the payment is late ("such mortgages," in line 242). "For love of the cross": i.e., for the money—
coins were marked with a cross—instead of for charity, which is the true meaning of the Cross.

I've more manors through forfeiture than through *miseretur
         et commodat.*"[3]
I've lent lords and ladies my wares
And been their broker afterwards and bought it back myself.[4] 245
Bills of exchange and borrowers' notes, that's my business,
And I lend money to people who lose a lip from every
         noble.*
And with Lombards' letters I delivered gold to Rome,
And procured it on credit here and counted out less there."[5]
"Did you ever lend to lords for love of their patronage?"   250
"Yes, I've lent to lords who loved me never after,
And I've made many a knight both mercer and draper[6]
That never paid for his apprenticeship a single pair of
         gloves."
"Do you have pity on poor men that borrow purely for
         need?"
"I've as much pity on poor men as a peddler has on cats   255
Who'd kill 'em if he could catch 'em because he craves their
         skins."
"Are you a generous man among your neighbors with your
         meat and drink?"
"I'm accounted as kindly," said he, "as a cur in the kitchen;
Especially with people living near me I'm reputed as such."
         "Now unless you repent properly," said Repentance,   260
"May God never give you grace to dispose your goods well,
Nor your heirs after you to have joy from what you win,
Nor your executors to bestow well the silver that you leave
         them;
And may what was won with wrong be spent by wicked men
For if I were a friar of that friary where good faith and
         charity are,   265
I'd not use your cash for copes or for the cost of church-
         repair,
Or take as my portion one penny of yours, for peril of my
         soul,
For the best book in our house though its leaves were
         burnished gold,
If I were surely persuaded that you are such as you say.

---

3. "[A good man] showeth favor and lendeth": Ps. 111.5—i.e., through compassionately help-
ing the needy without asking interest.
4. Another way of concealing interest-taking was to lend the borrower goods, not money, and
then buy the goods back at much less than their value (hence the reference in lines 252–53
to making knights into mercers and drapers).
5. Lombardy bankers developed an early equivalent of the international letter of credit; Sir
Harvey can get a letter of credit that is worth more in one place than he has to pay for it in
another.
6. One in the business of cloth-making. "Mercer": a dealer in textiles and cloth-making.

Greed for rich dishes makes you another's slave;
Eat your own bread: it will your freedom save.[7]

You're an unnatural creature: I cannot absolve you   270
Until you make restitution," said Repentance, "and have a
    reckoning with them all;
And until Reason enrolls it in the register of Heaven
That you've made every man good, I may not absolve you.
    The sin is not remitted until the theft has been returned.[8]
For any one who has any of your goods, as God has my
    troth,
Is obligated at the High Doom[9] to help you restore it.   275
And if any one believes I'm lying, look in the Psalter*-gloss,
In *Miserere mei Deus,*[1] whether my remarks are true.
    For behold thou hast loved truth, etc.[2]
Cum sancto sanctus eris:[3] construe that in English for me."
Then that wretch was overwhelmed with wanhope* and
    would have hanged himself
Except that Repentance swiftly consoled him in this way: 280
"Keep mercy in your mind and with your mouth beseech it.
    His mercy is over all his works, etc.[4]
And all the wickedness in this world that one could do or
    think
Is no more to the mercy of God than a spark amid the sea.
    *All iniquity compared to the mercy of God is like a spark in
        the middle of the sea.*[5]
Therefore have mercy in your mind, and as for merchandise,
    leave it,
For you haven't enough honest earnings to buy a loaf of
    bread   285
Unless you went to work with your tongue or with your
    hands.
For the goods you have gotten began all with falsehood.
And as long as you live with them you don't lighten your
    debt but borrow.
And if you can't remember to what man or where you must
    restore them,
Bear them to the bishop and beg him of his grace   290

7. No source for this Latin couplet has been found.
8. St. Augustine (see Gloss), Epistle 153, section 20.
9. Judgment, verdict; the "High Doom" is Doomsday, the Day of Judgment at the Second
Coming of Christ (Gloss).
1. "Have mercy on me, O God": Ps. 50.3.
2. Ps. 50.8.
3. "With the holy thou wilt be holy": Ps. 17.26.
4. Ps. 144.9.
5. Common statement.

To bestow them himself where it shall prove best for your
    soul.
For he shall answer for you at the High Doom —
For you and for many more that man shall give a reckoning
What lessons he taught you in Lent — believe nothing else —
And what he gave you of our Lord's goods to guard you
    from sin."   295
    Now Glutton begins to go to shrift
And takes his way towards the Church to tell his sins.
But Betty the brewer bade him good morning
And she asked him where he was going.
"To Holy Church," he said, "to hear Mass,   300
And then I shall be shriven and sin no more."
"I've got good ale, old friend," she said. "Glutton, will you
    try it?"
"Have you," he asked, "any hot spices?"
"I have pepper and peony and a pound of garlic,
A farthingworth* of fennel seed[6] for fasting days."   305
Then Glutton goes in, and great oaths after.
Cissy the seamstress was sitting on the bench,
Wat the warren-keeper[7] and his wife too,
Tim the tinker and two of his servants,
Hick the hackneyman and Hugh the needle-seller,   310
Clarice of Cock's Lane[8] and the clerk* of the church,
Sir Piers of Pridie and Parnel of Flanders,
Dave the ditch-digger and a dozen others,
A rebeck-player,[9] a rat-catcher, a street-raker of Cheapside,
A rope-maker, a redingking and Rose the dish vendor,   315
Godfrey of Garlickhithe and Griffin the Welshman,
A heap of old-clothesmen early in the morning
Gladly treated Glutton to drinks of good ale.
    Clement the cobbler took the cloak off his back
And put it up as a prize for a player of "New Fair."[1]   320

---

6. This herb was believed to be good for someone drinking on an empty stomach. "Peony":
considered a spice in the Middle Ages.
7. An official responsible for overseeing and protecting a game-preserve.
8. Clarice (and Parnel of the next line) are prostitutes.
9. Fiddle-player. "Street-raker": a scavenger — hence street-cleaner — of Cheapside, a section
of London. What a "redingking" (line 315) was is not known.
1. This was a game in which two participants exchanged items in their possession that were
not of equal value and hence involved a cash payment by the player who put up the less valuable
object. Clement puts up his cloak and Hick his hood; each chooses an agent to represent him
in the evaluation of the objects, which is conducted by peddlers. Hick is represented by Bart,
but since the evaluators are unable to agree, Robin is named as an umpire. It is decided that
Hick should have Clement's cloak and Clement Hick's hood, but that Clement should receive
a cup of ale as well, or perhaps the money for a cup of ale, which he would then share with
all the participants. A fine of further ale would be placed on either of the men who grumbled
at the exchange.

Then Hick the ostler[2] took off his hood
And bade Bart the butcher to be on his side.
Then peddlers were appointed to appraise the goods:
For his cloak Clement should get the hood plus
      compensation.
They went to work quickly and whispered together   325
And appraised these prize items apart by themselves.
There were heaps of oaths for any one to hear.
They couldn't in conscience come to an agreement
Till Robin the roper was requested to rise
And named as an umpire so no quarrel should break out.   330
Then Hick the ostler had the cloak
In covenant that Clement should have the cup filled
And have Hick the ostler's hood, and call it a deal;
The first to regret the agreement should get up straightway
And greet Sir Glutton with a gallon of ale.   335
There was laughing and louring and "Let go the cup!"
They began to make bets and bought more rounds
And sat so till evensong[3] and sang sometimes
Till Glutton had gulped down a gallon and a gill.[4]
His guts began to grumble like two greedy sows;   340
He pissed four pints in a Paternoster's length,[5]
And on the bugle of his backside he blew a fanfare
So that all that heard that horn held their noses after
And wished it had been waxed up[6] with a wisp of gorse.
He had no strength to stand before he had his staff in hand, 345
And then he made off moving like a minstrel's bitch[7]
Some times sideways and some times backwards,
Like some one laying lines to lime birds with.[8]
But as he started to step to the door his sight grew dim;
He fumbled for the threshold and fell on the ground.   350
Clement the cobbler caught him by the waist
To lift him aloft and laid him on his knees.
But Glutton was a large lout and a load to lift,
And he coughed up a custard in Clement's lap.
There's no hound so hungry in Hertfordshire   355
That would dare lap up that leaving, so unlovely the taste.
    With all the woe in this world his wife and his maid

---

2. I.e., stableman (called "hackneyman" above, implying a stable of horses primarily for hire).
3. Vespers, the evening prayer service said just before sunset.
4. A quarter pint.
5. I.e., the time it takes to say the Paternoster, the Lord's Prayer.
6. I.e., sealed. Gorse is a spiny shrub.
7. I.e., a trained dog performing some feat (probably walking on her hind legs) with difficulty.
8. Birds were caught by smearing a sticky substance ("lime") on strings or twigs; someone doing this systematically over an area would turn right and left or move forward and back.

Brought him to his bed and bundled him in it.
And after all this excess he had a fit of sloth
So that he slept Saturday and Sunday till the sun set.   360
When he was awake and wiped his eyes,
The first word he spoke was, "Where is the bowl?"
His spouse scolded him for his sin and wickedness,
And right so Repentance rebuked him at that time.
"As with words as well as with deeds you've done evil in
        your life,   365
Shrive yourself and be ashamed, and show it with your
        mouth."
"I, Glutton," he began, "admit I'm guilty of this:
That I've trespassed with my tongue, I can't tell how often;
Sworn by God's soul and his sides and 'So God help me!'
When there was no need for it nine hundred times.   370
And over-stuffed myself at supper and sometimes at midday,
So that I, Glutton, got rid of it before I'd gone a mile,
And spoiled what might have been saved and dispensed to
        the hungry;
Over-indulgently on feast days I've drunk and eaten both;
And sometimes sat so long there that I slept and ate at once; 375
To hear tales in taverns I've taken more drink;
Fed myself before noon on fasting days."
"This full confession," said Repentance, "will gain favor for
        you."
Then Glutton began to groan and to make great lament
For the life he had lived in so loathsome a way,   380
And vowed he would fast, what for hunger or for thirst:
"Shall never fish on Friday be fed to my belly
Till Abstinence my aunt has given me leave,
And yet I have hated her all my lifetime."
        Then came Sloth all beslobbered with two slimy eyes. 385
"I must sit to be shriven, or else I shall nap;
I can neither stand nor stoop nor kneel without a stool.
If I were tucked into my bed, unless my tail-end caused it,
No bell-ringing should make me rise before I was ready to
        dine."
He began *Benedicite*[9] with a belch and knocked his breast, 390
Stretched and sighed and snored at the last.
"What! Wake up, sir," said Repentance, "and speedily shrive
        yourself."
"If I should die on this day, my dread would be great.

---

9. "Bless me": the first words of a formal confession.

I can't say my Paternoster perfectly as the priest sings it,
But I know rhymes of Robin Hood and Randolph Earl of
    Chester,[1]   395
But neither of our Lord nor our Lady the least that was
    ever made.
I've made forty vows and forgotten them next morning.
I never performed the penance as the priest enjoined me,
Nor really sorry for my sins, so thrive I, I was never yet.
And if I pray any prayer that's not prompted by wrath   400
What I tell with my tongue is two miles from my heart.
I'm occupied every day, holy days and others,
With idle tales over ale and at other times in church;
God's pain and his passion I seldom put my mind on.
I never visited feeble men nor fettered men in prison.   405
I'd sooner hear scurrility or a summer game of shoemakers,[2]
Or lyings to laugh at and belie my neighbors,
Than all the books Mark ever made, Matthew, John, and
    Luke.
Vigils and fasting days, I forget them all,
And lie abed in Lent making love to my mistress   410
Till matins and Mass are done, and then must hurry to the
    friars;[3]
If I make it by *Ite missa est*[4] I feel meritorious.
Sometimes I'm not shriven, unless sickness causes it,
Twice in two years, and then I tell my sins by guess-work.
I've been a priest and parson passing thirty years now,   415
Yet I can't either sing or chant sol-fa[5] or read saint's lives;
But in a field or a furlong I can find a hare
Better than I can in *Beatus vir* or *Beati omnes*[6]
Construe clause by clause and make it clear to my
    parishioners.
I can hold lovedays* or hear a reeve's* reckoning   420
But neither in Canon[7] nor in Decretals can I read a line.

---

1. This is thought to be the first reference to vernacular narratives about Robin Hood. The context suggests that the "Earl of Chester" (there were several) is the one who became a popular hero about 1200 for resisting taxation.
2. Games were played to celebrate midsummer, but the reference to shoemakers has not been explained.
3. Friars offered late Masses and other services for those too lazy to attend regular parish services, another source of friction between friars and ordinary parish priests.
4. "Go, Mass is finished": the last words of the Mass.
5. "Sol-fa": the names of the fourth and fifth notes of the octave, which were used in teaching music; Sloth cannot learn to chant the various parts of the liturgy with their different cadences.
6. The first words of several instructive psalms: "Blessed [is] the man": Ps. 1 and 111; "Blessed [are] all [who]": Ps. 127.
7. Probably canon (or ecclesiastical) law, or possibly the canonical books of the Bible. "Decretals": collections of canon law by Gratian and by later authorities.

If I acquire something on credit, unless there's a clear
    record of it,
I disremember it immediately, and if a man asks me for it,
Six times or seven I swear it's not my debt.
And thus I trouble true men ten hundred times,   425
And my servants sometimes: their salary's in arrears;
It's heart-rending to hear the reckoning when we must read
    accounts:
Thus with such wicked will and wrath I pay my workmen's
    wages.
If any man does me a good turn or helps me at need,
I'm unkind in return for his courtesy and cannot understand
    it,   430
For I have and always have had some of a hawk's manners;
I'm not lured with love unless something's lying under the
    thumb.[8]
The kindness that my fellow-Christians accorded me years
    ago,
Sixty times since, I, Sloth, have forgotten it,
In speaking and in sparing to speak; I've spoiled many times   435
Both flesh and fish and many other victuals;
Both bread and ale, butter, milk, and cheese
For sloth went sour in my service till they could serve no
    one.
I ran about in youth and was a rebel against learning
And have ever since been a beggar because of my sloth."   440
    Alas, I repine   for a barren youth was mine.[9]
  "Do you repent?" said Repentance, and right away he
    swooned
Till *Vigilate*[1] the vigil-keeper fetched water from his eyes
And flicked it on his face and cried fast to him,
Saying, "Beware, for Wanhope* wants to betray you.
'I'm sorry for my sin,' say to yourself,   445
And beat yourself on the breast and beg him for grace,
For there's no guilt here so great but his goodness is more."
Then Sloth sat up and made the sign of the Cross,
And vowed before God, for his foul sloth,
"No Sunday shall pass for seven years, unless sickness
    causes it,   450
That I shall not direct my steps before daylight to the dear
    church

---

8. Trained hawks were used for hunting. They were recalled by whirling a lure on a line that indicated food in the falconer's hand.
9. A proverb used by Langland earlier: I.141a.
1. "Watch": Matt. 26.41.

And hear matins and Mass as if I'd taken a monk's vows.
Shall no ale after meals hold me away
Till I have heard evensong: I swear my oath to the Cross.
And yet I shall restore, if I still have so much,   455
All the ill gains I've got since I was first granted wits,
And though I lack livelihood I'll leave nothing undone
So that each man shall have what's his before I go hence;
And with the residue and the remnant, by the Rood of
      Chester,[2]
I shall seek Truth before I see Rome."   460
   Robert the Robber looked upon *Reddite*,[3]
And because he had nothing wherewith, he wept most
      sorrowfully.
But yet the sinful scoundrel said to himself,
"Christ that on Calvary on the Cross died,
When Dismas my brother begged thee for grace,   465
And thou haddest mercy on that man for *Memento*'s sake,[4]
So have ruth on this robber that has no *Reddere*,[5]
And never hopes to earn what he owes by honest labor;
But for thy much mercy I beseech mitigation:
Damn me not at Doomsday* because I did such evil."   470
What befell of this felon I cannot fully show.
Well I know he wept water with his eyes
And acknowledged himself culpable to Christ yet again,
That *Penitentia* should polish his pike[6] afresh
And leap with him over land all his lifetime,   475
For he had lain with *Latro*,[7] Lucifer's aunt.
   Then Repentance had pity and prayed them all to kneel.
"I shall beseech for all sinners our Savior for grace
To amend us for our misdeeds: grant mercy to us all,
God that of thy goodness gavest the world being,   480
And of nothing madest everything, and man most like
      thyself,
And then sufferedest him to sin, a sickness to us all,
And yet for the best, as I believe, whatever the Book says.
      O happy guilt, O necessary sin of Adam, etc.[8]
For through that sin thy son was sent to earth
And became man of a maid to save mankind,   485

2. A famous Cross ("Rood") on an island in the river Dee off Chester.
3. "Render [therefore to all their dues]": Rom. 13.7.
4. "Remember [me when thou comest into thy kingdom]": Luke 23.42; the words to Christ
on the Cross of the penitent thief, identified as Dismas in the apocryphal Gospel of Nicodemus.
5. "[Goods to] return": see line 461 above.
6. A staff with an iron point or spike, particularly associated with pilgrims. "*Penitentia*": penitence.
7. Thief.
8. From the Easter Eve liturgy.

And thou madest thyself with thy son like us sinful men;

> *Let us make man in our image and likeness; And elsewhere,*
> *Who dwelleth in love dwelleth in God and God in*
> *him.*[9]

And since then with thy own son thou sufferedest death in
our sect[1]

On Good Friday for man's sake at full time of the day,[2]

Where neither thyself nor thy son felt sorrow in death

But in our sect was the sorrow and thy son led it.   490

> *He led captivity captive.*[3]

The sun for sorrow of this lost sight for a time,

About midday when there's most light and mealtime of
saints;[4]

Thou feddest with thy fresh blood our forefathers in
darkness.

> *People that walked in darkness have seen a great light.*[5]

The light that leapt out of thee blinded Lucifer,

And blew all thy blessed into the bliss of Paradise.   495

The third day thereafter thou walkedest in our sect;

A sinful Mary[6] saw thee before Saint Mary thy mother,

And all to solace sinners thou sufferedest it so to be.

> *I came not to call the righteous but sinners to repentance.*[7]

And all that Mark made record of, Matthew, John, and
Luke,

About thy doughtiest deeds was done in our armor.   500

> *The Word was made flesh and dwelt among us.*[8]

And by so much, it seems, the more surely we may

Beg and beseech, if it be thy will,

Who art our father and our brother, be merciful to us,

And have ruth on these rogues that repent so sorely

That they ever angered thee on this earth in word, thought,
or deed."   505

---

9. (1) Gen. 1.26; (2) 1 John 4.16.

1. The expressions "in our sect" (i.e., as a member of our group—here and line 496) and "in our armor" (line 500) refer to Christ's putting on human nature in the Incarnation and acting as one of us.

2. The time of Christ's death (the "ninth hour" in the Gospels) had come to be identified with noon.

3. Eph. 4.8.

4. This image links the Crucifixion of Christ and the bread and wine of Communion (Lord's Supper), which is a re-enactment of it. Christ's blood was thought to have flowed into hell to rescue the patriarchs and prophets who lived before his coming ("our forefathers," line 493); Langland's image of this blood as food suggests not only Communion but a common image of the Atonement, the pelican that was believed to wound its breast to feed its children with its blood.

5. Isa. 9.2.

6. The repentant Mary Magdalene: Mark 16.9, John 20.1–18.

7. Luke 5.32.

8. John 1.14.

Then Hope took hold of a horn of *Deus tu conversus vivificabis*
    nos[9]
And blew it with *Beati quorum remissae sunt iniquitates*,[1]
So that all the saints sang for sinners at once,
"*Men and animals thou shalt save inasmuch as thou hast multiplied*
    thy mercy, O God."[2]

A thousand men then thronged together,   510
Cried upward to Christ and to his clean mother
To have grace to go to Truth—God grant they might!
But there was no one so wise as to know the way thither,
But they blundered forth like beasts over banks and hills
Till they met a man, many hours later,   515
Appareled like a pagan[3] in pilgrims' manner.
He bore a stout staff with a broad strap around it,
In the way of woodbine wound all about.
A bowl and a bag he bore by his side.
A hundred holy water phials were set on his hat,   520
Souvenirs of Sinai and shells of Galicia,
And many a Cross on his cloak and keys of Rome,
And the vernicle in front so folk should know
By seeing his signs what shrines he'd been to.[4]
These folk asked him fairly from whence he came.   525
"From Sinai," he said, "and from the Holy Sepulchre.
Bethlehem, Babylon, I've been to both;
In Armenia, in Alexandria,[5] in many other places.
You can tell by the tokens attached to my hat
That I've walked far and wide in wet and in dry   530
And sought out good saints for my soul's health."
"Did you ever see a saint," said they, "that men call Truth?
Could you point out a path to where that person lives?"
"No, so God save me," said the fellow then.
"I've never known a palmer* with knapsack or staff   535
To ask after him ere now in this place."

9. "O God, you will turn and give us life": from the Mass.
1. "Blessed [are they] whose transgressions are forgiven": Ps. 31.1.
2. Ps. 35.7–8.
3. I.e., outlandishly. (Langland's word, *paynym*, was especially associated with Saracens, i.e.,
Arabs.)
4. A pilgrim to Canterbury collected a phial of holy water from St. Thomas' shrine; collecting
another every time one passed through Canterbury was a mark of a professional pilgrim. "Sinai":
souvenirs from the Convent of St. Katharine on Sinai. "Shells": the emblem of St. James* at
Compostela, in Galicia; "Crosses": commemorating trips to the Holy Land. "Keys": the sign
of St. Peter's keys, from Rome. "Vernicle": a copy of the image of Christ's face preserved on
a cloth, another famous relic from Rome. It was believed to have appeared after Veronica gave
her head-cloth to Christ, as he was going to execution, to wipe his face on.
5. A church near Cairo on the site where Mary lived during the Flight into Egypt. "Armenia":
presumably to visit Mt. Ararat, where the Ark is said to have landed. "Alexandria": the site
of the martyrdom of St. Catherine and St. Mark.

"Peter!"[6] said a plowman, and put forth his head.
"We're as closely acquainted as a clerk and his books.
Conscience* and Kind Wit* coached me to his place
And persuaded me to swear to him I'd serve him forever,   540
Both to sow and set plants so long as I can work.
I have been his follower all these forty winters,
Both sowed his seed and overseen his cattle,
Indoors and outdoors taken heed for his profit,
Made ditches and dikes, done what he bids.   545
Sometimes I sow and sometimes I thresh,
In tailor's craft and tinker's, whatever Truth can devise.
I weave wool and wind it and do what Truth says.
For though I say it myself, I serve him to his satisfaction.
I get good pay from him, and now and again more.   550
He's the promptest payer that poor men know.
He withholds no worker's wages so he's without them by
          evening.
He's as lowly as a lamb and lovely of speech.
And if you'd like to learn where that lord dwells,
I'll direct you on the road right to his palace."   555
"Yes, friend Piers,"[7] said these pilgrims, and proffered him
          pay.
"No, by the peril of my soul!" said Piers, and swore an oath:
"I wouldn't take a farthing's fee for Saint Thomas' shrine.[8]
Truth would love me the less a long time after.

But you that are anxious to be off, here's how you go: 560
You must go through Meekness, both men and women,
Till you come into Conscience[9] that Christ knows the truth
That you love our Lord God of all loves the most,
And next to him your neighbors—in no way harm them,
Otherwise than you'd have them behave to you.   565
And so follow along a brook's bank, Be-Modest-Of-Speech,
Until you find a ford, Do-Your-Fathers-Honor;
          Honor thy father and thy mother, etc.[1]
Wade in that water and wash yourselves well there
And you'll leap the lighter all your lifetime.
So you shall see Swear-Not-Unless-It-Is-For-Need-   570

6. I.e., an oath "By St. Peter!"
7. I.e., Peter, hence the particular appropriateness of his swearing by St. Peter (line 537), a
connection that Langland will exploit in a variety of ways.
8. The shrine of St. Thomas at Canterbury was famous for the gold and jewels offered by
important pilgrims.
9. A good example of a place where the meaning "consciousness," rather than ethical "con-
science," is dominant (Gloss).
1. Exod. 20.12. Beginning in lines 563–64 with the two "great" commandments (Matt. 22.37–39),
Piers's directions include most of the Commandments of Exod. 20.

And-Namely-Never-Take-In-Vain-The-Name-Of-God-
    Almighty.
Then you'll come to a croft,[2] but don't come into it:
The croft is called Covet-Not-Men's-Cattle-Nor-Their-
    Wives-
And-None-Of-Your-Neighbor's-Serving-Men-So-As-To-
    Harm-Them.
See that you break no boughs there unless they belong to
    you.   575
Two wooden statues stand there, but don't stop for them:
They're called Steal-Not and Slay-Not: stay away from both;
Leave them on your left hand and don't look back.
And hold well your holiday until the high evening.[3]
Then you shall blench at a barrow,[4] Bear-No-False-Witness: 580
It's fenced in with florins and other fees aplenty.
See that you pluck no plant there for peril of your soul.
Then you shall see Speak-The-Truth-So-It-Must-Be-Done-
And-Not-In-Any-Other-Way-Not-For-Any-Man's-Asking.
Then you shall come to a castle shining clear as the sun. 585
The moat is made of mercy, all about the manor;
And all the walls are of wit* to hold will out.
The crenelations are of Christendom to save Christiankind,
Buttressed with Believe-So-Or-You-Won't-Be-Saved;
And all the houses are roofed, halls and chambers, 590
Not with lead but with Love-And-Lowness-As-Brothers-Of-
    One-Womb.
The bridge is of Pray-Properly-You-Will-Prosper-The-More.
Every pillar is of penance, of prayers to saints;
The hooks are of almsdeeds that the gates are hanging on.
The gate-keeper's name is Grace, a good man indeed; 595
His man is called Amend-Yourself, for he knows many men.
Say this sentence to him: 'Truth sees what's true;
I performed the penance the priest gave me to do
And I'm sorry for my sins and shall be so always
When I think thereon, though I were a pope.' 600
Pray Amend-Yourself mildly to ask his master once
To open wide the wicket-gate that the woman shut
When Adam and Eve ate unroasted apples.
    *Through Eve it was closed to all and through the Virgin
    Mary it was opened again.*[5]

2. A small enclosed field, or a small agricultural holding worked by a tenant.
3. A holiday—i.e., a holy day—lasted until sunset ("high evening"); it was not supposed to be used for work, and drinking and games were forbidden, at least until after attendance at church services.
4. A low hillock or a burial mound.
5. From a service commemorating the Virgin Mary.

For he keeps the latchkey though the king sleep.
And if Grace grants you to go in in this way   605
You shall see in yourself Truth sitting in your heart
In a chain of charity as though you were a child again,[6]
To suffer your sire's will and say nothing against it.
    But beware lest Anger ambush you, that arrant wretch,
For he has hatred for him who has his seat in your heart,   610
And he puffs you up with pride to praise yourself;
Confidence in your kind deeds makes you become blind
        then,
And so you'll be duly driven out and the door closed,
Latched and locked, to leave you outside,
Perhaps a hundred years before you enter again.   615
Thus you might lose his love through lauding yourself,
And get it back again through grace and through no gift
        else.
But there are seven sisters that serve Truth always
Who are guards of the gates that go into the place.
One is called Abstinence, Humility another;   620
Charity and Chastity are the chief maidens;
Patience and Peace proffer help to many people;
Largesse the lady lets in full many;
She has helped a thousand out of the Devil's pound.
But whoever is sib to these sisters, so God help me,   625
Is wonderfully welcomed and warmly received.
Unless you can claim kinship with some of these seven
It's very hard, by my head, for any of you all
To get admission at any gate unless grace prevails."
"By Christ," cried a pickpocket, "I have no kin there."   630
"Nor I," said an ape-trainer, "for anything I know."
"God knows," said a cake-seller, "if I were sure of this,
I wouldn't go a foot further for any friar's preaching."
"Yes!" said Piers Plowman, and prodded him for his good.
"Mercy is a maiden there that has dominion over them all,   635
And she is sib to all sinners, and her son as well,
And through the help of these two—think nothing else—
You might get grace there if you go in time."
"By Saint Paul!" said a pardoner,* "possibly I'm not known
        there;

6. Cf. Mark 10.15: "whosoever shall not receive the kingdom of God as a little child, he shall
not enter therein." This childlike quality is here envisaged as total submissiveness (line 608).
"In a chain of charity": either Truth is bound by (that is, constrained by) *caritas*, "love," or Truth
is enthroned, adorned with *caritas* like a chain of office.

I'll go fetch my box with my brevets[7] and a bull* with
    bishop's letters."   640
"By Christ!" said a common woman,[8] "I'll keep you
    company.
You shall say I am your sister." I don't know what became
    of them.

Passus VI

"This would be a bewildering way unless we had a guide
Who could trace our way foot by foot": thus these folk
    complained.
Said Perkin[1] the Plowman, "By Saint Peter of Rome!
I have a half-acre to plow by the highway;
If I had plowed this half-acre and afterwards sowed it,   5
I would walk along with you and show you the way to go."
"That would be a long delay," said a lady in a veil.
"What ought we women to work at meanwhile?"
"Some shall sew sacks to stop the wheat from spilling.
And you lovely ladies, with your long fingers,   10
See that you have silk and sendal to sew when you've time
Chasubles[2] for chaplains for the Church's honor.
Wives and widows, spin wool and flax;
Make cloth, I counsel you, and teach the craft to your
    daughters.
The needy and the naked, take note how they fare: 15
Keep them from cold with clothing, for so Truth wishes.
For I shall supply their sustenance unless the soil fails
As long as I live, for the Lord's love in Heaven.
And all sorts of folk that feed on farm products,
Busily abet him who brings forth your food."   20
    "By Christ!" exclaimed a knight then, "your counsel is the
    best.
But truly, how to drive a team has never been taught me.
But show me," said the knight, "and I shall study plowing."
"By Saint Paul," said Perkin, "since you proffer help so
    humbly,

---

7. Pardoner's credentials.
8. I.e., a prostitute.
1. A nickname for Piers, or, Peter.
2. Garments worn by priests to celebrate Mass. "Sendal": a thin, rich form of silk.

I shall sweat and strain and sow for us both,   25
And also labor for your love all my lifetime,
In exchange for your championing Holy Church and me
Against wasters and wicked men who would destroy me.
And go hunt hardily hares and foxes,
Boars and bucks that break down my hedges,   30
And have falcons at hand to hunt down the birds
That come to my croft[3] and crop my wheat."
Thoughtfully the knight then spoke these words:
"By my power, Piers, I pledge you my word
To uphold this obligation though I have to fight.   35
As long as I live I shall look after you."
"Yes, and yet another point," said Piers, "I pray you further:
See that you trouble no tenant unless Truth approves,
And though you may amerce[4] him, let Mercy set the fine,
And Meekness be your master no matter what Meed does.   40
And though poor men proffer you presents and gifts,
Don't accept them for it's uncertain that you deserve to
        have them.
For at some set time you'll have to restore them
In a most perilous place called purgatory.
And treat no bondman badly—you'll be the better for it;   45
Though here he is your underling, it could happen in
        Heaven
That he'll be awarded a worthier place, one with more bliss:
        Friend, go up higher.[5]
For in the charnelhouse[6] at church churls are hard to
        distinguish,
Or a knight from a knave: know this in your heart.
And see that you're true of your tongue, and as for tales—
        hate them   50
Unless they have wisdom and wit for your workmen's
        instruction.
Avoid foul-mouthed fellows and don't be friendly to their
        stories,
And especially at your repasts shun people like them,
For they tell the Fiend's fables—be very sure of that."
"I assent, by Saint James," said the knight then,   55
"To work by your word while my life lasts."
"And I shall apparel myself," said Perkin, "in pilgrims'
        fashion

3. A small enclosed field.
4. Punish with a fine the amount of which is at the discretion of the judge.
5. Luke 14.10.
6. A crypt for dead bodies.

And walk along the way with you till we find Truth."
He donned his working-dress, some darned, some whole,
His gaiters and his gloves to guard his limbs from cold,   60
And hung his seed-holder behind his back instead of a
  knapsack:
"Bring a bushel of bread-wheat for me to put in it,
For I shall sow it myself and set out afterwards
On a pilgrimage as palmers* do to procure pardon.
And whoever helps me plow or work in any way   65
Shall have leave, by our Lord, to glean my land in harvest-
  time,
And make merry with what he gets, no matter who
  grumbles.
And all kinds of craftsmen that can live in truth,
I shall provide food for those that faithfully live,
Except for Jack the juggler and Jonette from the brothel,   70
And Daniel the dice-player and Denot the pimp,
And Friar Faker and folk of his order,
And Robin the ribald for his rotten speech.
Truth told me once and bade me tell it abroad:
Deleantur de libro viventium:[7] I should have no dealings with
  them,   75
For Holy Church is under orders to ask no tithes[8] of them.
 For let them not be written with the righteous.[9]
Their good luck has left them, the Lord amend them now."
 Dame-Work-When-It's-Time-To was Piers's wife's name;
His daughter was called Do-Just-So-Or-Your-Dame-Will-
  Beat-You;
His son was named Suffer-Your-Sovereigns-To-Have-Their-
  Will-   80
Condemn-Them-Not-For-If-You-Do-You'll-Pay-A-Dear-
  Price-
Let-God-Have-His-Way-With-All-Things-For-So-His-Word-
  Teaches.
"For now I am old and hoary and have something of my
  own,
To penance and to pilgrimage I'll depart with these others;
Therefore I will, before I go away, have my will written: 85
'*In Dei nomine, amen,*[1] I make this myself.
He shall have my soul that has deserved it best,

---

7. "Let them be blotted out of the book of the living": Ps. 68.29.
8. Because the money they make is not legitimate income or increase derived from the earth;
therefore they do not owe the tithes, or 10 percent taxes, due the Church.
9. Ps. 68.29.
1. "In the name of God, amen": customary beginning of a will.

And defend it from the Fiend — for so I believe —
Till I come to his accounting, as my Creed teaches me —
To have release and remission I trust in his rent book.   90
The kirk* shall have my corpse and keep my bones,
For of my corn and cattle it craved the tithe:
I paid it promptly for peril of my soul;
It is obligated, I hope, to have me in mind
And commemorate me in its prayers among all Christians.   95
My wife shall have what I won with truth, and nothing else,
And parcel it out among my friends and my dear children.
For though I die today, my debts are paid;
I took back what I borrowed before I went to bed.'
As for the residue and the remnant, by the Rood of Lucca,[2]   100
I will worship Truth with it all my lifetime,
And be his pilgrim at the plow for poor men's sake.
My plowstaff shall be my pikestaff and push at the roots
And help my coulter to cut and cleanse the furrows."
　　Now Perkin and the pilgrims have put themselves to
　　　　plowing.   105
Many there helped him to plow his half-acre.
Ditchers and diggers dug up the ridges;
Perkin was pleased by this and praised them warmly.
There were other workmen who worked very hard:
Each man in his manner made himself a laborer,   110
And some to please Perkin pulled up the weeds.
At high prime[3] Piers let the plow stand
To oversee them himself; whoever worked best
Should be hired afterward, when harvest-time came.
Then some sat down and sang over ale   115
And helped plow the half-acre with "Ho! trolly-lolly!"[4]
"Now by the peril of my soul!" said Piers in pure wrath,
"Unless you get up again and begin working now,
No grain that grows here will gladden you at need,
And though once off the dole you die let the Devil care!"   120
Then fakers were afraid and feigned to be blind;
Some set their legs askew as such loafers can
And made their moan to Piers, how they might not work:
"We have no limbs to labor with, Lord, we thank you;

2. An ornate crucifix at Lucca in Italy was a popular object of pilgrimage. "Residue and remnant": land had to be left to one's natural heirs, though up to one third of personal property (the "residue and remnant") could be left to the Church for Masses for the testator or other purposes; the other two thirds had to go to the family, one to the widow and the other to the children. Piers's arrangements seem to leave the wife considerably more latitude.
3. Nine in the morning, or after a substantial part of the day's work has been done, since laborers start so early.
4. Presumably the refrain of a popular song. (Note similarly musical loafers in Pro.224-25.)

But we pray for you, Piers, and for your plow as well,   125
That God of his grace make your grain multiply,
And reward you for whatever alms you will give us here,
For we can't strain and sweat, such sickness afflicts us."
  "If what you say is so," said Piers, "I'll soon find out.
I know you're ne'er-do-wells, and Truth knows what's right,   130
And I'm his sworn servant and so should warn him
Which ones they are in this world that do his workmen
    harm.
You waste what men win with toil and trouble.
But Truth shall teach you how his team should be driven,
Or you'll eat barley bread and use the brook for drink;   135
Unless you're blind or broken-legged, or bolted[5] with iron—
Those shall eat as well as I do, so God help me,
Till God of his goodness gives them strength to arise.
But you could work as Truth wants you to and earn wages
    and bread
By keeping cows in the field, the corn from the cattle,   140
Making ditches or dikes or dinging on sheaves,
Or helping make mortar, or spreading muck afield.
You live in lies and lechery and in sloth too,
And it's only for suffrance that vengeance has not fallen on
    you.
But anchorites and hermits that eat only at noon   145
And nothing more before the morrow, they shall have my
    alms,
And buy copes at my cost—those that have cloisters and
    churches.
But Robert Runabout shall have no rag from me,
Nor 'Apostles' unless they can preach and have the bishop's
    permission.
They shall have bread and boiled greens and a bit extra
    besides,   150
For it's an unreasonable religious life that has no regular
    meals."
  Then Waster waxed angry and wanted to fight;
To Piers the Plowman he proffered his glove.
A Breton, a braggart, he bullied Piers too,
And told him to go piss with his plow, peevish wretch.   155
"Whether you're willing or unwilling, we will have our will
With your flour and your flesh, fetch it when we please,
And make merry with it, no matter what you do."

5. I.e., braced.

Then Piers the Plowman complained to the knight
To keep him safe, as their covenant was, from cursed rogues,   160
"And from these wolfish wasters that lay waste the world,
For they waste and win nothing, and there will never be
Plenty among the people while my plow stands idle."
Because he was born a courteous man the knight spoke
        kindly to Waster
And warned him he would have to behave himself better: 165
"Or you'll pay the penalty at law, I promise, by my order!"
"It's not my way to work," said Waster, "I won't begin now!"
And made light of the law and lighter of the knight,
And said Piers wasn't worth a pea or his plow either,
And menaced him and his men if they met again.   170
    "Now by the peril of my soul!" said Piers, "I'll punish you
    all."
And he whooped after Hunger who heard him at once.
"Avenge me on these vagabonds," said he, "that vex the
        whole world."
Then Hunger in haste took hold of Waster by the belly
And gripped him so about the guts that his eyes gushed
        water.   175
He buffeted the Breton about the cheeks
That he looked like a lantern all his life after.
He beat them both so that he almost broke their guts.
Had not Piers with a pease loaf[6] prayed him to leave off
They'd have been dead and buried deep, have no doubt
        about it.   180
"Let them live," he said, "and let them feed with hogs,
Or else on beans and bran baked together."
Fakers for fear fled into barns
And flogged sheaves with flails from morning till evening,
So that Hunger wouldn't be eager to cast his eye on them.   185
For a potful of peas that Piers had cooked
A heap of hermits laid hands on spades
And cut off their copes and made short coats of them
And went like workmen to weed and to mow,
And dug dirt and dung to drive off Hunger.   190
Blind and bedridden got better by the thousand;
Those who sat to beg silver were soon healed,
For what had been baked for Bayard[7] was boon to many
        hungry,

---

6. The cheapest and coarsest grade of bread, the food of those who cannot get better.
7. Generic name for a horse; a bread made of beans and bran, the coarsest category of bread, was used to feed horses and hounds, but was eaten by people when need was great.

And many a beggar for beans obediently labored,
And every poor man was well pleased to have peas for his
    wages,   195
And what Piers prayed them to do they did as sprightly as
    sparrowhawks.
And Piers was proud of this and put them to work,
And gave them meals and money as they might deserve.
   Then Piers had pity and prayed Hunger to take his way
Off to his own home and hold there forever.   200
"I'm well avenged on vagabonds by virtue of you.
But I pray you, before you part," said Piers to Hunger,
"With beggars and street-beadsmen[8] what's best to be done?
For well I know that once you're away, they will work badly;
Misfortune makes them so meek now,   205
And it's for lack of food that these folk obey me.
And they're my blood brothers, for God bought* us all.
Truth taught me once to love them every one
And help them with everything after their needs.
Now I'd like to learn, if you know, what line I should take   210
And how I might overmaster them and make them work."
"Hear now," said Hunger, "and hold it for wisdom:
Big bold beggars that can earn their bread,
With hounds' bread and horses' bread hold up their hearts,
And keep their bellies from swelling by stuffing them with
    beans—   215
And if they begin to grumble, tell them to get to work,
And they'll have sweeter suppers once they've deserved
    them.
And if you find any fellow-man that fortune has harmed
Through fire or through false men, befriend him if you can.
Comfort such at your own cost, for the love of Christ in
    Heaven;   220
Love them and relieve them—so the law of Kind[9] directs.
    Bear ye one another's burdens.[1]
And all manner of men that you may find
That are needy or naked and have nothing to spend,
With meals or with money make them the better.
Love them and don't malign them; let God take vengeance.   225
Though they behave ill, leave it all up to God
    Vengeance is mine and I will repay.[2]

8. Paid prayer-sayers.
9. Nature (Gloss).
1. Gal. 6.2.
2. Rom. 12.19.

And if you want to gratify God, do as the Gospel teaches,
And get yourself loved by lowly men: so you'll unloose his
    grace."
    Make to yourselves friends of the mammon of unrighteousness.[3]
  "I would not grieve God," said Piers, "for all the goods
    on earth!
Might I do as you say without sin?" said Piers then.   230
"Yes, I give you my oath," said Hunger, "or else the Bible
    lies:
Go to Genesis the giant, engenderer of us all:[4]
In sudore[5] and slaving you shall bring forth your food
And labor for your livelihood, and so our Lord commanded.
And Sapience* says the same—I saw it in the Bible.   235
Piger propter frigus[6] would plow no field;
He shall be a beggar and none abate his hunger.
Matthew with man's face[7] mouths these words:
'Entrusted with a talent, *servus nequam*[8] didn't try to use it,
And earned his master's ill-will for evermore after,   240
And he took away his talent who was too lazy to work,
And gave it to him in haste that had ten already;
And after he said so that his servants heard it,
He that has shall have, and help when he needs it,
And he that nothing has shall nothing have and no man
    help him,   245
And what he trusts he's entitled to I shall take away.'
Kind Wit* wants each one to work,
Either in teaching or tallying or toiling with his hands,
Contemplative life or active life; Christ wants it too.
The Psalter says in the Psalm of *Beati omnes*,[9]   250
The fellow that feeds himself with his faithful labor,
He is blessed by the Book in body and in soul."
    The labors of thy hands, etc.[1]
"Yet I pray you," said Piers, "*pour charité*,[2] if you know
Any modicum of medicine, teach me it, dear sir.

---

3. Luke 16.9.
4. This puzzling epithet has been explained on the grounds that Genesis is the longest book
(except for Psalms) in the Bible, and that it recounts the creation of mankind.
5. "In the sweat [of thy face shalt thou eat bread]": Gen. 3.19.
6. "The sluggard [will not plow] by reason of the cold": Prov. 20.4.
7. Each of the four Evangelists had his traditional pictorial image, derived partly from the faces
of the four creatures in Ezekiel's vision (Ezek. 1.5–12), and partly from those of the four beasts
of the Apocalypse (Rev. 4.7); Matthew was represented as a winged man, Mark, a lion, Luke,
a winged ox, and John, an eagle.
8. "The wicked servant": Luke 19.22; see 17–27. A talent is a unit of money.
9. "Blessed [are] all [who]": Ps. 127.1.
1. Ps. 127.2.
2. "For charity."

For some of my servants and myself as well   255
For a whole week do no work, we've such aches in our
    stomachs."
"I'm certain," said Hunger, "what sickness ails you.
You've munched down too much: that's what makes you
    groan,
But I assure you," said Hunger, "if you'd preserve your
    health,
You must not drink any day before you've dined on
    something.   260
Never eat, I urge you, ere Hunger comes upon you
And sends you some of his sauce to add savor to the food;
And keep some till suppertime, and don't sit too long;
Arise up ere Appetite has eaten his fill.
Let not Sir Surfeit sit at your table;   265
Love him not for he's a lecher whose delight is his tongue,
And for all sorts of seasoned stuff his stomach yearns.
And if you adopt this diet, I dare bet my arms
That Physic for his food will sell his furred hood
And his Calabrian[3] cloak with its clasps of gold,   270
And be content, by my troth, to retire from medicine
And learn to labor on the land lest livelihood fail him,
There are fewer physicians than frauds—reform them,
    Lord!—
Their drinks make men die before destiny ordains."
"By Saint Parnel,"[4] said Piers, "these are profitable words.   275
This is a lovely lesson; the Lord reward you for it!
Take your way when you will—may things be well with
    you always!"
    "My oath to God!" said Hunger, "I will not go away
Till I've dined this day and drunk as well."
"I've no penny," said Piers, "to purchase pullets,   280
And I can't get goose or pork; but I've got two green
    cheeses,
A few curds and cream and a cake of oatmeal,
A loaf of beans and bran baked for my children.
And yet I say, by my soul, I have no salt bacon
Nor any hen's egg, by Christ, to make ham and eggs,   285
But scallions aren't scarce, nor parsley, and I've scores of
    cabbages,

---

3. Of gray fur (a special imported squirrel fur).
4. Who St. Pernelle was is obscure; the A and B manuscripts and editions other than Kane-
Donaldson read, "By Saint Paul."

And also a cow and a calf, and a cart-mare
To draw dung to the field while the dry weather lasts.
By this livelihood I must live till Lammass[5] time
When I hope to have harvest in my garden.   290
Then I can manage a meal that will make you happy."
All the poor people fetched peasepods;[6]
Beans and baked apples they brought in their skirts,
Chives and chervils and ripe cherries aplenty,
And offered Piers this present to please Hunger with.   295
Hunger ate this in haste and asked for more.
Then poor folk for fear fed Hunger fast,
Proffering leeks and peas, thinking to appease him.
And now harvest drew near and new grain came to market.[7]
Then poor people were pleased and plied Hunger with the
        best;   300
With good ale as Glutton taught they got him to sleep.
Then Waster wouldn't work but wandered about,
And no beggar would eat bread that had beans in it,
But the best bread or the next best, or baked from pure
        wheat,
Nor drink any half-penny ale[8] in any circumstances,   305
But of the best and the brownest that barmaids sell.
Laborers that have no land to live on but their hands
Deign not to dine today on last night's cabbage.
No penny-ale can please them, nor any piece of bacon,
But it must be fresh flesh or else fried fish,   310
And that *chaud* or *plus chaud*[9] so it won't chill their bellies.
Unless he's hired at high wages he will otherwise complain;
That he was born to be a workman he'll blame the time.
Against Cato's* counsel he commences to murmur:
Remember to bear your burden of poverty patiently.[1]   315
He grows angry at God and grumbles against Reason,
And then curses the king and all the council after
Because they legislate laws that punish laboring men.[2]

---

5. The harvest festival, August 1 (the name derived from Old English *hlaf*, "loaf"), when a loaf made from the first wheat of the season was offered at Mass.
6. Peas in the pod. These, like most foods in the next lines, are early crops.
7. Presumably as the new harvest approaches, merchants who have been holding grain for the highest prices release it for sale, since prices are about to tumble.
8. Ale even weaker than Rose the retailer's watery pennyale; in line 309, laborers are too fussy and will no longer accept even penny-ale.
9. "Hot" or "very hot."
1. From Cato's *Distichs*, a collection of pithy phrases used to teach Latin to beginning students.
2. Like so many governments, later-fourteenth-century England responded to inflation and the bargaining power of the relatively scarce laborers with wage and price freezes, which had their usual lack of effect. One way landowners, desperate to obtain enough laborers, tried to get around the wage-laws was by offering food as well as cash.

But while Hunger was their master there would none of
    them complain
Or strive against the statute,[3] so sternly he looked.   320
But I warn you workmen, earn wages while you may,
For Hunger is hurrying hitherward fast.
With waters he'll awaken Waster's chastisement;
Before five years are fulfilled such famine shall arise.
Through flood and foul weather fruits shall fail,   325
And so Saturn[4] says and has sent to warn you:
When you see the moon amiss and two monks' heads,
And a maid have the mastery, and multiply by eight,[5]
Then shall Death withdraw and Dearth be justice,
And Daw the diker[6] die for hunger,   330
Unless God of his goodness grants us a truce.

Passus VII

   Truth heard tell of this and sent word to Piers
To take his team and till the earth,
And procured him a pardon *a poena et a culpa*,[1]
For him and for his heirs for evermore after;
And bade him hold at home and plow his land,   5
And any one who helped him plow or sow,
Or any kind of craft that could help Piers,
Pardon with Piers Plowman Truth has granted.
Kings and knights that keep Holy Kirk* safe
And in the realm rightfully rule the people   10
Have pardon to pass through purgatory quickly,
With patriarchs and prophets to be fellows in paradise.
Those who've been blessed as bishops, if they embody what
    they should,

3. I.e., anti-inflationary legislation.
4. Planet thought to influence the weather, generally perceived as hostile.
5. This cryptic prophecy, like the one at III.323–27, has never been satisfactorily explained; the basic point is that it is Apocalyptic.
6. A laborer who digs dikes and ditches.
1. This pardon has remained one of the most controversial elements of the poem. "From punishment and from guilt" is a formula indicating an absolute pardon. Strictly speaking, remissions obtained by pilgrimages (and pardons dispensed by pardoners in return for donations) could remit only the *punishment* for sin; note that even Truth's pardon does both only for some people (not, for example, for merchants, lines 18–19 below). Christ alone, through the Atonement, had the power to absolve repentant sinners from the *guilt* and delegated it to St. Peter and to the Church through the apostolic succession (lines 15–17 below) to be dispensed in the sacrament of confession and in penance. (This pardon also covers, according to another legal formula in the next line, Piers's heirs, which ordinary pardons could not.) The belief, however, that indulgences (especially those obtained from the Pope himself) absolved guilt as well as punishment was widespread.

And are expert in either law,[2] to preach each to the ignorant
And inasmuch as they may amend all sinners,   15
Are peers with the Apostles—thus Piers's pardon reads—
And on the Day of Doom* at their dais they will sit.
Merchants in the margin[3] had many years' grace
But the Pope would grant them no pardon *a poena et a culpa*,
Because they don't hold their holy days as Holy Church
        teaches,   20
And because they swear by their souls and "so may God
        help!" them
Against good conscience to get their goods sold.
But under his secret seal[4] Truth sent them a letter
And bade them buy boldly whatever best pleased them
And sell it again and save such profit as they made,   25
And have hospitals built with it to help the unfortunate,
Or apply it to repairing roads that are in poor condition,
Or to build bridges that have broken down,
Or marry off maidens or make them nuns,[5]
Poor people bedridden and prisoners in stocks,   30
Provide them with their food for our heavenly Lord's love,
Send scholars to school or set them to a craft,
Relieve religious orders and give them larger incomes.
"And I shall myself send you my angel Saint Michael
So that when you die no devil shall do you harm or scare
        you.   35
And if you will work thus, I'll ward off wanhope* from you
And send your souls in safety to my saints in joy."
Then merchants were merry; many wept for joy
And praised Piers the Plowman that procured them this
        bull.[6]
    Men of law had least pardon—believe nothing else!—   40
For the Psalter* grants no salvation to such as take gifts,
And especially from innocent people who purpose no evil.
        Thou shalt not take rewards against the innocent.[7]
Advocates should undertake to help them with their pleas.

---

2. Canon and civil law.
3. I.e., as a further clause added to the margin of an original document.
4. Personal, not public, seal authorizing a document, e.g., the stamp of a signet ring.
5. I.e., provide dowries without which a woman whose family cannot provide for her can neither marry nor enter a convent.
6. There was much debate about whether merchants exercised a legitimate function in society, since they did not create anything, but made money from redistributing the work of others. In the following lines, Langland takes the position that their trade has intrinsic moral hazards, but defends the function itself. "Bull" (Gloss).
7. Ps. 14.5.

Princes and prelates should pay for their labor:
> *From kings and princes will be their reward.*[8]

But many a justice and juror would for John do more   45
Than *pro Dei pietate*[9] plead at the bar.
But he that spends his speech speaking for the poor man
Who is innocent and has need and is harming no one,
He that comforts him in that case, covets no gifts from him,
But for our Lord's love expounds law for him,   50
No devil at his death-day shall do him any harm
So that he will not be surely safe; the Psalter bears witness,
> *Lord, who shall dwell in thy tabernacle?*[1]

But to buy water or wind or wit* or fire the fourth,
These four the Father of Heaven formed for this earth in
> common;

These are Truth's treasures to help true folk,   55
Which will never wax or wane without God's word.
When he draws near to death and would have indulgences,
His pardon is most paltry at his parting hence
That accepts from poor people any pay for his pleading.
You lawyers and legal experts, if I lie blame Matthew.   60
> *Whatsoever ye would that men should do to you, do ye to*
> *them.*[2]

  All living laborers that live by their hands
That truly take and truly earn
And live in love and in law, for their low hearts
Had the same absolution that was sent to Piers.
Of beggars and street-beadsmen[3] the bull makes no mention   65
Unless there's a real reason that renders them beggars.
For whoever asks for alms, unless he has need,
Is as false as the Fiend and defrauds the needy,
And also beguiles the giver against his will.
For if he were aware he was not needy he would give his
> alms   70

To another that was more needy; thus the neediest should
> have help.

Cato* counsels me thus, as does the Clerk of the *Historia*.[4]
Cui des videto[5] is Cato's teaching.

---

8. Source unknown, but cf. Ecclus. 38.2.
9. "For love of God." "John" (line 45): a representative commoner; "justice and juror" will "do more" for him: presumably because he will pay (unlike the "poor man" in line 47).
1. Ps. 14.1.
2. Matt. 7.12.
3. Paid prayer-sayers.
4. *Historia Scholastica* (Scholastic History) of Peter Comestor, an account of major events in the Bible.
5. "See to whom you give."

And in the *Historia* he tells how to bestow your alms:

Let your alms remain in your hand until you are sure to whom you
      are giving.   75

But Gregory was a good man and bade us give to every
    one

That asks us for his love that gives us everything.

    Do not choose whom you pity lest by chance you pass over
        him who deserves to receive, since it is uncertain for
        whose sake you will please God more.[6]

For you never know who is worthy, but God knows who
    has need.

The treachery is in him that takes, if betrayal is involved.

For giving presents is repayment that brings the giver peace
    of mind;   80

But the beggar is a borrower who brings more debt on
    himself.

For beggars are borrowers whose bond is God almighty

To pay their debts to their donors, and in addition interest.

    Wherefore then gavest thou not my money into the bank, that
        at my coming I might have required it with usury?[7]

Therefore beg not, you beggars, unless it be for need;

For whoever has wherewith to buy bread, the Book bears
    witness,   85

He has enough who has bread enough, though he has
    nothing more.

    He is rich enough who does not lack bread.[8]

(It's a comforting custom to read accounts of saints.)[9]

The Book curses all beggars and blames them in this way:

I have been young and now have become old; and I have not seen the
    righteous forsaken nor his seed begging bread.[1]

For they live in no love and think no law binds them;   90

They wed no women with whom they deal

But like wild beasts with "weehee!" mount and go to work,

And bring forth a brood that bear the name of bastard;

Or they break a child's back, or a bone, in his youth,

And go forth as fakers with their brats for evermore after.   95

There are more misshapen people among these beggars

Than among all other manner of men that move upon this
    earth.

---

6. Not from Pope Gregory the Great* but from St. Jerome's* Commentary on Eccl. 11.6.
7. Luke 19.23.
8. From St. Jerome's Epistles.
9. Presumably because they show how God provides for those whose trust in him is complete.
1. Ps. 36.25.

Thus they that lead their lives so may loathe the time
That they were ever made men when they must go hence.
But men old and hoary that are helpless of strength,   100
And women with child for whom work is impossible,
Blind and bedridden and broken-limbed people
Who take their misery meekly, leper-men and others,
Have as plenary pardon[2] as the plowman himself;
For love of their low hearts our Lord has granted them   105
Their penance and their purgatory in full plenty on earth.
    "Piers," said a priest then, "your pardon must I read,
For I'll explain each paragraph to you and put it in English."
And Piers unfolds the pardon at the priest's prayer,
And I behind them both beheld all the bull.*   110
In two lines it lay, and not a letter more,
And was worded this way in witness of truth:
They that have done good shall go into life everlasting;
And they that have done evil into everlasting fire.[3]
"Peter!" said the priest then, "I can find no pardon here—   115
Only 'Do well, and have well,' and God will have your soul,
And 'Do evil, and have evil,' and hope nothing else
But that after your death-day the Devil will have your soul."
And Piers for pure wrath pulled it in two
And said, "*Though I walk in the midst of the shadow of death*   120
I will fear no evil; for thou art with me.[4]
I shall cease my sowing and not work so hard,
Nor be henceforth so busy about my livelihood.
My plow shall be of penance and of prayers hereafter,
And I'll weep when I should work, though wheat bread fails
         me.   125
The prophet[5] ate his portion in penance and sorrow
As the Psalter says, and so did many others.
Who loves God loyally, his livelihood comes easy.
    My tears have been my bread day and night.[6]
And unless Luke lies, he finds another lesson for us
In birds that are not busy about their belly-joy: 130
'*Ne soliciti sitis,*'[7] he says in the Gospel,
And shows us examples by which to school ourselves.
The fowls in the firmament, who feeds them in winter?
When the frost freezes they forage for food,

---

2. As complete a pardon (i.e., *a poena et a culpa*) as Piers.
3. From the Athanasian Creed, based on Matt. 25.31–46.
4. Ps. 22.4.
5. David, whose Psalm is quoted below.
6. Ps. 41.4.
7. "Take no thought [for your life]": Matt. 6.25; also Luke 12.22.

They have no granary to go to, but God feeds them all."   135
"What!" said the priest to Perkin, "Peter, it would seem
You are lettered a little. Who lessoned you in books?"
"Abstinence the abbess taught me my a b c,
And Conscience* came after and counseled me better."
"If you were a priest, Piers," said he, "you might preach
    when you pleased   140
As a doctor of divinity, with *Dixit insipiens*[8] as your text."
"Unlearned lout!" said Piers, "you know little of the Bible;
Solomon's sayings are seldom your reading."

    Cast out the scorners and contentions with them, lest they
       increase.[9]

The priest and Perkin opposed each other,
And through their words I awoke and looked everywhere
    about,   145
And saw the sun sit due south at that time,
Meatless and moneyless on Malvern Hills.
Musing on my dream, I walked a mile-way.
Many a time my dream has made me study
What I saw sleeping, if it might so be,   150
And for love of Piers the Plowman most pensive in heart,
And what a pardon Piers had for the people's comfort,
And how the priest impugned it with two proper words.
But I've no delight in dream-lore, for it lets us down often.
Cato* and canon-lawyers counsel us to cease   155
Assigning certainty to dream-lore, for "*Somnia ne cures.*"[1]
But because the Bible book bears witness
How Daniel divined the dreams of a king—
Nebuchadnezzar,[2] as these clerks name him—
Daniel said, "Sir King, your dream signifies   160
That strange soldiers shall come to seize your kingdom:
Among lower lords your land will be divided."
As Daniel divined, in deed it happened after:
The King lost his lordship and lesser men had it.
Moreover, Joseph dreamed marvelously how the moon and
    the sun   165
And the eleven stars all hailed him.
Then Jacob judged Joseph's dream:
"*Beau fils,*"[3] said his father, "for famine we shall—

8. "The fool hath said [in his heart, There is no God]": Ps. 13.1.
9. Prov. 22.10.
1. "Pay no attention to dreams."
2. Daniel interpreted dreams for Nebuchadnezzar in Dan. 2 and 4 and for his son Belshazzar
in Dan. 5; the poet seems to be conflating the two (or three) incidents.
3. "Fair son."

I myself and my sons—seek you for need."
It befell as his father said in Pharaoh's time　　　170
That Joseph was justice with jurisdiction over Egypt;
It befell as his father said, his friends sought him there.[4]

　All this makes me muse on dreams
And how the priest proved no pardon to Do-Well,
And deemed that Do-Well by-passes indulgences,[5]　　175
Biennial Masses and triennial Masses and bishops' letters.[6]—
Do-Well at the Day of Doom* is deferentially received:
He passes by all the pardon of Saint Peter's church!
Now does the Pope possess power to grant such a pardon
That people may pass without penance to joy?　　　180
This is a leaf of our belief, as lettered men teach us.

> *Whatsoever thou shalt bind on earth shall be bound in*
> *Heaven, etc.*[7]

And so I believe loyally—Lord forbid otherwise!—
That pardon and penance and prayers will save
Souls that have sinned seven times deadly.
But to trust to these triennials, truly, I think　　　185
Is not so certain for the soul, surely, as is Do-Well.
Therefore I admonish you men that have money on earth
And trust through your treasure to have triennials,
Be you never the bolder to break the Ten Commandments,
And mainly you masters, mayors and judges,　　　190
That have the wealth of this world—and are thought to be
　　　wise men—
To purchase pardon and the Pope's bulls,
At the dreadful doom* when dead men shall arise
And all come before Christ and account to him,
How you led your life here and kept the letter of the law,　195
What you did day by day the doom will record.
A poke full of pardon there, nor Provincial's letters,[8]
Though you're found in the fraternity among the four
　　　orders[9]

---

4. Joseph's dream occurs in Gen. 37.9–10, but the interpretation the poet attributes to Jacob is based on subsequent events, not on Jacob's reaction at the time.
5. Formal remissions of the temporal or purgatorial punishment for sin (not the *guilt*—see VII.3, note), issued by pardoners or earned by pilgrimage or certain acts of worship.
6. Letters authorizing pardoners to preach indulgences (like the pardoner in Pro.72–82). "Biennial" and "triennial" Masses were said for the soul of a deceased person for two, or for three, years after the death of the beneficiary.
7. Matt. 16.19.
8. Letters from the Provincial, or head of a province (i.e., of a regional group of houses of a religious order), which appointed a lay person a "confrater," or honorary brother, of the order within that region, and conferred the privileges of the order on him or her or, sometimes, on whole families. "Poke": a small bag or sack, especially those carried by poor travelers, pilgrims, or beggars.
9. In Langland's day there were four orders of friars in England: Franciscans, Dominicans, Carmelites, and Augustinians.

And have indulgences doublefold, unless Do-Well helps you,
I count your patents and your pardon not worth a pie's
    heel.[1]   200
Therefore I counsel all Christians to cry to God for mercy,
And to Mary his mother to be our mean between,
That God give us grace before we go hence
To work such works while we are here
That after our death-day Do-Well will report   205
At the Day of Doom we did what he bade.

Passus VIII

Thus robed in russet[1] I roamed about
A whole summer season searching for Do-Well,
And I asked very frequently of folk that I met
If any one knew where Do-Well made his home,
And many a man I asked what man he might be.   5
There was never any one as I went that was able to tell me
Where that fellow could be found, not the first inkling,
Till it befell on a Friday I fell in with two friars,
Masters* of the Minorites,[2] men of great intelligence.
I hailed them as handsomely as I had been taught   10
And prayed them, *pour charité*,[3] before they parted from me,
If they knew any neighborhood, near or far,
"Where Do-Well dwells, do please tell me.
For you walk most widely of worldly men,
And know countries and courts and many kinds of places,   15
Both princes' palaces and poor men's cottages,
And Do-Well and Do-Evil, where they dwell both."
"Mary!" said the masters, "he dwells among us,
And always has, as I hope, and always will hereafter."
"*Contra!*"[4] said I like a clerk and commenced to argue.   20
    "*Seven times a day falleth the just man*.[5]
Seven times, says the Book, sins the righteous;
And if someone sins, I say, it seems certain to me

---

1. The crust left at the broad end of the slice when the rest has been eaten. "Patents": papal licenses or indulgences.
1. Coarse woolen cloth, commonly reddish, worn by workers and by those, such as hermits, adopting an ascetic life; this fits with the clothes the Dreamer puts on in the Prologue "as I'd become a sheep" (or a shepherd).
2. The Friars Minor or Franciscans.
3. "For charity."
4. "On the contrary": a technical term of objection in scholarly argument.
5. Prov. 24.16.

That Do-Well and Do-Evil cannot dwell together.
Ergo[6] he is not always at home among you friars.
He's occupied at times elsewhere, educating the people."   25
    "I shall show you, my son," said the friar then,
"How the steadiest man sins seven times a day.
By an example," said the friar, "I shall show you clearly.
Let a man be brought in a boat amid a broad expanse of
        water:
The wind and the water and the wobbling of the boat   30
Will make the man many a time fall and stand.
For though he stands ever so stiffly, he stumbles from the
        motion,
And yet he is safe and sound, and so it behooves him be,
For if he doesn't arise right away and reach for the helm,
The wind and the water will overwhelm the boat.   35
Then the man's life would be lost through his laziness alone.
Just so it fares," said the friar, "with folk here on earth.
The water that wanes and waxes is likened to the world;
The goods of this ground are like the great waves,
For like water in the wind they welter about.   40
The boat is likened to the body that is brittle by nature,
So that through the Fiend and the flesh and the false world
The steadfast man sins seven times a day.
But he does not do deadly sin for Do-Well helps him,
That is charity the champion, chief help against sin.   45
For he strengthens you to stand and steers your soul
So that though your body turns about like a boat in the
        water,
Your soul is always safe unless you yourself will
Follow your flesh's will and the Fiend's as well,
And do deadly sin and drown yourself.   50
God will gladly suffer your sloth if you yourself wish it,
For he gave you a New Year's gift with which to guide
        yourself,
Wit* and free will, to every wight[7] a portion,
To flying fowls, to fishes, and to beasts,
But man has most of it and is most to blame,   55
Unless he works well with it as Do-Well teaches."
    "I have no natural knowledge,"* said I, "to understand
        your words,
But if I may live and go on looking, I shall learn better."

6. "Therefore": technical term of resolution in scholarly argument.
7. Creature.

"I commend you to Christ," said he, "who was crucified on
    Cross."
And I said, "The same save you from misfortune   60
And give you grace on this ground to become good men."
    Thus I fared far and wide trying to find Do-Well,
And as I went by a wood, walking alone,
The merry melody of birds made me abide,
And on a lea under a linden I lay down a while   65
To learn the lays the lovely fowls made.
Mirth of their mouths made me go to sleep.
The most marvelous dream came to me then
That ever any hero had in danger, I think.
A large man who looked to me much like myself   70
Came and called me by my christened name.
"Who are you," I asked then, "who know my name?"
"That you know well enough," said he, "and no one better."
"Do I know who you are?" I asked. "Thought," said he then.
"I've pursued you seven years; haven't you seen me before?"   75
"Are you Thought?" said I then. "I think you could tell me
Where Do-Well dwells and direct me to him."
    "Do-Well," said he, "and Do-Better and Do-Best the third
Are three fair virtues and are not far to find.
Whoever is meek of his mouth, mild of his speech,   80
True of his tongue and of his two hands,
And through his labor or his land earns his livelihood,
Trustworthy of his tail-end, takes only what is his,[8]
And is not drunken or disdainful, Do-Well is with him.
Do-Better does the same, but he does much more.   85
He's lowly as a lamb, lovely of speech;
While he has anything of his own he helps where there's
    need.
The bags and the strongboxes, he's broken them all,
That the Earl Avarice had, or his heirs,
And with Mammon's[9] money he has made himself friends,   90
And has taken residence in religious houses and has
    rendered the Bible,
And preaches to the people Saint Paul's words:
Ye suffer fools gladly, seeing ye yourselves are wise.[1]
'You wise ones, allow the unwise to live with you
And with glad will do them good, for so God commands.'   95

---

8. This line is based on an untranslatable pun: *tailende/tail-ende*. The first means "talleying,
keeping accounts"; the second, "tail-end," is a sexual allusion.
9. In the New Testament, riches, often personified as the demon of greed (a basic passage is
Luke 16.1–13).
1. 2 Cor. 11.19.

Do-Best is above both and bears a bishop's crozier
That has a hook at one end to hold men in good lives.
A spike is on that staff to shove down the wicked
That lie in wait devising villainy with which to vex Do-Well.
And as Do-Well and Do-Better decided between them,   100
They have crowned one to be king and keep watch over
      them all,
That if Do-Well and Do-Better did anything against Do-Best,
And were disobedient to his bidding and bold to do evil,
Then the king should come and cast them in prison,
Put them there in penance without pity or grace,   105
Unless Do-Best recommends mercy, to remain there forever.
Thus Do-Well and Do-Better and Do-Best the third
Crowned one to be king: their counsel would guide him.
And he should rule the realm by direction of them all,
And not in any other way but as those three agreed."   110
   I thanked Thought then that he thus taught me.
"But still I've no savor in your sayings, so help me God:
More natural knowledge I need to learn,
How Do-Well, Do-Better, and Do-Best do among the
      people."
"Unless Wit* can tell you this," said Thought, "where those
      three live,   115
Otherwise no one knows that is now alive."
Thought and I thus three days we walked
Debating about Do-Well day after day.
But before we were aware we met with Wit.
He was long and lean, like no one else;   120
There was no pride in his apparel nor poorness either;
Of a soft speech and sober of appearance.
I dared mention no matter that would make him wrangle,
But I bade Thought then to be an intermediary between us,
And to put forth some proposition that would prove his wits, 125
How Do-Well differed from Do-Better and Do-Best from
      them both.
Then at that time Thought said these words:
"Where Do-Well and Do-Better and Do-Best live in the
      country,
Here is Will who'd wish to learn if Wit knew how to teach
      him;
And whether he is man or no man this man would
      discover,   130
And work as they three would wish; this is his intention."

Passus IX

"Sir Do-Well dwells," said Wit, "not a day from here,
In a castle that Kind made of four kinds of things.[1]
It is made of earth and of air all mingled together,
With wind and with water woven cleverly together.
Kind has enclosed therein, cunningly enough,   5
A lady he loves who's like himself:
Anima[2] is her name: there lusts after her
A haughty horseman of France, *princeps huius mundi*,[3]
Who would win her away with wiles if he could.
Kind, knowing this, keeps most careful watch over her,   10
And has domiciled her with Sir Do-Well, duke of these
        borders;
Do-Better is her damsel, Sir Do-Well's daughter,
And serves this lady loyally both late and early.
Do-Best is above both, a bishop's peer:
What he bids must be done; he emboldens them all;   15
What Dame Anima does is at Do-Best's instruction.
But the constable[4] of the castle, who keeps guard over them
        all
Is a wise knight withal; Sir Inwit[5] is his name.
He has five fair sons by his first wife:
Sir See-Well, and Say-Well, and Hear-Well the courteous,   20
Sir Work-Well-With-Your-Hands, a man of wondrous
        strength,
And Sir Godfrey Go-Well, great lords all.
To these six is assigned the safety of Lady Anima
Till Kind come or send for her to keep her himself."

    "What kind of thing is Kind?" said I. "Can you tell me?"   25
"Kind," said he, "is creator of all kinds of beasts,
Father and former, the first of all things,
And that is the great God that had beginning never,
Lord of life and of light, of relief and of pain.
Angels and all things are at his command,   30
But man is most like him in mien and in shape.
For beasts came into being by the breath of his word,

---

1. The four basic elements — earth, air, fire, and water — out of which the creation is made. "Kind" (Gloss).
2. The soul (Gloss). The line above is untranslatably ambiguous and could also mean "A lady he loves as much as himself."
3. "The prince of this world" (a title for the Devil).
4. The governor or warden of a royal castle.
5. Basically, "mind, understanding, rational power," but often "moral awareness, conscience" as well (Gloss).

And they all as he willed had life at his speech,
>   *He spoke and they were created,*[6]
Except man that he made in the image of himself
And Eve of Adam's rib-bone without any intermediary.   35
For he was singular himself and said '*Faciamus*,'[7]
As if to say, 'There must be more for this than my word
>   alone.
My might* must help along with my speech.'
Just as a lord would write a letter, but if he lacked paper,
Though he could write ever so readably and had a pen
>   ready to hand,   40
The letter, for all his literacy, I believe would not be written.
And so it seems to have been with him when he said in the
>   Bible,
Let us make man in our image.
He must both work with his word and show his wit as well.
And in this manner man was made through the might of
>   God almighty,   45
With his word and with his workmanship, and with life to
>   last.
And thus God gave him a soul from the Godhead of Heaven,
And of his great grace granted him bliss,
Life that shall last forever, and all his lineage as well.
That is the castle that Kind made: *Caro*[8] is its name,   50
Which is to mean as much as man with a soul.
Both with work and with word he created him;
Through the might of the majesty man was made.
Inwit* and all wits* are enclosed therein,
For love of that lady Anima, as life is called.   55
She walks and wanders everywhere in man's body,
But in his heart is her home and her chief place of rest;
But Inwit is in the head, and he looks to the heart:
Whether Anima is lief[9] or loath, he leads her at his will;
For after the grace of God the greatest is Inwit.   60
>   Much woe has that man who misuses his inwit,
And such are gluttons, guzzlers—their god is their belly.
>   *Whose God is their belly.*[1]
Since they serve Satan he shall have their souls;
Those who live sinful lives here, their souls are like the
>   Devil;

---

6. Ps. 148.5.
7. "Let us make [man in our image]": Gen. 1.26; the whole sentence appears in line 43.
8. Literally, "Flesh"; by extension, a human being.
9. Willing, glad.
1. Phil. 3.19.

And all who lead good lives here are like God almighty.   65
    He that dwelleth in love dwelleth in God, etc.[2]
Alas, that drink shall destroy what God dearly paid for,
And cause him to cast off those he created in his likeness.
    Verily I say unto you, I know you not; And elsewhere,
        And I gave them up unto their own lusts.[3]
Infants and idiots in whom inwit is lacking,[4]
Holy Church is obligated to help and save them
And provide them with what they fail in — and fatherless
    children,   70
And widows that have nothing wherewith to win their food,
Mad men and maidens that would be helpless:
All these lack inwit and must have direction.
Of this matter I might make a long story,
And find sufficient texts among the four doctors;[5]   75
And that this lesson is no lie, Luke bears witness.[6]
Godfathers and godmothers who see their godchildren
In misfortune and in mischance and yet might assist them
Shall get penance in purgatory unless they provide help.
For more belongs to the little child before he learns the law   80
Than being named with a name,[7] and he never the wiser.
No Christian creature would cry at the gate
Or be deprived of bread and pottage if prelates did as they
    should.
A Jew would not see a Jew go chattering for need
For all the goods on this ground if he might give him help.   85
Alas, that any Christian creature should be unkind to his
    fellow
Since Jews that we judge Judas' fellows,
Each of them helps the other with whatever he needs.
Why are we Christians not as kind with Christ's goods?
That Jews should show us good examples is a shame to us
    all!   90
It will cost the commons* dear for their unkindness,* I fear;
Bishops shall be blamed for beggars' sakes.

---

2. 1 John 4.16.
3. Matt. 25.12; Ps. 80.13.
4. Wit moves on from drunks who have voluntarily destroyed their *inwit* to other groups who lack rational understanding through no fault of their own and must be provided for. Here *inwit* cannot mean "conscience" (Gloss).
5. St. Ambrose* (340?-397), St. Augustine* (354-430), St. Jerome* (340?-420), and St. Gregory the Great* (540?-604) were considered the four major early theologians and commentators of the Western Church (Gloss).
6. There is nothing pertinent in Luke; Langland may have had in mind Acts 6.1 or Jas. 1.27.
7. I.e., christened.

He is judged with Judas that gives a jester silver
And bids the beggar be off for his bedraggled clothing.
>   *A traitor with Judas is the prelate who fails to distribute*
>   *Christ's patrimony; And elsewhere, He is a pernicious*
>   *steward who wastes the things of Christ's poor.*[8]
He does not well that does this, nor dreads God almighty,   95
Nor loves the sayings of Solomon in his Sapience-Book.
>   *The fear of the Lord is the beginning of wisdom.*[9]
Who dreads God, he does well; who dreads him for love
And dreads him not for dread of vengeance does thereby
>   better.
He does best who desists, day and night,
From squandering any speech or any space of time.   100
>   *Who offends in one point is guilty of all.*[1]
And Truth knows what's true: time that is wasted
On earth is most hated by those who are in Heaven,
And then the squandering of speech, which is the sprout of
>   grace,
And God's music-maker, and a merriment of Heaven.
The faithful father would never wish that his fiddle were
>   untuned!   105
Nor his gleeman[2] a gadabout, a goer to taverns.
All sincere and steady men who desire to work,
Our Lord loves them and allows, great or small,
Grace to go with them and let them gain their livelihood.
>   *They that seek the Lord shall not want any good thing.*[3]
Do-Well in this world is wedded people who live truly,   110
For they must toil to take their bread and to sustain the
>   world.
For those who are called confessors come of their kind,
Kings and kaisers,[4] clerks and knights;
Maidens and martyrs from one man have their being.
The woman was made meet[5] to help the man work.   115
And thus marriage was made with an intermediate person's
>   help[6]
First by the father's will and the friends' counsel,
And then by their own assent as they two might agree.

---

8. Religious maxims of conjectural origin.
9. Ps. 110.10; Ecclus. 1.16.
1. Jas. 2.10.
2. Minstrel (*glee*: music, melody).
3. Ps. 33.11.
4. Emperors (from Latin *Caesar*). "Confessor": one who heroically makes an avowal of faith.
5. Suitable, fitting. "One man": i.e., Adam.
6. I.e., arranging a marriage must start with negotiations between intermediaries, relatives and friends if not an actual go-between; the consent of the parties themselves (line 118) is the last step, rather than the first. "Thus" here means "in the following manner."

And in this way wedlock was wrought, and it was God who
    made it.
Its Heaven is on earth, as he himself bore witness.[7]   120
But false folk, faithless, thieves and liars,
Wasters and worthless men, out of wedlock, I think,
Are conceived in cursed time, as Cain was on Eve
After Adam and she had eaten the apple.[8]
Of such sinful scoundrels the Psalter makes mention.   125
    He hath conceived sorrow and brought forth injustice.[9]
And all that came from that Cain came to evil ends.
    For God sent to Seth[1] and said by an angel,
'I will that you wed your issue with your issue,
And that your kin with Cain's be not coupled nor married.'
Yet Seth against the stricture of our Savior in Heaven   130
Coupled his kin with the kin of Cain,
Till God grew angry with their behavior and uttered this
    sentence:
'That I made man it now makes me sorry.'
    I repent that I made man.[2]
And he came to Noah anon and bade him not delay:
'Quickly go build a boat of boards and planks.   135
Yourself and your three sons and also your wives,
Set yourselves up in that ship and stay inside it
Till forty days have been fulfilled and the flood has washed
Clean away the cursed blood that Cain has made.
Beasts that now breathe shall upbraid the time   140
That ever cursed Cain came upon earth.
All shall die for his deeds on downs and hills,
And the fowls that fly forth along with other beasts,
Save for a single couple of every sort that there is
That in the shingled ship shall be saved.'   145
Here the grandchild was made guilty for the grandfather's
    sins,
And all for his forefather fared the worse.

---

7. Behind this line lie God's creation of Eve (Gen. 2.18–25) and Christ's first miracle, changing water into wine, at the wedding at Cana (John 2.1–11). It is more specifically based, however, on the wedding Mass, which states both that God "hallowed wedlock by a great sacrament, thereby foreshadowing, in the marriage bond, Christ's union with the Church," and that God "endowed this primal fellowship of [Adam and Eve] with the one and only blessing not forfeited either in the punishment of the first sin or under sentence of the flood."
8. Medieval legend, such as that reflected in an apocryphal *Life of Adam and Eve* (source unclear), held that Cain was conceived during a time of penitence and fasting; sexual intercourse was just as definitely forbidden at such times as it was outside of marriage.
9. Ps. 7.15.
1. God's command to Seth, Adam's third son, is not in Genesis, but appears in Peter Comestor's *Historia*, an account of major events in the Bible. Biblical commentators, however, interpreted the forbidden marriages in Gen. 6 between "the sons of God" and "the daughters of men" as between Seth's kin and Cain's.
2. Gen. 6.7. The lines following refer to Gen. 6–7.

The Gospel is against this in some degree, I find:

The son shall not bear the iniquity of the father, neither shall the
father bear the iniquity of the son.[3]

But I find if the father is false and a scoundrel,   150
That to some degree the son shall have his sire's faults.
Graft applewood on an alder and if your apple is sweet
It would seem to me most marvelous, and more so if a
        scoundrel
Should bring forth any brat who does not behave the same
And smack of his sire — you seldom see otherwise.   155

Men never gather grapes of thorns nor figs of thistles.[4]

And thus through cursed Cain care came upon earth,
And all for marriages they made against the commands of
        God.
    Therefore those have misfortune in marriages that thus
        marry off their children.
For some as I see now, to speak the truth,
In hope of making money marry unnaturally.   160
Care-ridden conception comes of such marriages,
As befell the folk that I before spoke of.
For good folk should wed good folk though goods they have
        none.
'I am *via et veritas*,'[5] says Christ, 'I can advance you all.'
It is an uncomely couple, by Christ, I think,   165
When a young wench is wedded to a worn-out gaffer,
Or any widow wedded for the wealth she possesses,
Who will never bear a baby unless it be in her arms.
In jealousy, joyless, and in jangling abed
Many a pair since the pestilence have pledged their vows.   170
The fruit that they bring forth are foul words;
They have no children but chafing and exchanges of blows.
Though they dare go to Dunmow, unless the Devil helps
        them,
To vie for the flitch, they'll never fetch it home;
Unless they both lie under oath they'll lose that bacon.[6]   175
Therefore I counsel all Christians not to crave to be married
For a fat fortune or family connections.
But virgins and virgins should make vows with one another,
And widowers and widows should wed in the same way.

3. Not the Gospel but Ezek. 18.20.
4. Matt. 7.16.
5. "The way and the truth": John 14.6.
6. The Dunmow flitch (a cured side of bacon) was awarded to the couple who after a year
of marriage could claim no quarrels, no regrets, and the desire, if freed from their vows, to
remarry one another.

For no lands but for love look to it that you marry,   180
And then you'll get the grace of God and goods enough to
      live with.
And every manner of secular man that cannot remain
      continent
Wisely go wed and ward off sin,
For fantasies of the flesh are the Fiend's lures.
While you're young and yeasty and your weapon yet keen,   185
Work it out in wiving if you would be excused.
> *While you've strength galore,   don't waste it on a whore.*
> *For o'er the door is writ this lore: 'A whore is death's*
>   *door.'*[7]
When you've wedded, be wary and work in season,
Not as Adam and Eve when Cain was engendered.
For truly in unfitting time between men and women
There should be no bed-games; unless they're both clean   190
Of life and of love and of law as well,
The deed done in the dark should be done by no one.
But if they lead their lives thus, it delights God almighty,
For he first devised marriage and referred to it himself:
> *It is good for every man to have his own wife on account of*
>   *fornication.*[8]
Those conceived outside wedlock are considered worthless,   195
False folk, foundlings, fakers and liars
Without grace to gain property or get people's love,
Wander like wolves, wasting what they may;
Against Do-Well they do evil and give the Devil pleasure,
And after their death-day will go dwell with him,   200
Unless God gives them grace to amend themselves here.
    Do-Well, my dear sir, is to do as law teaches,
To behave lovingly and humbly and harm no person;
But to love and to lend aid, believe me, that's Do-Better;
To protect and provide for people young and old,   205
To heal them and to help them, is Do-Best of all.
Then is Do-Well to dread, and Do-Better to suffer,
And so Do-Best comes about and brings down Obstinate,
And that is wicked will who spoils work constantly
And drives away Do-Well with deadly sins."   210

---

7. The Latin couplet is traditional. Cf. Prov. 29.3, 7.27.
8. 1 Cor. 7.2.

Passus X

Then Wit had a wife—her name was Dame Study—
Who was lowly of look and lean of her body.
She was very vexed that Wit informed me thus,
And scowling Dame Study sternly said:
"Well, aren't you wise, Wit," she said, "to speak any wisdom   5
To flatterers or fools that are frenzied in their wits?"
And upbraided him and blamed him and bade him be still,
And to stop speaking to sots such wise words,
And said, "*Nolite mittere*, man, margery-pearls[1]
Among hogs that have husks at their will.   10
All they do is dirty them; they'd rather have swill
Than all the precious pearls that Paradise grows.
I say it of such," she said, "that show by their actions
That they'd liefer have[2] land and lordship on earth,
Or riches, or revenue, or rest when they please,   15
Than all the true saws Solomon spoke in his life.
Wisdom and wit now are not worth a rush
Unless they're carded with covetousness as cloth-makers
          card wool.[3]
Whoever can construct frauds and conspire in wrongs
And direct a loveday* to disable the truth,   20
Whoever's capable of such craft is called to council;
They influence lords with lies and make liars of the facts.
Job the gentle* generalizes in his story
That wicked men wield the wealth of this world,
And that those who live outside the law are lords of every
          land.   25
          *Wherefore do the wicked live? Wherefore are all they happy
          that deal very treacherously?*[4]
The Psalter* says the same of such as do evil.
          *Behold these are the sinners who prosper in the world; they
          increase in riches.*[5]
'See,' says Holy Scripture, 'what sorts of lords these
          scoundrels are!'
Those whom God gives most to, the least they give in turn,

---

1. "Cast not [pearls before swine]": Matt. 7.6. *Margery* (Latin *margarita*) means "pearl"; Langland's
repetition suggests "fine pearls."
2. Prefer.
3. Wool is carded before spinning with a comb-like tool that gets out debris and separates and
orders the fibers; similarly, wit and wisdom are valued only if they have been sorted out and
neatened up by greed to serve the user's purpose. "Rush": a straw, a trifle.
4. Job 21.7; Jer. 12.1.
5. Ps. 72.12.

And the most unkind to the community are those with most
    money.
> *What thou hast made they have destroyed; but the just man,
>   etc.*[6]

Ribalds for their ribaldry may relish their gifts,   30
And jesters and jugglers and jabberers of tales,
But he who has Holy Writ always in his mouth,
And can tell of Tobit[7] and of the twelve Apostles,
Or preach of the pain that Pilate caused
To Jesu the gentle whom the Jews stretched   35
Upon a Cross on Calvary, as clerks teach us,[8]
Little is he loved or listened to that teaches such a lesson,
Or caressed or comforted, I call God to witness.
But those who feign to be fools and get a fraudulent living
Against the law of our Lord, and lie about themselves,   40
Spit and spew and speak foul words,
Drink and drivel and draw men's guffaws,
Caricature people and calumniate those who don't care to
    tip them,
They know no more minstrelsy nor music to gladden men
Than Mund the miller knows of *Multa fecit Deus.*[9]   45
If lewdness didn't lend its aid, the Lord have my troth,
Would never king nor knight nor canon of Saint Paul's[1]
Give them a New Year's gift of a groat's* value.
But minstrelsy and mirth among men nowadays
Are filthiness, flatteries, and foolish tales;   50
Gluttony and great oaths—these are games nowadays,
But if they discourse of Christ, these clerks and laymen,
At meals in their mirth when minstrels are still,
Then they tell of the Trinity how two slew the third,[2]
And bring a threadbare argument to bear, take Bernard* to
    witness,   55
And proffer an assumed probability as a proof of the truth.

---

6. Ps. 10.4.
7. The Book of Tobias, included in the Catholic Bible but regarded as apocryphal by Protestants.
8. Langland here seems to take for granted the anti-Semitic portrayal of Jews, especially in accounts of the Crucifixion, which became increasingly virulent in the late Middle Ages; elsewhere, as in IX.84ff., he includes passages that speak positively of Jews.
9. "God hath done many things": Ps. 39.6.
1. The cathedral of the city of London. "Canon": one of a group of privileged (and well-paid) priests attached to a cathedral and constituting its ruling body under a dean.
2. Academic disputes of the day, pursued by educated laity as well as by clerics, played with the possibilities on opposing sides of problems arising from the biblical text, as an integral part of serious theological training. Here, however, the possibility that the Crucifixion is the murder of one member of the Trinity by the other two is being made a blasphemous after-dinner joke, which some scribes were shocked enough to edit out of their copies of *Piers Plowman*.

Thus they drivel on the dais[3] a definition of Godhead,
And set their teeth in God's gorge when their guts are full.
But the care-worn may cry and clamor at the gate,
Famished and faint with thirst, and freezing for cold;   60
There is no one to ask him in nor offer help for his harm,
But they curse him like a cur and bid him clear out.
Little does he love that Lord who lends him all that bliss
That parcels out to the poor such a portion in his need.
If there weren't more mercy in low men than among the rich   65
Mendicants might go meatless to bed.
God is much in the gullet of these great masters,*
But among lowly men are his mercy and his works.
And so the Psalter says: seek it in *Memento*.[4]
 Lo, we heard of it at Ephratah; we found it[5] *in the fields*
  of the wood.
Clerks and clever men converse glibly of God   70
And have him much in their mouths—but lowly men in
 heart.
 Friars and frauds have devised such questions
To please proud men with since the pestilence time;
And they preach at Saint Paul's[6] in pure envy of the clergy
So that folk are not firm in their faith nor free with their
 goods,   75
Nor are sorry for their sins, so has pride increased
In religious orders and in all the realm, among rich and
 poor,
That prayers have no power to prevent these pestilences.
For God is deaf nowadays and does not deign to hear us,
So that for our guilts he grinds girls and boys to death.   80
And yet worldly wretches will not beware from watching
 others,
Nor for dread of the Death withdraw their pride,
Nor give plentifully to the poor as pure charity asks,
But in gluttony and gay living guzzle down their wealth,
And break no bread for the beggar as the Book teaches.   85
 Deal thy bread to the hungry, etc.[7]

3. The important people were seated at the head table on a raised dais at the end of the hall in which meals were served. As the fourteenth century began to place more importance on privacy (and on fireplaces), meals were less often served in this communal manner, as Langland complains in lines 97–102.
4. "Remember": Ps. 131.1.
5. I.e., a place for the Lord (Ps. 131.6).
6. Many important sermons were preached out-of-doors to large crowds; the Cross outside St. Paul's Cathedral was a major preaching place in London. Langland suggests that friars compete with ordinary clerical preaching by popularizing intellectual paradoxes—"such questions" (line 72)—like those he criticizes above.
7. Isa. 58.7.

And the more he wins and wields worldly riches
And lords it over his landsmen, the less good he gives.
Tobit teaches not so: take heed, you rich,
How the Bible-Book bears witness of him:

> *If thou hast abundance, give thine alms accordingly; if thou*
> *hast but a little, take care even so to bestow that*
> *willingly.*[8]

Whoever has received much should bestow much, so says
    Tobit,   90
And whoever's been allotted little, limit himself accordingly,
For we've no document that defines the duration of our life.
Such lessons lords should love to hear,
And how they might most liberally look after the largest
    household,
And not fare like a fiddler or friar seeking feasts,   95
At home in other men's houses and hating his own.
Unhappy is the hall, every day in the week,
Where the lord and the lady have no liking to sit.
Now has each rich man a rule to eat by himself
In a private parlor to avoid poor men,   100
Or in a chamber with a chimney-corner, and leave the chief
    hall empty
That was made for men to eat their meals in.
And all to spare and to save what some one else will spend.
   I have heard high-born men, eating at the table,
Discourse like clerks on Christ and his powers,   105
And impute faults to the Father that formed us all,
And carp against clergy with crabbed words:
'Why would our Savior suffer such a worm in his bliss
That fooled the female and her fellow after,
Through which work and will they went to hell,   110
And all their seed for that sin suffered the same death?
Here your learning lies,' these lords start to argue,
'If what you clerks claim is true of Christ in the Gospel:
The son shall not bear the iniquity of the father, etc.[9]
Why should we who live now for the works of Adam   115
Go to rot and ruin? Reason forbids it!'

> *Every man shall bear his own burden, etc.*[1]

Such matters they mouth, these masters,[2] in their boasting,

---

8. Tob. 4.9.
9. Ezek. 18.20: repeats IX.149.
1. Gal. 6.5.
2. The term "master" is ironic here; Langland means the lay lords who are pretending to authority in matters of divinity.

And make men believe amiss who muse on their words.
Imaginative hereafter[3] shall answer to your purpose.
Such arguers Augustine* answers with this text: 120
Know no more than is necessary.[4]
Never wish to learn why it was God's will
To suffer Satan to deceive his seed,
But believe loyally in the lore of Holy Church,
And pray him for penance and pardon in your lifetime,   125
And that for the muchness of his mercy he may amend us
         here.
For any one who wants to learn the whys of God almighty,
I wish his eye were in his arse, and his heel as well —
Whoever again wants to know why it was God's wish
To suffer Satan to deceive his seed   130
Or Judas the Jew to prepare Jesus' betrayal.
All was as he willed — Lord, worship be unto you! —
And all will be as you wish whatever we say.
And whoever tries these tactics to trick men's minds
How Do-Well differs from Do-Better, now deafness come
         upon him,   135
Since he's eager to understand who they all are.
Unless he lives in the lowest degree that belongs to Do-Well,
I'll boldly put up a bond for him that he'll Do-Better never,
Though day after day Do-Best aim at him."
      And when Wit was aware what his wife was saying,   140
He became so confused he couldn't speak,
And as dumb as a doornail drew to the side.
And for no words I knew, nor for kneeling to the ground,
I might garner no grain of his great wits,
But all grinning he grimaced and glanced at Study   145
As a sign that I should beseech her of grace.
And when I was aware what he wanted I knelt to his wife
And said, "Mercy, madam, your man shall I be
As long as I live, both late and early,
And work your will while my life lasts,   150
If you consent to counsel me how I may comprehend
         Do-Well naturally."*
      "For your meekness, man," said she, "and for your mild
         speech,
I shall acquaint you with my cousin — Clergy* is his name.
He has wedded a wife within these six weeks

3. Imaginative is the principal character in *Passus* XII; he first appears at XI.410.
4. No exact source in Augustine is known, but see Rom. 12.3.

Who is sib to the seven arts; she is called Scripture.[5]   155
These two, as I hope, after my request
Will direct you to Do-Well, I dare well warrant it."
   Then was I as blithe as a bird on bright morning,
Merrier than a minstrel whom men have given gold,
And asked her the highway to where Clergy dwelt.   160
"And tell me how to introduce myself, for it's time I went."
   "Ask for the highway," said she, "from here to Suffer-
Both-Welfare-And-Woe, if you wish to learn;
And ride on past Riches—don't rest there,
For if you keep company with him, you'll never come to
           Clergy.   165
And also the long pastureland, Lechery by name,
Leave it on your left hand a long mile or more
Till you come to a castle, Keep-Well-Your-Tongue-
From-Lies-And-Loose-Speech-And-Delicious-Drinks.
Then you shall see Sobriety and Sincerity-Of-Speech,   170
So that every one will be willing to share his wits with you.
Then you will come to Clergy who knows many kinds of
           things.
Repeat this password: I put him in school;
And that you bring best wishes for his wife—I wrote the
           Bible for her,
And set her studying *Sapientia*[6] and the Psalter* gloss.   175
She learned logic from me, and all the law after,
And with all the measures in music I made her acquainted.
Plato the Poet,[7] I put him first to reading;
Aristotle and many others too I taught how to argue.
Grammar books for brats I first brought into being,   180
And beat them with a broom, anybody who wouldn't learn.
For all kinds of crafts I contrived tools,
For carpenters and carvers; I first counseled masons

---

5. "Clergy": book-learning in general and, as here, theological knowledge in particular; the term also means "clerics," the class of persons who (traditionally at least) had such knowledge. Theology was the culminating science in medieval university training and was based on the interpretation of scripture. Knowledge of scripture, in turn, as Study explains in more detail below, presupposed the "seven arts" that formed the basic curriculum in medieval education and that are therefore Scripture's siblings. They consist of the trivium, comprising grammar, rhetoric, and logic, which teach language and rational discourse, and the quadrivium, comprising arithmetic, geometry, astronomy, and music. Why Clergy has been married only six weeks (or, according to many manuscripts, six months) has not been explained.
6. "[The Book of] Wisdom": in the Vulgate Bible, thought to have been written by Solomon, along with the other books of Wisdom literature (Prov., Eccl., Ecclus.). Portions of these books, together with the Psalms and Cato's *Distichs*, formed the elementary core for studying Latin grammar.
7. I.e., the writer (though Plato did actually write poetry as well as philosophical dialogues). Plato (437?–337 B.C.) and Aristotle (384–322 B.C.) are the major Greek philosophers whose work underlies subsequent Western thought.

And taught them level and line, though my sight's a little
　　　dim.
　　But Theology has troubled me ten score times.   185
The more I muse on it, the mistier it seems,
And the deeper I divined, the darker I thought it;
It's surely no science to argue subtly in;
If it weren't for the love that lies in it, it would be a lame
　　　study.
But since it allows so much to Love, I love it the better,   190
For wherever Love is leader, there's no lack of grace.
Be sure to love loyally if you'd like to Do-Well,
For Do-Better and Do-Best are drawn from Love's school.
In other sciences it says (I saw it in Cato*):
If some one dissembles in words and is not a good friend at heart,   195
You do the same: thus art's deceived by art.[8]
'If some one glozes[9] as the guileful do, give him back the
　　　same;
And thus you'll fool folk who are faithless and false.'
This is Cato's counsel to clerks he teaches.
But Theology does not teach this, if you take heed;   200
He counsels us the contrary, against Cato's words,
And bids us be like brothers and bless our enemies,
And love those that lie about us, and lend them help at
　　　need,
And do good against evil; God himself commands it.
　　　While we have time, let us do good unto all men, especially
　　　　　unto them who are of the household of faith.[1]
Paul[2] who loved perfectness preached the people   205
To do good for God's love and give to men who asked,
And especially to such as subscribe to our Creed.
And our Lord teaches us to love all that lie about us or
　　　slander us,
And not to grieve them that grieve us: God forbids that.
　　　Vengeance is mine and I will repay.[3]
Therefore look to it that you love as long as you last,   210
For no science under sun is so salutary for the soul.
　　But astrology is a hard subject, not easy to understand;
Geometry and geomancy[4] are full of juggling terms;

---

8. From Cato's *Distichs*.
9. Interprets.
1. Gal. 6.10.
2. I.e., St. Paul.
3. Rom. 12.19; cf. Deut. 32.35.
4. Divination by means of lines and figures, such as those derived from random patterns in
dirt or in dots on a page.

Whoever thinks to work with those three thrives full late,
For sorcery is the sovereign book those sciences deal with.   215
Yet there is claptrap bound in covers composed by many
    men,
Experiments of alchemy of Albert's devising,
Nigromancy and perimancy[5] to make the Devil appear.
If you're disposed to Do-Well, never deal with these.
All these sciences I myself established and developed,   220
And was their first founder, that they might fool people.
Tell these tokens to Clergy, and to Scripture as well,
That they will answer to your asking how inwardly to know
    Do-Well."
  I said, "Many thanks, madam," and meekly saluted her,
And went quickly on my way without further delay,   225
And before I came to Clergy I could never stop.
I greeted the good man as the good wife taught me,
And afterwards his wife — I was respectful to both,
And told her the tokens that had been taught to me.
Never man that moved on this earth, since God made
    Heaven,   230
Was made more warmly welcome or more wonderfully at
    ease
Than I myself surely, as soon as he knew
That I was of Wit's house and with his wife Dame Study.
Courteously Clergy kissed and embraced me,
And asked how Wit was and his wife Study.   235
I told them truly that I'd been sent to them
To learn of Do-Well and Do-Better and Do-Best too.
  "It's a common[6] life," declared Clergy, "to believe in Holy
    Church
With all the articles of faith that ought to be known.
And that is to believe loyally, both learned and layman,   240
In the great God that had no beginning ever,
And in the soothfast[7] Son that saved mankind
From the deadly death and the Devil's power
Through the help of the Holy Ghost, who is of both;
Three perfect persons, but not in plural number,   245
For all are but one God and each is God himself:
    God the Father, God the Son, and God the Holy Ghost.[8]

5. "Nigromancy" (i.e., necromancy) and "perimancy" (i.e., pyromancy) in the next line are
forms of magic based on contacts with the dead and on patterns in fire, respectively. Albert the
Great (1193?–1280): a major scholastic philosopher and teacher of St. Thomas (1225?–1274):
his major work in the sciences gave him the reputation of being a magician.
6. In common, communal, i.e., not peculiar to particular individuals.
7. Truthful, honest; true or real.
8. From the Athanasian Creed.

God the Father, God the Son, God Holy Ghost of both,
Maker of man and his mate and of animals too.
Augustine* the old hereof made books,
And he himself established this to make us sure in our faith. 250
Who was his authority? All the four Evangelists,
And Christ called himself so, the Scripture bears witness.

> *I am in the Father, and the Father in me, and he that seeth*
> *me seeth also my Father.*[9]

All the clerks under Christ could not explain this,
But so it belongs to the belief of unlettered men that wish
         to do well,
For no clerk ever had wit acute enough to discuss faith's
         reasons,   255
And man would have no merit if it might be proved.

> *Faith has no merit where human reason supplies the proof.*[1]

   So Do-Better is to suffer for your soul's health
All that the Book bids by Holy Church's teaching.
And that is, man, according to your might, for mercy's sake,
See to it that you put into practice what's proclaimed by
         your word;   260
Such as you seem to sight, be found in assay,

> *Seem what you are and be what you seem.*[2]

And let nobody be beguiled by your behavior,
But be such in your soul as you seem outside.
Then is Do-Best to be bold in blaming the guilty,
Since you see yourself to be clean in soul;   265
But never blame anybody if you are blameworthy;

> *If you wish to blame,   see that you're free of shame;*
> *Your teaching fails   when your own sin prevails.*[3]

God in the Gospel grimly reproves
All who find fault with others and have faults themselves.

> *Why beholdest thou the mote that is in thy brother's eye, but*
> *considerest not the beam that is in thine own eye?*[4]

'What makes you mad about a mote in your brother's eye
When your own bears a beam that is blinding you—   270

> *First cast the beam out of thine own eye—*

And stopping you from seeing things small or large?'

---

9. John 14.9–11.
1. The Latin pronouncement is St. Gregory's.*
2. Saying quoted by such well-known biblical commentators of the Middle Ages as Thomas Aquinas.
3. Source unknown. Literally this line, which the editors have translated, reads, "Your teaching is foul when your sin gnaws at you."
4. Matt. 7.3; the quotation three lines below is verse 5. "Mote": a speck. "Beam": a large piece of wood.

I advise every blind booby to better himself,
Such as parsons or parish priests that should preach and
        teach
And amend all manner of men as much as they can.
This text was told you so that before teaching you'd make
        sure   275
You were such as you said when you offer salve to others.
Yet God's word would not be wasted, for it works always.
Though it meant nothing to the community, it might avail
        yourselves.
But surely it seems now to the sight of the world
That God's word is not working on wise men or on ignorant 280
Except in such a manner as Matthew mentions in the
        Gospel.
        If the blind lead the blind both shall fall into the ditch.[5]
Unlettered people may apply this parable to you: the beam
        lies in your eyes,
And for your misbehavior the mote has made blind
All kinds of human creatures because of cursed priests.
    The Bible bears witness that everybody in Israel   285
Paid a bitter price for two bad priests' guilts,
Hophni and Phinehas; for their covetousness
Mishap befell *Archa Dei*,[6] and Ely broke his neck.
Therefore you correctors, clutch this hard and correct
        yourselves first,
And then you may say sturdily, as David's Psalter puts it, 290
*Thou thoughtest unjustly that I would be such an one as thyself, but
        I will reprove thee and set them in order before thy face.*[7]
Then shall bare-witted clerks be abashed to blame or vex
        you,
And to carp as they carp now, and call you dumb hounds:
        Dogs not able to bark.[8]
And be afraid to anger you with any word that hinders
        your works,
And move more promptly at your prayer than for a pound
        of nobles,*   295
And all for your holiness; hold this in heart.
Among righteous religious orders this rule should be kept.
Gregory the great clerk* and the good Pope
Rehearses in his *Moralia*[9] the rule of religious orders

---

5. Matt. 15.14.
6. "The Ark of God": 1 Sam. 4.11, 18.
7. Ps. 49.21.
8. Isa. 56.10.
9. One of his best-known works, a commentary on Job pointing moral applications.

And says this as an example that they should act on: 300
'When fishes leave the salt flood or the fresh water,
They die for drought, lying on the dry ground;
Right so religious, they rot and die
When they crave to escape life in cloister and convent.'
For if Heaven be on this earth and ease to any soul,   305
It is in cloister or in school, on many counts I find.
For in cloister no man comes to quarrel or to fight,
But there all is obedience and books, to read and to learn.
There is scorn in school if a clerk will not learn,
And great love and liking, for each bows low to the other. 310
But now Religion* is a rider, a runner through the streets,
A leader of lovedays* and a land-buyer,
One who pricks his palfrey from market place to manor,
A heap of hounds at his arse as if he were a lord,
And unless his body-servant bend his knee when he brings
      him the cup,   315
He glowers at him and grumbles, Where did he get his
      manners?
Lords were of little wisdom to take land from their heirs
For religious who have no ruth though it rain on their altars.
In many places where they are parsons, if they have peace
      and comfort,
They have no pity on the poor, and that's their plenary
      charter.[1]   320
And they behave like lords, their lands stretch so far.
  But there shall come a king and confess you religious,
And beat you as the Bible tells, for breaking your rule,
And amend members of your orders, monks, nuns, and
      canons,
And put them to their penance, *Ad pristinum statum ire*;[2] 325
And barons with earls shall beat them with *Beatus vir's*
      teaching;

---

1. A deed conferring absolute ownership. Clergy here attacks monks who become absentee
parish priests when lay lords leave landed property to monastic orders. The donation often
included the parish church with its income from tithes, which was supposed to be used to
discharge parish responsibilities. Under such circumstances the order could get away with
pocketing the money, letting the church building go to ruin, providing inadequately for the
religious duties, and ignoring its responsibility for the poor of the parish.
2. "To go [back] to their original state": i.e., the state of the primitive church before it owned
wealth and property. There was controversy in Langland's time over proposals to reform the
Church by having the secular government take over its property and supply only the funds
needed for services actually carried out. After the Reformation, this passage was read as a
prophecy of Henry VIII, who dissolved the monasteries, confiscated their property, and made
himself head of a reformed church. (Such Reformation readers found confirmation in the
reference in line 331 to the "Abbot of Abingdon," head of a particularly wealthy and ancient
abbey that was to be among those dispossessed.) *Beatus vir*: "Blessed [is] the man" (Ps. 1.1).

Confiscate what their children[3] claim and condemn you
     foully.
> *Some trust themselves to chariots and some to horses, etc.*[4]

And then friars in their refectory shall find a key
To Constantine's coffers that contain the money
That Gregory's godchildren have ungodly dispended.[5]   330
And then the Abbot of Abingdon and all his issue forever
Shall have a cut from a king, and incurable the wound.
That this shall turn out true, test it, you frequent readers
     of the Bible:

> *How hath the oppressor ceased! the tribute ceased! The Lord*
>   *hath broken the staff of the wicked and the sceptre of*
>   *the rulers who cut with an incurable wound.*[6]

And before that king comes Cain shall awake,
But Do-Well shall dash him down and destroy his might."   335
   "Then is Do-Well and Do-Better," said I, "*dominus*[7] and
     knighthood?"
   "I'll not be scornful," said Scripture; "unless legal sticklers
     lie,
Can neither kinghood nor knighthood, as far as I can see,
Help at all toward Heaven when one's hour comes,
Nor riches, nor revenue, nor royal lord's estate.   340
Paul proves it impossible, rich men in Heaven;[8]
Solomon also says that silver is the worst thing to love.
> *There is not a more wicked thing than to love money.*[9]

And Cato counsels us not to covet it except as need teaches.
> *Love the penny but be sparing of love for its beauty.*[1]

And patriarchs and prophets and poets too
Wrote works to warn us not to wish for riches   345
And praised poverty with patience; the Apostle bears witness[2]
That the poor have heritage in Heaven, and by true right,
While rich men may not claim right, but only mercy and
     grace."
   "*Contra!*"* I cried, "by Christ, that I can refute!

---

3. The heirs who were passed over in order that monasteries might be endowed.

4. Ps. 19.8–9; the verses continue, "but we shall call upon the name of the Lord our God. They have been bound and have fallen, but we have risen."

5. "Constantine": the Emperor who allegedly gave the Pope temporal rulership and lands when he made Christianity the official religion of the Roman Empire. "Gregory's godchildren": monks, so called because Gregory the Great* was a monk before being drafted to the papacy. Presumably Clergy means that if friars, too, had a fixed income for their services they would not be dependent on begging and no longer need to compete with the parish clergy.

6. Isa. 14.4–6.

7. Lord[ship].

8. No such passage has been identified.

9. Ecclus. 10.10.

1. From Cato's *Distichs*.

2. There is no consensus on what passages Langland had in mind here or in line 350 below.

And prove it by the Epistle that bears Peter's name: 350
Whoever is baptized will be saved, be he rich or poor."
    "That is *in extremis*,"[3] said Scripture. "Saracens and Jews
May be saved so, and so we believe;
Non-Christians may in that case christen a heathen,
And for his loyal belief, when his life is lost,   355
He may have heritage in Heaven like a high Christian.
But Christians cannot without something more come to
        Heaven,
Because Christ died for Christian men and confirmed the law
That whoever wishes and wills to arise with Christ
        If ye be risen with Christ, etc.[4]
He should love and lend help and fulfill the law's commands.   360
That is, love your Lord God as dearest love of all,
And then all Christian creatures, in common each man
        other;
And thus it behooves him to love that hopes to be saved.
And unless we do this in deed before the Day of Doom,*
The silver that we save will beset us most sourly,   365
And our overcoats that are moth-eaten, while we behold
        beggars go naked,
Or delight in wine and wild fowl when we're aware of one
        in need.
For all Christian creatures should be kind to each other,
And then help heathen in hope of amending them.
God orders both high and low that no one hurt another,   370
And says, 'Slay none that is similar to my own likeness
Unless I send you some token,' and says, '*Non moechaberis*,'[5]
That is, slay not but suffer, for so is the best,
For *vengeance is mine and I will repay.*[6]
'I shall punish in purgatory or in the pit of hell   375
Each man for his misdeeds unless mercy prevents it.' "
    "This is a long lesson," said I, "and I'm little the wiser;
Where Do-Well is or Do-Better you disclose darkly.
Many tales you tell that are taught by Theology,
And that I was made man and my name entered   380
In the ledger of life long before I was,
Or else unwritten for doing wrong as Holy Writ witnesses.
        *No man hath ascended up to Heaven but he that came down
            from Heaven.*[7]

---

3. "At the point of death."
4. Col. 3.1.
5. "Thou shalt not commit adultery," which Langland renders "slay not" in the next line, thus conflating the fifth and sixth commandments: Exod. 20.13–14, Luke 18.20.
6. Rom. 12.19; cf. Deut. 32.35.
7. John 3.13.

I believe this well, by our Lord, and no letter better.
For Solomon the sage that wrote *Sapientia*,[8]
God gave him grace of wit and all goods as well   385
To rule the realm and make rich his people;
He judged well and wisely as Holy Writ tells;
Aristotle* and he, who taught men better?
Masters that teach men and preach God's mercy to them
Instruct us with their sayings as for the sagest in their time, 390
And all Holy Church holds them both in hell![9]
And if I should work by their words to win myself Heaven,
Who for their works and wit are now walled up in hell,
Then I'd be working unwisely, whatever you preach.
But of many wise men, in truth, little marvel I have   395
That their spirits have no power by which to please God.
For many men on this earth more set their hearts
On goods than in God; therefore grace fails them —
At the moment of greatest misery mercy would be best,
When they must leave life, a lump of God's grace —   400
As it was with Solomon and such others as showed great
        intelligence,
But their works, as Holy Writ witnesses, were always the
        contrary.
Therefore wise-witted men and well-learned clerks
As they say themselves seldom act accordingly
        In Moses' seat, etc.[1]
    But I think it is with a number now as it was in Noah's
        time   405
When he built that boat of boards and planks:
No carpenter who came to work on it was saved, nor any
        kind of workman,
But birds and beasts and the blessed Noah,
And his wife and his sons and also their wives;
None of the carpenters who constructed it came to be saved; 410
God forbid it fare thus with the folk who teach the faith
Of Holy Church, our harborage, and God's house to save
And shield us from shame as Noah's ship did beasts —
And that the men who made it amid the sea drowned.

8. "[The Book of] Wisdom." The "masters" of line 389 are non-Christian sages, like Solomon
and Aristotle,* born before the coming of Christ.
9. The fate of the "Righteous Heathen," a category that includes righteous pagans and biblical
figures who lived before Christ, was a recurrent concern in the Middle Ages, to which Langland
returns throughout the Life of Do-Well.
1. Matt. 23.2: the verse continues, "have sat the Scribes and the Pharisees." The next verse
in Matthew observes the discrepancy between the high-minded words of such men and their
self-serving actions.

The *culorum*[2] of this clause refers to ecclesiastics   415
Who are carpenters to build Holy Kirk* for Christ's own
    beasts:
    O Lord, thou preservest men and beasts, etc.[3]
At Doomsday will come a deluge of death and fire together;
Therefore I counsel you clerks, carpenters of Holy Church,
Work the way you've seen it written, lest you not be one
    who's in it.

    On Good Friday, I find, a felon was saved   420
That had lived all his life with lies and theft,
And because he confessed on the Cross and shrove himself
    to Christ
He was sooner saved than Saint John the Baptist
Or Adam or Isaiah or any of the prophets
That had lain with Lucifer many long years.   425
A robber was ransomed rather than them all
Without punishment in purgatory to perpetual bliss.[4]
Than Mary Magdalene who might do worse?[5]
Or who did worse than David who devised Uriah's death,
Or Paul the Apostle who pitilessly   430
Killed all kinds of Christian people?[6]
But now such are sovereigns with saints in Heaven,
Those who worked most wickedly when they were on earth,
And those who spoke their minds most wisely and wrote
    many books
Of wit and wisdom dwell with damned souls.   435
What Solomon says I think is true and certain of us all:
    There are righteous and wise men and their works are in the
        hand of God.[7]
'There are witty and well-living but their works are hidden
In the hands of almighty God' and he knows the truth

2. "Conclusion": from *saeculorum*, which, in the phrase "*in saecula saeculorum*," "for ever and ever,"
concludes many prayers.
3. Ps. 35.7.
4. Luke 23.39–43. St. John the Baptist is listed with the Old Testament figures because, though
he baptized Christ (Matt. 3), he was killed by Herod before Christ saved mankind (Matt.
14.1–12), and, as Christ said (Matt. 11.11–15), though he is the greatest of human beings yet
born, still "the least in the kingdom of Heaven is greater than he."
5. Seven devils (traditionally interpreted as the Seven Deadly Sins) were cast out of Mary
Magdalene (Luke 8.2); she was assumed by medieval readers to be the same person as the "sinner"
Jesus was rebuked for allowing to anoint his feet (Luke 7.37–50) and as the sister of Lazarus
and of Martha, whom Jesus praised because she chose "the better part" of sitting at his feet
(Luke 10.38–42). She was regarded as the archetypal corrupt but repentant woman, who came
to represent the contemplative life.
6. King David, when he desired Bathsheba, orchestrated things so that her husband Uriah
was killed in battle (2 Sam. 11). Before his conversion to Christianity, St. Paul was a zealous
persecutor of Christians, especially the first martyr, Stephen (Acts 7.57–59).
7. Eccl. 9.1.

Whether a man will be let in there[8] for love and for his
    loyal deeds,
Or else for his evil will and envy of heart   440
And let in[9] because he lived so: for by the wicked men
    learn the good;
And whereby would men know what white is if everything
    were black,
And what a good man was like unless there were some
    scoundrels?
Therefore let's live along with evil men; I believe few are
    good,
For 'when necessity comes near, there's nothing to do but
    suffer.'[1]   445
And may he that amends everything have mercy on us all.
For the most certain thing God ever said was when he said
    Nemo bonus.[2]
    And yet further I've forgotten from five wits'[3] teaching
That Clergy[4] was ever commended by Christ's words,
For he said to Saint Peter and such as he loved,   450
    When you shall stand before rulers and kings take no
        thought.[5]
'Though you come before kings and clerks of the law,
Be not afraid of that folk, for I shall lend you tongue,
Cunning and clergy to confound them all.'
David makes mention he spoke among kings
And no king could overcome him in cunning of speech.[6]   455
But neither wit nor wisdom ever won a victory
When man was in misfortune without the more grace.
The doughtiest doctor and diviner of the Trinity
Was Augustine the old,* and highest of the four;[7]
He said this in a sermon — I saw it written once —   460
'Behold the ignorant themselves seize Heaven while we wise men are
    sunk in hell.'[8]
And this is to mean to Englishmen, the mighty and the
    small,
Are none more readily ravished from the right belief

---

8. I.e., into Heaven.
9. I.e., let in elsewhere, to hell. "Or else": i.e., or, alternatively.
1. This saying, which Langland gives in a mixture of Latin and French, is proverbial.
2. "No one [is] good [save one, that is, God]": Luke 18.19.
3. The five senses: sight, hearing, touch, taste, and smell.
4. Here the meaning "learning" is clearly dominant over "clerics," though not divorced from
it (Gloss).
5. Mark 13.9, 11.
6. Ps. 118.46.
7. The four doctors: St. Ambrose,* St. Augustine,* St. Jerome,* and St. Gregory the Great.*
8. Not from a sermon by Augustine, but from his *Confessions*, VIII, 8.

Than are these clever clerks that quote many books,
Or none sooner saved or surer in their faith   465
Than plowmen and pasture-men and poor common laborers,
Shoemakers and shepherds: such ignorant dolts
Pierce with a Paternoster* the palace of Heaven,
And pass through purgatory penanceless at their parting
    hence
Into the perfect bliss of Paradise for their pure faith   470
Who led imperfect lives here and had little knowledge.
Aye, men recall clerks who have cursed the time
That they ever cared to construe more in a book than *Credo
    in Deum Patrem*[9]
And especially their Paternoster; many a parson has wished
    it.
I see examples myself, and so may many others,   475
That servants who serve lords seldom fall in arrears,
But those who keep the lord's accounts, such as clerks and
    reeves.*
Just so unlettered laborers and of little knowing
Seldom fall so foully and so far into sin
As clerks of Holy Kirk that keep Christ's treasure,   480
Which is man's-soul-to-save, as God says in the Gospel.
    Go ye into my vineyard."[1]

Passus XI

Then Scripture scorned me and spoke her mind,
And belittled me in Latin, and made light of me,
And said, "*Many men know many things and don't know
    themselves.*"[1]
Then I wept at her words, for woe and for anger,
And grew drowsy and dozed off into a deep sleep.[2]   5
    A most marvelous dream came to me then
That I was fetched away forcibly — Fortune seized me
And into the land of longing and love she brought me,
And made me look into a mirror called Middle Earth.
Afterwards she said to me, "In this you might see wonders,   10
And recognize what you really want and reach it, perhaps."

9. "I believe in God, the Father [Almighty]": the beginning of the Apostles' Creed.
1. Matt. 20.4; the line invokes Jesus' parable of the laborers in the vineyard, in which the laborers
hired late in the day are paid the same as those hired early.
1. The opening of a popular meditation on penance and forgiveness.
2. Here begins a dream within a dream, which runs to XI.405.

Then Fortune had following her two fair damsels;
Concupiscentia-Carnis[3] men called the elder maid,
And Covetousness-of-Eyes the other was called.
Pride-of-Perfect-Living pursued them both   15
And said that for appearance's sake I should pay small heed
    to Clergy.*
Concupiscentia-Carnis clasped me about the neck
And said, "You are young and yeasty and have years
    enough ahead
To live a long life and make love to ladies,
And in this mirror you might see mirths by the score   20
That will lead you to delight all your lifetime."
The second said the same: "I shall serve your pleasure;
Till you're a lord and have land I'll not leave you ever,
But will follow in your fellowship if Fortune pleases."
"He shall find me his friend," said Fortune then;   25
"The fellow that followed my will never failed to have bliss."
Then was there one called Old Age that was unhappy of
    countenance:
"Man," said he, "if I meet you, by Mary of Heaven,
You'll find Fortune failing you at your greatest need,
And *Concupiscentia-Carnis* will clean forsake you;   30
Your curses will be bitter, both day and night,
For Covetousness-of-Eyes, that ever you knew her;
And Pride-of-Perfect-Living will put you in great danger."
    "Yes? Don't take him seriously," said Recklessness,
        standing forth in ragged clothes.
"Follow whatever Fortune wills; you've far to go till Age.   35
It's time enough for a man to stoop when he starts going
    bald.
'*Man proposes*,' said a poet then, and Plato was his name,
'And *the Deity disposes*,'[4] said he; let God do his will.
If Truth will witness it's well done to follow Fortune,
Concupiscentia-Carnis and Covetousness-of-Eyes   40
Will not grieve you greatly nor, unless you wish, beguile
    you."
"Yes, farewell, Phip,"[5] said Childishness, and drew me forth
    with him
Till *Concupiscentia-Carnis* accorded to all my deeds.
"Oh, alas!" said Old Age and Holiness both,

3. "Lust of the Flesh": 1 John 2.16 warns against "the lust of the flesh and the lust of the eyes, and the pride of life, . . . [which are] not of the Father, but . . . of the world."
4. Proverbial, ultimately deriving from Prov. 16.9. "Plato": Plato wrote poetry as well as philosophical dialogues.
5. A childish form of Philip; perhaps also, as it was later, a name for a sparrow.

"That wit will turn to wretchedness so Will may have his
        pleasure!"   45
Covetousness-of-Eyes comforted me straightway
And followed me forty winters and a fifth more,
So that I didn't give a damn for Do-Well and Do-Better.
I had no liking, believe me, to learn the least thing about
        them.
Covetousness-of-Eyes came more often in my mind   50
Than Do-Well or Do-Better did among all my doings.
Covetousness-of-Eyes comforted me often.
"Have no scruple," she said, "how you succeed to wealth.
Go find some friar to confess to, and fill him with your sins.
For while Fortune is your friend, friars will love you,   55
And embrace you in their brotherhood and ask a boon for
        you
From their Prior Provincial to get a pardon for you,
And they'll pray for you pate by pate if you're *pecuniosus*."[6]
        Pecunial punishment does not suffice for spiritual sins.[7]
     So sweet were this wench's words I did what she said
Till my young days were done and I'd drifted into age.   60
And then Fortune was my foe for all her fair promises,
And poverty pursued me and put me low.
And then I found the friar afraid and fickle, too,
Contrary to our first compact, because I said I wouldn't
Be buried at their house but at my parish church.[8]   65
For I had heard once how Conscience said it:
A man's body should be rightly buried at the church he
        was baptized in.
And since I said this to friars, they considered me a fool,
And loved me the less for my legitimate speech.
And yet I confronted my confessor who fancied himself so
        clever,   70
"By my faith, friar," I said, "I find you like a wooer
Who will wed no woman before her wealth's in his control.
Just so, by the Cross, you couldn't possibly care less
Whose earth covered my corpse once you'd acquired my
        silver.
I am much amazed at you, and so are many others,   75

---

6. "Rich." "Pate by pate": i.e., head by head, each friar individually. "Prior Provincial": head
of a regional group of houses of a religious order.
7. Based on canon law.
8. The friars competed with the parish priest for donations by cornering the market in con-
fessions and burials, which brought good pickings, and by avoiding the ongoing work of the
community, such as the apparently less lucrative baptisms and preparation for confirmation.

Why your fraternity prefers to confess men and bury them
Rather than christen converts and other fit candidates.
Baptizing and burying, both are necessary,
But there's much more merit, it seems to me, in baptizing.
For a baptized man may, as masters* relate,   80
Through contrition come clean to the high Heaven,
    Contrition alone destroys sin.[9]
But without baptism a baby may not be saved:
    Unless a man be reborn.[1]
Look, you learned men, whether I lie or not."
  And Lewte* laughed at me because I was louring at the
    friar.
"Why are you louring?" said Lewte, and looked at me hard.   85
"If I only dared," I declared, "tell this dream among men!"
"Yes, by Peter and by Paul!" said he, and took them both
    to witness:
"*Thou shalt not hate the brothers secretly in thy heart, but rebuke
    them publicly.*"[2]
"They'll produce a passage too," said I, "a proof from the
    Gospel:
Do not judge any one."[3]   90
"And what purpose does law possess," said Lewte, "if no one
    reproves them —
Falseness and fraudulence? For that's why the Apostle said,
Thou shalt not hate the brother [*secretly*].
And in the Psalter also says David the prophet,
Thou thoughtest unjustly that I would be such an one as thyself, etc.[4] 95
It's *licitum*[5] for laymen to allege what's true
If they'd like to and elect to — every law allows it
Except for parsons and priests and prelates of Holy Church.
It's not proper for such people to publish any stories —
Even though the tale were true — if it touched on sin.   100
What the whole world's aware of, why should you hesitate
To write about it in a book to rebuke deadly sin?
But never be the first to blame bad behavior;
Though you see evil don't be the first to say so; be sorry
    it's not amended.
A matter that's not manifest, don't you make it known.   105

---

9. Theological tenet.
1. John 3.5.
2. Lev. 19.17.
3. Matt. 7.1.
4. Ps. 49.21.
5. "Licit, lawful."

Neither laud it for love nor belittle it for malice.
  Be spare in your praise; be more spare in your blame."[6]
"He speaks the truth," said Scripture then, and skipped on
  high and preached.[7]
But the topic that she treated, if untaught men knew it,
The less, I believe, their love would be
For the belief of our Lord that lettered men teach.   110
This was her topic and her text—I took careful note—
"*Multi* were bidden to a marriage, to take meat at the feast,
And when the folk were fully assembled the porter unfastened
  the gate
And passed *pauci*[8] in privately and let the rest go packing."
All troubled by her text I trembled at heart   115
And grew gloomy in mind and began to argue with myself
Whether I was chosen or not chosen; Holy Church, I
  thought,
Had befriended me at the font for one of God's chosen.
For Christ called us all, come if we would,
Saracens and schismatics and also the Jews,   120
  O all ye that thirst come, etc.[9]
And bade them for their sins suck safety at his breast,
And drink remedy for wrong-doing, revel in it who would.
"Then may all Christians come," said I, "and claim entry
  there
By the blood that he bought us with, and through baptism
  after:
  He that believeth and is baptized, etc.[1]
For though a Christian man craved to deny his Christianity, 125
Reason would never acknowledge that he might deny it
  rightfully.
For no churl may make a charter or put his chattels up for
  sale
Without leave of his lord: no law will grant it.
But he may run in arrears and go roving from home
And roam around recklessly like a runaway prisoner.   130
But Reason shall have a reckoning with him and rebuke
  him in the end,
And Conscience account with him and convict him of debt,

---

6. From the Roman Seneca, a Stoic philosopher and dramatist, a number of whose sayings
were widely quoted in the Middle Ages.
7. The scene shifts with dream-suddenness back to the encounter with Scripture broken off
in XI.4, though remaining within the dream within a dream.
8. "Few": Matt. 22.1-14; the Latin words occur in verse 14, "Many are called, but few are
chosen." "*Multi* " (line 112): many.
9. Isa. 55.1. "Saracens": a general word for pagans, not just Moslems. "Schismatics": heretics.
1. Mark 16.16.

And then put him in prison — to burn in purgatory;
And reward him there for his arrears, right to the Day of
    Doom,*
Unless Contrition will come and cry in his lifetime   135
For mercy for his misdeeds, with mouth and with heart."
    "That is true," said Scripture; "no sin may prevent
Mercy from amending everything if Meekness go with her;
For they are both, as our books say, above God's works:
    His mercy is above all his works."[2]
"Yeah? Bah for books," said one who'd broken out of hell,   140
"I, Trajan,[3] a true knight, take witness of a pope
How I was dead and damned to dwell in torment
As an unchristian creature; clerks know the truth
That all the clergy* under Christ couldn't snatch me from
    hell,
But only love and lawfulness and my law-abiding judgments.   145
Gregory was well aware of this and willed to my soul
Salvation for the steadfast truth he saw in my deeds.
And because he wept and wished that I would be saved,
Grace was granted me for the great force of his wishes.
Without special prayers his plea was heeded,   150
And I saved, as you may see, without singing of Masses,
By love and by his learning of my living in truth.
This plucked me out of bitter pain where no praying might."[4]
    Lo, you lords, what lawfulness did for an Emperor of
    Rome
That was an unchristian creature, as clerks* find in books;   155
Not through prayer of a pope, but purely for his truth
Was that Saracen saved,[5] as Saint Gregory bears witness.
Well ought you lords that keep the laws have this lesson in
    mind
And think of Trajan's truth, and administer truth to the
    people.
This matter is murky for many, but, men of Holy Church,   160
The *Legenda Sanctorum*[6] tells the lesson at greater length than I.

2. Ps. 144.9.
3. The Roman Emperor Trajan was renowned for his dedication to justice. The story of his being saved, even though a pagan, by the intervention of St. Gregory the Great* was widely told in the Middle Ages as a solution to the problem of how God deals with the "righteous pagan," and as proof that pagans who are sufficiently dedicated to virtues known to them can be saved by the special mercy of God.
4. Where Trajan's speech stops and a different one begins (by a speaker who quotes Trajan in line 171) is unclear. The present translation concludes Trajan's speech proper here. Who the next speaker is and why Langland is so vague about identifying him will be treated, where appropriate, in a later note.
5. In most versions of the story, Trajan was brought back to life and baptized, so he could be saved; Langland omits this.
6. A popular collection of saints' lives (literally, "Readings of Saints").

But thus lawful love and living in truth
Pulled out of pain a pagan of Rome.
Blessed be truth that so broke hell's gates
And saved the Saracen from Satan's power,   165
Where no clergy could, nor competence in law.
Love with lawfulness is a reliable science,
For they are the blessed book of bliss and of joy.
God first fashioned it and with his own finger wrote it,
And gave it to Moses on the mountain that all men might
    learn it.[7]   170
"Law without love," said Trajan, "that's worth less than a
    bean!"
Or any science under sun, the seven arts[8] and all,
Unless they're learned for our Lord's love, the labor's all lost,
Not for some craft to acquire silver by, or to be called a
    master,*
But all for the love of our Lord and to love the people
    better.   175
For Saint John said it, and his sayings are true:
    Who loveth not abideth in death.[9]
Whoever loves not, believe me, he lives in death-dying.
And let folk of all factions, whether friends or enemies,
Love each other and help each other as they would
    themselves.
Whoever lends no help loves not, the Lord knows the truth,   180
And he commands every creature to conform himself to love
Other Christians as himself and his enemies as well.
For whoever hates us it's our merit to love,
And especially poor people; their prayers may help us.
For our joy and our jewel, Jesus Christ of Heaven,   185
In a poor man's apparel pursues us always,
And looks on us in their likeness—and with lovely
    countenance—
To find out by our friendly heart and on whom we fix our
    eyes
Whether we love the lords here before the Lord of bliss;
And he urges us in the Evangel that when we hold feasts   190
We should not ask our kin to come, nor any kind of rich
    men:
    When thou makest feasts call not thy friends.[1]

7. God gave the Ten Commandments to Moses on Mt. Sinai, written by him on two tablets
of stone (Exod. 32.15–16).
8. Grammar, rhetoric, logic, arithmetic, geometry, astronomy, and music (Gloss under "clergy").
9. 1 John 3.14.
1. Luke 14.12; Langland's next four lines are based on Luke 14.13–14.

"But call the care-worn to them, the crippled and the poor;
For your friends will feed you, find ways to pay you back,
For your feasting and fair gift; each friend thus repays the
    other.
But I shall pay for the poor, and requite the pains they take   195
Who give them meals and money and love men for my
    sake."
   God might have made all men rich if he'd wished,
But it's for the best that some be rich and some beggars
    and poor.
For we are all Christ's creatures and his coffers make us
    rich,
And brothers of one blood, as well beggars as earls.   200
For of Christ's blood on Calvary Christendom sprang,
And we became blood brothers there in the body that won
    us,
As *quasi modo geniti*[2] gentlemen all,
No beggar or blackguard is among us unless he were bred
    by sin:
      Whosoever committeth sin is the servant of sin.[3]
In the Old Law, as the letter tells, men called us "Men's
    sons"
                                               205
Of Adam's issue and of Eve, always till God-man died;
And after his resurrection *Redemptor*[4] was his name,
And we his brothers, bought by him, both rich and poor.
Therefore let us love like dear children, each man laughing
    with the other,
And with what each man may spare, amend where there's
    need,   210
And every man help other, for we all must go hence:
      Bear ye one another's burdens.[5]
And let us not be miserly of our money, nor of our minds
    either,
For no man knows how near's the time he'll be denied both.
Therefore blame nobody else though he has better Latin,
And rebuke no one bitterly, for nobody's without fault.   215
For whatever comment clerks make on Christendom and
    such,
Christ said to a common woman who'd come in at a feast

---

2. "As newborn babes": 1 Pet. 2.2. This text opens the Introit, or beginning of the main part
of the Mass, for the Sunday Mass after Easter.
3. John 8.34.
4. "Redeemer."
5. Gal. 6.2.

That *fides sua*[6] should save her and absolve her of her sins.
Then belief is a reliable help, more than logic or law.
For logic and for law in *Legenda Sanctorum*   220
Is little allowance made, unless belief assists them;
For it's overlong before logic resolves a lesson's meaning,
And law is loath to love before he lays hand on silver.
Both logic and law, if you do not love to lie,
I counsel all Christians not to cling to them too hard,   225
For I find a phrase written that was of Faith's teaching,
That saved sinful men, as Saint John bears witness:
With the same measure ye mete, it shall be measured to you.[7]
Therefore let's learn the law of love as our Lord taught;
And as Saint Gregory* said, for man's soul's health   230
It is better to examine our sins than the natures of things.[8]

 Why I'm making much of this matter is mostly for the
   poor;
For in their likeness our Lord has often let himself be seen.
Witness in Easter week, when he went to Emmaus;
Cleophas could not tell that it was Christ who came   235
Because of his poor apparel and pilgrim's clothes,
Till he blessed and broke the bread that they ate.[9]
Thus by his works they became aware that he was Jesus,
But by clothing they could not recognize him, he came
   dressed so wretchedly.
And this was all an example, surely, to us sinful here   240
That we should be lowly and loving, and loyal to each other,
And patient like pilgrims, for pilgrims are we all.
And in the apparel of a poor man and in pilgrim's likeness
Many a time God has been met among needy people,
Where none ever encountered him clad in the costume of
   the rich.   245
Saint John and other saints were seen in poor clothing,
And as poor pilgrims prayed men for their goods.
Jesus Christ alighted in a Jew's daughter, and though she
   was a gentle woman
She was a most impoverished maid and married to a poor
   man.[1]
Martha made a great complaint about Mary Magdalene   250
And to our Savior himself said these words:

---

6. "Her faith": Luke 7.50 (which reads, "thy faith").
7. Not John but Matt. 7.2.
8. A common maxim, for which no exact source in Gregory has been identified.
9. This appearance of the resurrected Christ is recounted in Luke 24.13–32.
1. The account of the Annunciation is in Luke 1.26–38, but the notion that Mary was genteel and poor comes from medieval tradition.

"*Lord, dost thou not care that my sister hath left me to serve alone?*"[2]
And God answered hastily, allowing each her way,
Both Martha and Mary, as Matthew bears witness.
But poverty God placed ahead, and praised it for the better: 255
> "*Mary hath chosen the best part, which shall not be taken
>   away from her.*"
And all the wise men that ever were, from what I can tell,
Praise poverty as the best life if patience accompany it,
And both better and blesseder by many times than riches.
Although it's sour to suffer, there comes a sweetness
          afterward.
As on a walnut on the outside is a bitter bark,   260
And under that bitter bark, once the shell's been removed,
Is a kernel of comfort that can restore health.
So it is after poverty or penance have been patiently
          suffered:
They make a man put his mind on God and move him to
          wish eagerly
To weep and to pray well, from which there wells up mercy, 265
Of which Christ is a kernel to comfort the soul.
And far sounder sleep is sent to the poor man,
And he dreads death less, and darkness with its robbers
Than he that wields much wealth; let the witness be Reason:
> *I, the poor man, play while you, the rich, are anxious.*[3]
          Although Solomon said, as folk see in the Bible,   270
Neither riches nor poverty, etc.[4]
A man wiser than Solomon was bore witness and taught
That perfect poverty was to have no possessions,
And a life that God likes most, as Luke bears witness;
> *If thou wilt be perfect, go and sell, etc.*[5]
And this means to men that move over this earth,   275
Whoever wishes to be wholly perfect has to give up all his
          possessions,
Or sell them, as the Book says, and dispense his silver
To beggars who for God's love beg and bid their prayers.
For meat never failed any man who served mighty* God;
As David says in the Psalter,* such as desire   280
To serve God goodly are grieved by no penance:
> *Nothing shall be impossible to him who desires,*[6]

---

2. Luke 10.40 (line 255a is from Luke 10.42). Langland follows the tradition that Mary of
Bethany, sister of Martha and Lazarus, is identical with Mary Magdalene.
3. Proverbial.
4. Prov. 30.8: the verse reads, "give me neither poverty nor riches. . . ."
5. Not Luke but Matt. 19.21; the "wiser man" in line 272 is Jesus.
6. Matt. 17.19.

Nor does he ever lack livelihood, linen or woolen:
> But they that seek the Lord shall not be deprived of any good
> thing.[7]

If priests were wise, they would take no silver
For Masses or for matins*—nor take meat from usurers,
Nor either kirtle[8] or coat, though the cold killed them,   285
If they did their duty, as David says in the Psalter:
> Judge me, O God, and distinguish my cause.[9]

Spera in deo[1] speaks of priests that have no silver to spend,
That if they toil truly and trust in God almighty,
They should lack no livelihood, neither linen nor woolen.
And the title that you take in orders tells that you've been
preferred.   290
Then you need accept no silver for singing Masses,
For he should award you your wages who awarded you
your title,
Or else the bishop that blessed you and put balm on your
fingers.[2]
For a king would make no man a knight unless he'd money
to spend
As was fitting for a knight, or else he'd fund him for his
prowess.   295
It's an uneasy knight, made by an ignoble king,
That has no property or rich parentage or prowess of his
deeds.
I say the same, be sure, of all such priests
That have neither keen minds nor kindred, but a tonsured
crown only,
And a title, a useless trifle, to trust to when one's needy.   300
He ought to rely on no more livelihood, I believe, because
of his tonsure,
Than a church-living for his learning and for being "allowed
of good behavior."[3]

7. Ps. 33.11.
8. A knee-length tunic.
9. Ps. 42.1.
1. "Trust in God": Ps. 36.3.
2. The question of whether priests should be paid for their services (and, if so, by whom) was a burning issue in Langland's time and a focus of discussion about the need to reform the Church among radical and conservative thinkers alike. Langland's speaker takes the position here that the *function* of priest should be financed by the authorities responsible for appointing him to carry out his activities, rather than that the "consumers" of his specific services should "pay by the piece" (i.e., for the singing of a Mass or the baptizing of a child). The person who awarded the priest his particular "title" (line 292) would be most often a lay lord appointing a priest to a parish under his control; the person responsible for certifying his fitness to be a priest and consecrating him as such ("blessed you and put balm on your fingers"—line 293) would be the bishop.
3. Being certified as of good behavior—often the most shameless formality—was the only ethical or spiritual test a candidate for a parish had to meet.

A charter is challengeable before a chief justice
If false Latin is in the language, the law impugns it,
Or if there's lettering between the lines, or passages left out.   305
Whoever handles a charter so is held to be a goose.
So is he a goose, by God, that's faulty in Gospel-reading,
Or makes any mistake in Mass or in matins:
Who offends in one point is guilty in all.[4]
And also in the Psalter David says to over-skippers: 310
*Sing praise to our God; sing praise since the king of the world is the
        God of Israel; sing praises wisely.*[5]
The bishop shall be blamed before God, I believe,
That names those as God's knights who cannot *sapienter*[6]
Sing or read Psalms or say a Mass of the day.[7]
But neither shall be blameless, the bishop or the chaplain;[8]   315
For each one is an offender and the charge is *Ignorantia
Non excusat episcopos nec* uneducated priests.[9]
This look at unlearned priests has made me leap away from
        poverty
Which I praise, when it's in patience's company, as more
        perfect than riches.
    Yet much more in my dream some one[1] thus argued with
        me, ·
                                                                        320
And sleeping I saw all this, and soon Kind* came
And named me by name and bade me note carefully
And through the wonders of this world my wits should be
        sharpened.
And on a mountain called Middle Earth — as it seemed to
        me then —
I was lifted aloft, to learn by examples   325
To love Kind my creator through every creature of his.
I saw the sun and the sea and the sand after

4. Jas. 2.10.
5. Ps. 46.7–8.
6. "Wisely."
7. Each daily Mass contains parts common to all Masses and parts that vary according to the day; putting together the specific Mass for a particular date requires considerable knowledge.
8. I.e., neither the appointer (the bishop) nor the appointee (the incompetent "chaplain" or priest) can avoid responsibility.
9. The Middle English word translated as "uneducated" is actually *ydiotes*, "idiots." The Latin means "Ignorance does not excuse bishops nor" (no known source).
1. As was noted earlier, Trajan's speech ends somewhere around line 153, though Trajan is quoted at line 171. The identity of "someone," the next speaker, is controversial, and therefore the speech has not been put within quotation marks. Much of its content is unsuited to Trajan, and various speakers have been suggested, including Scripture (whom Trajan originally interrupted) and "Recklessness," a character who appears only briefly in this version of the poem (XI.34), but who is given much of this material in the subsequent version, the C-text. Recklessness is an ambiguous character whose meaning includes "carelessness" in the modern sense and the biblical "take no thought for the morrow," conceived of as a positive quality, radical trust in God.

And where birds and beasts moved beside their mates,
Wild worms in woods and wonderful fowls
With flecked feathers and of various colors.   330
Man and his mate I might see both,
Poverty and plenty, both peace and war,
Bliss and bitterness, both I saw at once,
And how men took Meed* and dismissed Mercy.
I saw how steadily Reason stayed with all beasts,   335
In eating, in drinking, in engendering of species,
And after intercourse caused conception, they took scant
      heed of each other,
As when he'd ridden her in rutting time at once they rested
      thereafter;
Males withdrew with males all mourning by themselves,
And females with females flocked and herded.   340
There was no cow or cow-kind that had conceived in her
      womb
That would bellow for a bull—nor boar for a sow.
Both horses and hounds and all other beasts
Would not meddle with their mates, save man alone.
I beheld birds building nests in bushes—   345
No man's imagination could make a match for the simplest.
I wondered from whom and where the magpie
Learned to lay the sticks in which she lays and breeds.
No carpenter could, I think, copy her nest correctly;
If any mason made a mold for it, it would be most
      wonderful.   350
Yet I marveled more of many other birds
How secretly they screened and concealed their eggs
So that folk should not find them when they flew away.
In marshes and on moors many hid their eggs
For fear of other fowls and for wild beasts.   355
And some trod, I took note, on trees where they bred,
And brought forth their birdlings high above the ground.
And some birds brought about conception by breathing
      through their bills,
And some copulated by cauking;[2] I noticed how peacocks
      bred.
I marveled much what master they had,   360
And who brought them to build nests on branches so high
That their birdlings were above the reach both of beasts
      and men.

---

2. Copulating or "treading" as birds do, with the male mounting the female's back.

And later I looked upon the sea and so aloft to the stars;
I saw many marvels I must not speak of now.
I saw flowers in the field and their fair colors   365
And how among the green grass grew so many hues,
And some sour and some sweet; it seemed wonderful to me.
To discuss their kinds and colors would keep me too long.
  But what most moved me and changed my mood
Was that Reason respected and ruled all beasts   370
But man and his mate; many times, I thought,
No reason ruled them, neither rich nor poor.[3]
And then I rebuked Reason and said right to his face,
"It seems strange to me why you, who are considered so
          intelligent,
Don't follow man and his mate so they don't misbehave."   375
And Reason scolded me, and said, "It's no concern of yours
What I permit and don't permit: mind your own business.
You amend whatever you may, for my time is yet to come.
Sufferance is a sovereign virtue and a swift vengeance.
Who suffers more than God?" he asked. "No man, as I
          believe.[4]   380
He might in a minute's time amend all that is amiss.
But he suffers for some man's sake, and so it's better for us.
Holy Scripture," said that person, "instructs men to suffer.
       Be ye subject to every creature for God's sake.[5]
Frenchmen and good family men thus try to fashion their
          children:[6]
Forbearance is a virtue fair;   malediction but a vengeance spare;   385
Pleasant mien and answer kind   bring the forbearing peace of mind.[7]
Therefore I direct you," said Reason, "to rule your tongue
          better.
And before you belittle my life see that your life merits
          praise.
For there is no creature under Christ that can form himself,
And if a man might make himself wholly without fault,   390
Everybody would be blameless—believe nothing else.

---

3. Langland is playing here on the traditional medieval definition of a human being as *animal rationale*, an animal who differs from other animals in having reason. Here human beings differ from other animals in being unreasonable.
4. Langland puns here on the double meaning of "suffer," "to permit" and "to undergo pain." God does both in relation to his creation: he permits, or even enables, good and evil to happen (thus making himself responsible for evil), and, as Jesus, he endures the pain and abandonment that evil brings about.
5. 1 Pet. 2.13.
6. At this date, upper-class Englishmen were still speakers of French and took French culture in many respects as a norm of cultivation.
7. These French verses are evidently contemporary.

And you'll find but a few who feel happy to hear
A list of their foul faults reviewed in their presence.
The wise and the witty once wrote in the Bible:
In a thing that does not trouble you strive not.[8]   395
For whether a man is foul or fair, it's not fitting to libel
The favor or the form that God fashioned himself.
For all he wrought was well wrought, as Holy Writ
   witnesses,
   And God saw all things that he had made, and they were
    very good.[9]
And he commanded every creature to increase in its kind,
All to make man merry who must suffer woe   400
From the tempting of the flesh and from the Fiend as well.
For man was made from such a matter that he may not
   escape
So that some times it betides him to follow his nature.
Cato accords with this: *Nemo sine crimine vivit.*"[1]
 Then at once my face flushed and I began to feel
   ashamed,   405
And awaked therewith;[2] I was woeful then
That I might have learned a larger lesson as I lay dreaming.
Then I said to myself, "Sleeping, I had grace
To learn what Do-Well is, but waking, never."
And as I lifted my eyes aloft, some one was looking at me.   410
"What is Do-Well?" said that person. "Well, sir," I said,
"To see much and suffer more surely is Do-Well."
"If you'd suffered," he said, "when you were sleeping just
   now,
You would have acquired Clergy's knowledge, and conceived
   more through Reason.
For Reason would have reviewed all that Clergy revealed to
   you;   415
But for your interference you have been forsaken.
   You would have been a philosopher if you had remained
    silent.[3]
While Adam held his tongue, he had Paradise to play in,
But when he fussed about food and fancied he might learn
The wisdom and the wit of God, he was turned away from
   bliss.

---

8. Ecclus. 11.9.
9. Gen. 1.31.
1. "No one lives without fault": Cato's *Distichs*.
2. The dream within a dream ends here.
3. Boethius (480?–524), *The Consolation of Philosophy*, II, prose 7. The *Consolation* was one of the most influential philosophical treatises in the Middle Ages.

And Reason behaved right so with you: you with rude
    speech   420
Praised and dispraised things of which you were not a
    proper judge.
Then he felt small satisfaction in instructing you further.
Now pride and presumption will perhaps bring charges
    against you,
So that Clergy will no longer care to keep company with
    you.
Never shall challenging and chiding chasten a man so
    quickly   425
As shame will, and shatter him, and make him shape up.
For if a drunken fool falls in a ditch,
Let him lie, don't look at him, till he feels like getting up,
For though Reason rebuked him then, he'd not react to it;
For Clergy and his counsel he couldn't care less.   430
To blame him or to beat him then were but a waste of time.
But when necessity snatches him up, lest he expire for need,
And shame scrapes his clothes and washes his shins clean,
Then finally the drunken fool feels why he is to blame."
"You speak truth!" said I. "I've seen it often.   435
Nothing strikes as sharply or smells as foul
As shame: where he shows up he's shunned by everybody.
Why you counsel me thus," I declared, "was because I
    rebuked Reason."
"Certainly," he said, "that is so," and started to walk,
And I arose right then and reverently addressed him,   440
And if it were his will, he would tell me his name.

Passus XII

"I am Imaginative,"[1] said he; "I was never idle
Though I sit by myself, in sickness nor in health,
I've followed you, in faith, these forty-five winters
And many times have moved you to have mind on your
    end,[2]
And how many are your yesteryears, and so few yet to
    come,   5

1. Not "imagination" in the modern sense, but the power to form mental images of things in the exterior world or in the past. "Imaginative" takes the data given by experience and interiorizes them so that the rational powers of the mind can work on them. Medieval psychology associated this aspect of the mind with memory and with the capacity to make analogies, rather than with the creation of art (Gloss).
2. I.e., think about your mortality.

And of your wild wantonness when you were young —
To amend it in your middle age lest might* fail you
In your old age that ill can endure
Poverty or penance, or pray to good effect:
  If not in the first watch nor in the second, etc.[3]
Amend yourself while you may — you have been warned often   10
By pangs of pestilence, by poverty and ailments;
And with these bitter brooms God beats his dear children:
  Whom I love I castigate, etc.[4]
And in the Psalter* David says of such as love Jesus,
  Thy rod and thy staff, they comforted me.[5]
'Although you strike me with your staff, with stick or with
    rod,
It's merely mirth to me, to amend my soul.'   15
And you meddle with making verse and might go say your
    Psalter,
And pray for them that provide your bread, for there are
    plenty of books
To tell men what Do-Well is, Do-Better and Do-Best both
And preachers to explain it all, of many a pair of friars."
  I saw well he spoke the truth, and somewhat to excuse
    myself   20
Said, "Cato* comforted his son, clerk* though he was,
To solace himself sometimes: so I do when I write.
  Interpose some pleasures at times among your cares.[6]
And I've heard it said of holy men, how they now and then
Played to be more perfect in their prayers afterward.
But if there were any one who would tell me   25
What Do-Well and Do-Better were, and Do-Best at the last,
I would never do any work but wend to Holy Church
And stay there saying prayers save when I ate or slept."[7]
  "Paul in his Epistle," said he, "explains what Do-Well is:
  Faith, hope, charity, and the greatest of these, etc.[8]

3. Cf. Luke 12.38: the idea is that the Lord *will* come and should find his servants ready.
4. Rev. 3.19; cf. Prov. 3.12.
5. Ps. 22.4: here the Old Testament is taken, as it often is by Langland and medieval readers generally, to anticipate the New Testament.
6. From Cato's* *Distichs.*
7. The narrator defends the writing of poetry on the grounds that the process, however idle it may seem, is necessary to his discovering something he can learn in no other way; such a view is extraordinary, if not unique, in medieval thinking. Poetry was generally viewed as doing the reader good by transmitting known truths or stories in a form attractive enough that he or she will remember them (the "sugar-coated pill" view of art, in which benefit comes from the moral content, and the poet creates only the pleasing form). As in the narrator's response to Holy Church (I.138) and to the friars (VIII.57), he insists that the fact his society offers him true and already discovered answers to his questions does not dispense him from his own inquiry.
8. 1 Cor. 13.13.

'Faith, hope, and charity, and all are good,   30
And save men sundry times, but none so soon as charity.'
For he does well, without doubt, who does what Lewte*
    teaches.
That is, if you're a married man, you must love your mate
And live as law requires as long as you both live.
Right so, if you're a religious,* never run any further   35
To Rome or to Rochemadour,[9] save as your rule teaches,
And hold yourself under obedience that's highway to Heaven.
And if you're man or maid unmarried and might well
    continue so,
Seek no saint further for your soul's health.
Lo, what made Lucifer lose the high Heaven,   40
Or Solomon his sapience, or Samson his strength?[1]
Job the Jew bought his joy dearly;
Aristotle and others too, Hippocrates and Virgil,
Alexander who won everything—all ended badly.
Wealth and Kind Wit* weakened them all.[2]   45
Felicia for her fairness fell into contempt
And Rosamond right so ruinously employed
The beauty of her body—in badness she squandered it.[3]
Of many such I may read, of men and of women,
That could speak wise words, and worked the contrary;   50
    They are worthless men speaking well of virtue.[4]
And just so prosperous people pile up money and hoard it.
And those men that they most hate administer it in the
    end.
And since they let themselves see so many needy folk
And don't love them as our Lord bade, they lose their souls.
    Give, and it shall be given unto you.[5]
So wealth and Kind Wit weaken many—   55
Woe to him who has them unless he employ them well!
    Those who know and act not they shall beat with many
    whips.[6]

9. These were popular pilgrimage places; Roquemadour in France was a famous shrine of the
Virgin.
1. Solomon was led by his foreign wives into building shrines to pagan gods (1 Kings 11.2–4);
Samson was betrayed by Delilah (Judg. 16.4–21).
2. This enigmatic comment is explained below (lines 55ff.).
3. The prosperity of Job led God to permit Satan to test him by taking everything from him
and inflicting undeserved suffering on him. Aristotle* was believed to have committed suicide,
Hippocrates (the famous Greek physician) to have died of dysentery as a punishment for murder,
and the poet Virgil to have died in an unsuccessful experiment in sorcery. Alexander the Great
was said to have died of poison. Felice, the heroine of a popular romance, died of grief after
the hero's death. Rosamond, the mistress of Henry II, was poisoned by his wife.
4. From a Latin epigram that had become proverbial in Langland's time.
5. Luke 6.38.
6. Luke 12.47.

Sapience, the Book says, swells a man's soul:
> *Knowledge puffeth up, etc.*[7]

And right so do riches unless they rise from a true root.
But grace is a herb-grass therefor that gives relief for these
    ailments.
But grace does not grow until good will brings rain;   60
Patience-And-Poverty is the place where it grows,
And in men who live lives lawful and holy,
And through the gift of the Holy Ghost as the Gospel tells:
> *The spirit bloweth where it will.*[8]

  Clergy* and Kind Wit come of seeing and studying
As the Book bears witness to anybody who can read: 65
> *We speak what we know, we testify what we have seen.*[9]

Of *quod scimus* comes Clergy, heavenly comprehension,
And of *quod vidimus* comes Kind Wit, of what various men
    have seen.
But grace is a gift of God and springs from great love;
No clerk ever knew how it comes forth, nor Kind Wit its
    ways.
> *No one knoweth whence it cometh or whither it goeth.*[1]

Yet Clergy is to be commended, and Kind Wit too,   70
And especially Clergy, for love of Christ who's Clergy's root.
For Moses records that God wrote to direct the people
In the Old Law as the letter tells, that was the law of Jews,
That whatever woman was taken in adultery, whether rich
    or poor,
Men should strike her with stones and stone her to death.[2]   75
A woman as we find was guilty of that deed,
But Christ of his courtesy used Clergy to save her.[3]
For through the characters that Christ wrote the Jews
    confessed themselves
Guiltier before God, and more gravely in sin,
Than the woman that was there, and went away for shame.   80
Thus Clergy there comforted the woman.
Holy Church recognizes that by his writing Christ rescued
    her;
So Clergy is comfort to creatures that repent,
And to unremorseful men mischief at their ending.
For God's body could not be of bread without Clergy,   85

7. 1 Cor. 8.1.
8. John 3.8.
9. John 3.11: "what we know" (*quod scimus*), "what we have seen" (*quod vidimus*).
1. John 3.8.
2. Deut. 22.23–24.
3. John 8.3–11.

And that body is both betterment to the righteous
And death and damnation to those who die wicked,
As Christ's characters both comforted, and convicted of guilt,
The woman whom the Jews judged that Jesus thought to
     save.
    Judge not and ye will not be judged.[4]
Just so God's body, brethren, unless it be worthily taken   90
Damns us at the Day of Doom* as the characters did the
     Jews.
Therefore I counsel you for Christ's sake to give Clergy
     your love;
For Kind Wit is of his kindred, and both close cousins
Of our Lord, believe me; therefore love them, I say.
For both are like looking-glasses in which we learn to cure
     our faults   95
And leaders for unlearned men and lettered men as well.
  Therefore do not belittle logic, law, nor its customs,
Nor contradict clerks, I counsel you forever.
For as a man may not see who is missing his eyesight,
No more can any clerk know unless he acquired it first in
     books.   100
Although men made books, the master was God,
And the Holy Spirit the exemplar who said what men
     should write.
And just as sight serves a man so he can see the high street,
Just so by literature[5] unlearned men learn to reason.
And as a blind man in battle who bears a weapon to fight   105
Has no luck with his axe to hit his enemy,
No more can a kind-witted man, unless clerks teach him,
Come for all his kind wit to Christendom and be saved.
And that's the coffer of Christ's treasure, and clerks have
     the keys,
To unlock it when they like, and to unlearned people   110
Give mercy for their misdeeds if men will request it
Humbly and whole-heartedly, and ask it of grace.
Levites in the Old Law looked after *Archa Dei.*[6]
No unlearned man had leave to lay hand on that chest,
Unless he were a priest or a priest's son, patriarch or
     prophet.   115

4. Matt. 7.1.
5. I.e., "letters," writing.
6. "The Ark of God"; see 1 Sam. 13.12 on Saul (line 116 below) and 2 Sam. 6.6–7 on the
unsanctified touching of the sacred Ark containing the stone tablets God gave Moses, on which
the Ten Commandments were written (lines 118–20).

Because Saul performed a sacrifice, sorrow came upon him,
And his sons also suffered from that sin;
And many more men, too, who were not Levites,
Who walked with *Archa Dei* in worship and reverence,
And laid hand on it to lift it, lost their lives afterward. 120
   Therefore I counsel all Christians not to condemn Clergy,
Nor make light of clerks' learning, no matter what the
     clerks are like themselves.
Let's assume their words are worthy, for they're witnessed
     by truth.
And let's not meddle with them much to move anyone to
     wrath,
Lest ill will so heat us all that we hit out at one another. 125
     Touch not mine anointed.[7]
For Clergy is caretaker under Christ of Heaven:
There could never be king nor knight unless Clergy made
     him.
But Kind Wit* comes of all kinds of observations,
Of birds and of beasts, of bits of truth.
Diviners before our time surveyed and made note 130
Of the strange things they saw to teach their sons about
     them.
And considered it a high science, the skill they possessed;
But through such science, in truth, was never one soul saved
Nor brought by their books to bliss or to joy.
For all their natural knowledge came from nothing but
     observations. 135
Patriarchs and prophets reproved their science
And said their words and their wisdom were merely folly;
Compared to Christ's Clergy they accounted it as trifling:
     The wisdom of this world is foolishness with God.[8]
   For the high Holy Ghost shall hew through Heaven[9]
And love shall leap out into this low earth, 140
And cleanness shall catch it, and clerks shall find it:
The shepherds were talking one to another.[1]
He makes no mention of rich men there nor of men of
     common sense,
Nor of lords that were unlettered, but of the most learned
     anywhere:
     There came wise men from the east.[2]

7. Ps. 104.15.
8. 1 Cor. 3.19.
9. I.e., break his way out.
1. Luke 2.15.
2. Matt. 2.1.

If any friar was found there, I'll bet five shillings   145
That that baby was not born in a beggar's cottage
But in a burgess'* house, the best in Bethlehem.
> *But there was no room for him in the inn, and a poor man
> has no inn.*[3]

To shepherds and sages the angel showed himself
And ordered them on to Bethlehem to honor God's birth,
And they sang a song of solace, *Gloria in excelsis Deo.*[4]   150
Rich men then were sound asleep, snoring in their beds,
When it shone to shepherds, a shower of bliss.
Clerks were well aware what it was and came with their
    presents
And did their homage honorably to him who was almighty.
   Why I have told you all this, I took careful note   155
How you contradicted Clergy with crabbed words,
How with less difficulty than learned men unlearned men
    were saved,
More easily than clerks or kind-witted men of Christian
    people.[5]
And you spoke the truth of some, but see in what manner.
Take two strong men and toss them in the Thames,[6]   160
And both naked as a needle, neither sturdier than the other;
One has acquired competence—he can swim and dive.
The other does not know how—he never learned to swim.
Which of those two do you think feels most threatened in
    the Thames,
He who has no notion of swimming and never dived,   165
Or the swimmer, who is safe so long as he himself pleases,
While his companion's carried on as the current pleases,
And is in dread of drowning, the one that never did swim?"
"The one who can't swim," I said, "it seems to my wits."
"Precisely," said that personage, "so it appears by reason   170
That he that's had a clerk's education can sooner arise
Out of sin and be safe, though he sins often,
If he feels it urgent upon him, than uneducated people.

---

3. Luke 2.7; that a poor man cannot afford an inn (and that, therefore, if Joseph and Mary were trying to get a room, they cannot have been poor) is Langland's addition. The passage reflects a major controversy in Langland's time about whether Christ was poor. Friars, especially the more extreme Franciscans, claimed that their commitment to radical poverty and to begging as a means of support was justified by the example of Christ, who was, they claimed, equally poor; this claim was challenged by more conservative churchmen who thought the financial basis of the whole institutional Church was at stake. The controversy was the more embittered because friars were widely criticized as hypocrites who were in fact quite wealthy; see, for example, the corrupt friar in Chaucer's *Canterbury Tales.*
4. "Glory to God in the highest": Luke 2.14.
5. In X.448–82.
6. The river along which London is situated.

For if the clerk is clever he can tell what sin is,
And how contrition without confession comforts the soul,   175
As you see in the Psalter in a Psalm or two
How contrition is commended, for it clears away sin:

> Blessed are they whose transgressions are forgiven, and whose
> [sins] are covered.[7]

And this comforts each clerk* and recalls him from
      wanhope*
Which is the flood in which the Fiend fastens hardest on a
      man,
While the unlearned man lies still and looks toward Lent,   180
And has no contrition before he comes to confession, and
      can then tell but little,
But what his instructor teaches he trusts and believes,
And that's from a parson or parish priest, and perhaps
      incompetent
To give lessons to unlearned men, as Luke bears witness:
When the blind lead the blind, etc.[8]   185
Woe was marked out for him that must go wading with the
      ignorant!
A young man may much thank him who first made him
      read books,
So that living by written lore delivered him body and soul:
Dominus pars hereditatis meae[9] is a merry little verse
That has taken out of Tyburn twenty flagrant thieves.[1]   190
While unlettered thieves are locked up, look how they're set
      free!
The thief that had grace of God on Good Friday, as you
      mentioned,[2]
— That was because he yielded himself conquered to Christ
      and acknowledged his guilts,
And prayed God for grace, who always readily grants it
To those that humbly ask for it and are in will to amend
      themselves.   195
But though that thief had Heaven, he had no high bliss,
Such as Saint John and other saints who had deserved
      better.

7. Ps. 31.1.
8. Matt. 15.14, but Luke 6.39 is similar.
9. "The Lord is the portion of mine inheritance": Ps. 15.5.
1. Langland refers to the "neck verse"; if a criminal could read a passage in a Latin Bible, usually a Psalm, his life (or neck) was spared. The ability to read Latin, which implied learning, had legal implications in the eyes of the secular authority, since anyone who could thus claim classification as a cleric was accountable to the Church, not to the State's criminal law. "Tyburn": place of public execution in London.
2. In X.420–27 and also in V.461–70.

Just as some man might give me food and set me in the
    middle of the floor;
I would have more than enough meat, but not so much
    honor
As those that sat at the side table or held sway in the hall, 200
But like a beggar, not at the board but by myself on the
    ground.
So it fares with that felon that won salvation on Good
    Friday:
He sits neither with Saint John, Simon, nor Jude,[3]
Nor with maidens nor with martyrs nor with meek widows,
But by himself solitary, and served on the earth. 205
For he who has been once a thief is evermore in danger,
And as law likes, to live or to die:
    Be not without fear for a sin propitiated.[4]
And to serve a saint and such a thief together,
It would be neither reasonable nor right to regard them
    both alike.
And just as Trajan the true knight was not entombed so
    deep in hell 210
So that our Lord didn't have him lightly out, so I believe
    the thief is in Heaven.
For he is lodged in the lowest part of Heaven, if our belief
    is true,
And most loosely he loiters there by the law of Holy Church:
    Since he rendereth to each according to his works.[5]
But why that one thief on the Cross there yielded himself
    recreant
Rather than that other thief, though you demand an answer, 215
All the clerks under Christ couldn't give the reason:
    Why did it please him? Because he wished it.[6]
    And so I say of you, who seek for the whys,
And adduce reasons against Reason — rebuke him, as it were,
And want to know about birds and beasts, and of their
    breeding habits,
Why some stay low and some go aloft you'd like to learn; 220
And of the flowers in the field and of their fair hues,
Whence they come by their colors, so clear and so bright,
And of the stones and of the stars; you study, I believe,
How every beast or bird has such brilliant wits.

---

3. These saints were among the original twelve Apostles.
4. Ecclus. 5.5.
5. Ps. 61.13.
6. Cf. Ps. 134.6: "Whatsoever the Lord wished [*voluit*], that did he."

Clergy or Kind Wit could never know the cause,   225
But Kind* knows the cause himself, no creature else.
He is the magpie's patron and put it in her ear
To build and to breed where the thorn bush is thickest;
And Kind taught the peacock to copulate in such a way.
Kind caused Adam to be conscious of his privy parts,   230
And taught him and Eve to hide them with leaves.
Many times ignorant men demand of masters*
Why Adam didn't first hide his mouth that ate the apple
Rather than his body below: ignorant men thus badger
          clerks.
Kind can tell why he did so, and no clerk else.   235
But from birds and beasts men born in former times
Derived patterns and parables, as these poets tell,
And that the fairest fowl breeds in the foulest manner,
And is the feeblest fowl of flight of those that fly or swim.
And that is the peacock and the peahen with their proud
          feathers,   240
Which represent rich men who reign here on earth.
For if you pursue a peacock or a peahen so as to catch them,
They may not fly far nor very high either;
For the trailing of his tail he is overtaken quickly.
And his flesh is foul flesh, and his feet foul too,   245
And his language is unlovely, loathsome to hear.
Right so the rich man, if he keeps his riches hoarded up
And does not dole them out until his death-day, the tail[7] is
          of sorrow.
Just as the plumes of the peacock impede him in his flight,
So there is an impediment in possession of pennies* and
          nobles*   250
To all those who hold on to them until their tails are
          plucked.
And though the rich man repent then and start to rue the
          time
That he ever gathered such a great amount and gave away
          so little,
Though he cry to Christ then with keen will, I believe
His language will sound in our Lord's ear like a magpie's
          chattering.   255
And when his corpse comes to be enclosed in the grave
I believe it will infect foully all the field around it,

---

7. Langland plays on the pun *tail/tale*, including the three meanings of the Middle English word: "tail," "tale," and "tally."

And all the others where it lies will be imbued with its
    poison.
By the peacock's feet are figured, as I have found in
    Avienus,[8]
Executors, false friends that don't fulfill his will   260
Which was written, and they were witnesses, for them to
    work as it directed;
Thus the poet points out the peacock for his feathers;
So is the rich man reverenced by reason of his goods.
The lark that is a littler bird is more lovely of voice,
And far away of wing swifter than the peacock,   265
And fatter of flesh, and many times more flavorsome.
The lark is likened to low-living men.
Aristotle* the great scholar tells stories such as these.
Thus in his *Logic*[9] he draws this likeness from the littlest
    fowl there is.
And whether he is saved or not saved is surely known to no
    Clergy,   270
Nor of Socrates[1] nor of Solomon no scripture can tell.
But God is so good, I hope that since he gave them wits
With which to make us men wise who wish to be saved—
And we are obliged by their books the better to pray—
That God of his grace give their souls rest,   275
For learned men would be unlettered still if it weren't for
    the lore of their books."
    "All these clerks," I declared then, "that believe in Christ's
    teaching,
Say in their sermons that neither Saracens nor Jews
Nor any creature of Christ's likeness can be saved without
    Christendom."
    "*Contra!*"* exclaimed Imaginative then, and commenced
    to frown,   280
And said, "*Salvabitur vix justus in die judicii;*
Ergo salvabitur,"[2] said he, and spoke no more Latin.
"Trajan was a true knight and never took Christendom,
And he is safe, the book says, and his soul in Heaven.
For there is baptism both at the font and by blood-shedding, 285

---

8. A writer of Latin fables (fourth century), though his name had come to signify collections
of such material generally. Where the discussion of the peacock's feet actually comes from is
unknown.
9. Not in the *Logic*; in the *Historia Animalium* he mentions that the lark is edible.
1. The Greek philosopher (470?–399 B.C.) and leading figure in the Dialogues of his pupil Plato.
2. "The righteous man will scarcely be saved in the day of judgment; therefore he *will* be saved":
line 281 comes from 1 Peter 4.18. Langland interprets this apparently discouraging biblical
verse in an imaginatively positive light.

And through fire there is baptism, and that's our firm belief:

> *Then came a divine fire, not burning but illuminating, etc.*[3]

But truth[4] that never trespassed nor transgressed against his
   law,
But lives as his law teaches, and believes there is no better,
And if there were he would adopt it, and in such a will
   dies —
Would never true God wish but true truth were allowed.[5]   290
And whether it's witness of truth or not, the worth of belief
   is great,
And a hope is hanging in it to have reward for his truth;
For *DEUS* is to say D*ans* E*ternam* U*itam* S*uis*,[6] that is, to the
   faithful.

> *And elsewhere, If I walk through the midst of the shadow of
> death.*[7]

The gloss upon that verse grants a great reward to truth.
And wit and wisdom," said that man, "was once a treasure   295
To keep a community with: no capital was held better,
And such mirth and manhood."[8] And with that he vanished.

---

3. From the liturgy for Pentecost; the line refers to the tongues of fire in which the Holy Ghost descended on the Apostles: Acts 2.1-4. The "baptism" of blood is martyrdom, the suffering prophesied by Christ (Luke 12.50ff.); the "baptism" of fire is direct illumination by the Holy Ghost, foretold by John the Baptist: "I indeed baptize you with water unto repentance, but he who cometh after me is mightier than I . . . ; he shall baptize you with the Holy Ghost, and with fire" (Matt. 3.11). In this passage Imaginative reconciles the logically contradictory doctrines that, on the one hand, faith in Christ and baptism are necessary to salvation and that, on the other, Christ died for all men and seeks their salvation, and will not condemn anyone except for that person's own unrepented faults.

4. I.e., a true person, a person of integrity.

5. The translation of this line accurately reflects Langland's contorted way of putting his point, since he is trying so hard to express it within the limits of orthodoxy and without claiming it is directly authorized by Scripture; the line may be paraphrased, "The true God couldn't possibly want anything other than that real integrity be recognized and provided for."

6. "God"; "giving eternal life to his own": in medieval spelling, which is retained here, the *v* with which *vitam* ("life") begins is represented by a *u*; the initial letters of the Latin phrase spell out the acrostic *Deus*, or "God."

7. Ps. 22.4: the verse continues, "I will fear no evil: for thou art with me." In the next line, the "gloss" is the *Glossa Ordinaria*, the traditional medieval commentary on the Bible, which explains "with me" as "that is, in the heart, by faith, so that after the shadow of death I will be with thee."

8. I.e., humanity (here "manhood" carries no connotation of machismo).

Passus XIII

And with that I woke up, my wits almost gone,
And like some one under a spell I started to walk
In the manner of a mendicant,[1] many a year after.
And about this dream of mine many times I had much
      thought,
First how Fortune failed me at my greatest need,   5
And how Old Age menaced me, if we might ever meet;
And how friars followed after folk that were rich,
And people that were poor they prized but little,
And in their kirks* or kirkyard no corpse was buried
Unless while alive he left them something or helped lighten
      their debts,   10
And how this covetousness overcame clerks* and priests,
And how laymen are led, unless our Lord helps them,
Through incompetent curates[2] to incurable pains;
And how Imaginative told me in my dream
Of Kind* and of his cleverness, and how courteous he is to
      beasts,   15
And how loving he is to every creature alive, on land and
      on water —
He allots to no living thing more or less than to another,
For all creatures that creep or walk of Kind are engendered;
And so on to how Imaginative said, *"Vix salvabitur justus,"*[3]
And when he had said so how suddenly he vanished.   20
  I lay long in this thought, and at the last I slept,
And as Christ willed there came Conscience* to comfort me
      then,
And bade me come to his court, to dine in company with
      Clergy.*
And because Conscience mentioned Clergy I came all the
      sooner.
And there I met a Master* — I'd no idea what man he was —   25
Who bowed down deeply and deferentially to Scripture.
Conscience was well acquainted with him and welcomed
      him warmly.
They washed their hands and wiped them and then went to
      dinner.

---

1. A friar, who lives by begging; one of the implications of their vow of collective poverty was that they did all their traveling on foot.
2. Assistant or deputy priests.
3. "The righteous man will scarcely be saved." In XII.281-82.

But Patience stood in the palace yard in pilgrim's clothes
And prayed for food *pour charité*[4] for a poor hermit.   30
Conscience called him in and courteously said,
"Welcome, sir, go and wash, we shall sit soon."
   This Master was made to sit in the place of most honor,
And then Clergy and Conscience and Patience came after.
Patience and I were placed as companions for dinner,   35
And sat by ourselves at a side table.
Conscience called for food, and then came Scripture
And served them thus soon with many sorts of dishes,
Of Augustine,* of Ambrose,* of all the four Evangelists.
       Eating and drinking what things are among them.[5]
But of these men this Master nor his man ate no manner
       of flesh,   40
But fed on food more costly, viands stewed and thick soups.[6]
With what men miswon they made themselves easy,
But their sauce was oversour and unsavorly ground
In a mortar *Post mortem*[7] of many bitter pains,
Unless they sing for those souls and weep salt tears: 45
       You who feast upon men's sins, unless you pour out tears
              and prayers for them, you shall vomit up among
              torments the food which you feast on now among
              pleasures.[8]
   Conscience courteously then commanded Scripture
To bring bread before Patience, seated below them,
And to me his messmate more sorts of food as well.
He set a sour loaf before us and said, "*Agite poenitentiam*,"[9]
And then he drew us drink, *Diu perseverans*,[1]   50
"As long," said he, "as life lasts and body draws breath."
"This is proper service," said Patience. "No prince could
       fare better."
And he brought us some *beati quorum* made by *Beatus Vir*,[2]

---

4. "For charity."
5. Luke 10.7.
6. The point here is that the Master, while sticking to the letter of his rule not to eat flesh,
is actually wolfing down far more luxurious dishes. Exactly what Langland actually wrote here
is a matter of controversy—most manuscripts give the Master a servant who is not mentioned except
in lines 41–44 and who would presumably not be at the high table in any case. The
translation here combines some of the Kane-Donaldson edition's conjecture about a solution
with more common, if puzzling, components of the line.
7. "After death."
8. Source unknown.
9. "Do penance": Matt. 3.2. It is not clear why Scripture, who earlier was Clergy's wife and
here seems to act as hostess, has become male, but the manuscripts all agree on this.
1. "Persevering a long while," i.e., to the end: cf. Matt. 10.22.
2. "Blessed [are they] whose [transgressions are forgiven]"; "Blessed [is] the man [unto whom
the Lord imputeth not sin]": Ps. 31.1–2; line 54a also comes from the first verse of this Psalm.

And then a serving of another mixture made by *Miserere*
    Mei Deus,[3]
    And whose sins are covered,
In a salver of secret shrift, *Dixi et confitebor tibi*.[4]   55
"Bring Patience an extra portion privately," said Conscience,
And then Patience had a portion, *Pro hac orabit ad te omnis*
    sanctus in tempore opportuno;[5]
And Conscience comforted us with his cheerful conversation:
    A contrite and humbled heart, O God, thou wilt not despise.[6]
  Patience was proud of that proper service
And made merry at his meal, but I mourned ever   60
Because this Doctor* on the high dais[7] drank wine so fast:
    Woe to you that are mighty to drink wine![8]
He munched many sorts of foods, mutton stews and
    puddings,
Eggs fried in fat, and tripe, and flesh of wild boar.
Then I said to myself so that Patience heard me,
"It was not four days ago that this friar, before the Dean of
    Paul's,[9]   65
Preached of penances that Paul the Apostle suffered:
In fame et frigore[1] and flailings with whips.
    Thrice was I beaten and of the Jews five times forty, etc.
But one verse they always leap over whenever they preach
That Paul in his Epistle told the people everywhere:
There is danger in false brothers.[2]   70
Holy Writ directs men to beware — I will not write it here
In English lest perhaps it should be too often repeated,
And thereby grieve those that are good — but grammarians
    shall read:
    Let each one guard himself from a brother, as it is said that
      there is danger in false brothers.
But I never knew a fellow dressed as a friar before men in
    English
Take this as his text and talk about it without glozing.[3]   75

---

3. "Have mercy on me, God": Ps. 50.3.
4. "I have said and I will confess to thee": Ps. 31.5.
5. "For this shall every one that is holy pray unto thee in an opportune time": Ps. 31.6.
6. Ps. 50.19.
7. Important people sat at the head table on a raised dais at the end of the hall in which meals were served.
8. Isa. 5.22.
9. The cathedral of the city of London. The head of the group of priests assigned to a cathedral was called the dean.
1. "In hunger and thirst": 2 Cor. 11.27; the next line is 2 Cor. 11.24–25.
2. 2 Cor. 11.26. The pun on "brother" and "friar" (Latin *frater*), on which Langland plays in this line and in line 73a, was well established.
3. Interpreting (in a twisted way).

They preach that penance is profitable to the soul,
And what strong pain and distress Christ stood for man's
       sake,
But this God's glutton," said I, "with his great cheeks
Has no pity on us poor—he performs badly
What he preaches and practices no patience," I said,   80
And I hoped most heartily, with a full hateful will,
That the platters and plate placed before this Doctor
Would turn to molten lead in his midriff—and Mahoun[4] in
       the midst.
"I shall prate to this pisspot with his plump belly,
And press him to say what penance is, of which he preached
       earlier."   85
Patience perceived what my purpose was, and winked at
       me to be still,
And said, "You will see soon enough, when he can eat no
       more,
He will have a penance in his paunch, and puff at every
       word,
And then his guts will grumble, and he'll begin to belch.
For now he's drunk so deep he'll soon start divining for us,   90
And prove it by their Apocalypse and the passion of Saint
       Aurea[5]
That neither bacon nor brawn, blankmanger[6] nor stew,
Is either fish or flesh, but food for a penitent;
And then he'll testify of a Trinity[7] and take his fellow to
       witness
What he found in some volume about a friar's way of life,   95
And unless the first line is a lie, believe me never.
And that's the moment for your move to make him give an
       answer
About Do-Well and Do-Better, and whether Do-Best is any
       penance."
    And I sat still as Patience said, and soon this Doctor
(As red as a rose reddened his cheeks)   100

---

4. I.e., Mohammed: a name for the Devil, because of popular belief that Mohammed was the
Moslems' God rather than their prophet.
5. The "Apocalypse of Gluttons" of Walter Mapes was a satire on greed, a parody of the Book
of Revelation; Langland's puzzling "Seint Avereys" is translated as Saint Aurea, who, accord-
ing to Vincent of Beauvais' popular medieval Encyclopedia, drank only "what she could distil
from cinders."
6. This popular dish seems to have contained eggs, cream, and sugar and probably (especially
in view of the next line) chicken and almonds. It was a specialty of the Cook in the *Canterbury
Tales*. Langland's point here is that foods which are actually luxuries are being claimed by the
Doctor as constituting a specially ascetic diet because they do not fit into the usual categories
of foods forbidden during a fast.
7. It is not clear what this or the reference in line 102 means, but X.54 appears to treat a similar
topic.

Coughed and cleared his throat, and Conscience heard him
And told him of a Trinity and looked toward us.
"What is Do-Well, sir Doctor?"* said I. "Is Do-Best[8] any
      penance?"
"Do-Well," said this Doctor, and drank after,
"Perform no injury to your fellow-Christians, as far as you
      can avoid it."   105
"By this day, sir Doctor," said I, "then you don't Do-Well!
For you have harmed us two in that you ate the pudding,
Marrow bones and other meat—and no morsel for us.
And if that's how you behave in your hospital, I'd think it a
      wonder
If charity's not changed to contention there, if young children
      dared complain.   110
I'd like to replace my penance with yours, for I'm in purpose
      to Do-Well."
    Then Conscience courteously cast a glance in my direction
And winked at Patience to imply he should pray me to
      keep quiet,
And said himself, "Sir Doctor, if it is your will,
What is Do-Well and Do-Better? You divines know."   115
"Do-Well," said this Doctor, "do as clerks teach;
Whoever tries to teach others, I take that for Do-Better;
And Do-Best does himself just so as he says and preaches:
        Who shall do and teach he shall be called great in the kingdom
          of Heaven."[9]
"Now, Clergy," said Conscience, "you declare what Do-Well
      is."
"I have seven sons,"[1] he said, "who serve in a castle   120
Where the Lord of Life lives, so they may learn Do-Well.
Until I see those seven and myself agree,
I am unconfident," said he, "to define it for any one.
For one Piers the Plowman has impugned us all
And says no study is worth a straw except for love alone,   125
And takes no text to sustain his case
But *Dilige Deum* and *Domine, quis habitabit*,[2]
And declares that Do-Well and Do-Better are two unfinished
      things,[3]

8. Most manuscripts have "Do-Well" here.
9. Matt. 5.19.
1. The seven liberal arts (Gloss under "Clergy").
2. "Love God": Matt. 22.37; "Lord, who shall dwell": Ps. 14.1.
3. In Middle English, "infinites": this word, which to us connotes an unlimited and therefore
admirable state, meant to medievals an open-ended and therefore incomplete and ultimately
unsatisfactory state (see Middleton's article mentioned in the Acknowledgments).

Which unfinished things with a faith will find out Do-Best,
Which will save man's soul: thus says Piers the Plowman."   130
"I know nothing of this," said Conscience, "but I know
          Piers.
He will not argue against Holy Writ, I dare answer for it."
"Then let this pass until Piers comes and explains it in
          person.
Patience has been in many places and perhaps he knows
What no clerk can, as Christ bears witness: 135
          The patient overcome, etc."[4]
     "At your prayer," said Patience then, "provided it
          displeases no one,
Disce," said he, "*doce, dilige inimicos.*[5]
Disce and Do-Well, *doce* and Do-Better, *dilige* and Do-Best:
I learned this from a lover once—Love was her name.
'With words and with works,' she said, 'and will of your
          heart,   140
Look that you love your soul faithfully all your lifetime.
And so learn to love, for the Lord of Heaven's sake,
Your enemy in every way even as you love yourself.[6]
Cast coals on his head of all kind speech;
Both with work and with word strive to win his love;   145
And lay on him with love until he laughs with you.
And unless he bows for this beating, let blindness come
          upon him!'
But to fare thus with your friend would be folly indeed,
For he who loves you loyally wants little that is yours.
Natural love needs no return but speech.   150
With half a lamp-line in Latin, *Ex vi transitionis*,
I bear in a box, fast bound there, Do-Well
In a sign of the Saturday that first started the calendar,
And all the wit of the Wednesday of the next week after;
The middle of the moon is the might of both.[7]   155
And herewith I am welcome, when I have it with me.
Undo it; let this Doctor see if Do-Well is inside.

---

4. Proverbial, but cf. Matt. 10.22.
5. "Learn, teach, love your enemies"; cf. Luke 6.35.
6. See Matt. 5.43–48; for line 144, Prov. 25.21–22 and Rom. 12.20–21.
7. Patience's riddle (he calls it that himself in line 167), like several earlier enigmatic prophecies, has never been fully explained; nor does the reader have to figure it out, since we will learn what is in Patience's bundle in the next *Passus*, when Patience will open it to display the contents. The basic meaning—see line 163a—is clearly that "Do-Well" is "charity," unleashed by the suffering and resurrection of Christ. The word translated "box," *bouste*, means a special container for such precious things as salves or the Host, the wafer consecrated in the Mass. *Ex vi transitionis*: "by the power of the transition (or transitivity)"; the term *transitionis* is grammatical and refers to the power by which a verb controls its object but may also allude to transition in the sense of "passage," as in such changes as Passover, baptism, or transubstantiation, or

For by him that made me, might never poverty,
Misease nor mischief nor man with his tongue,
Cold nor care, nor company of thieves,   160
Nor either heat or hail or any Devil of hell,
Nor either fire or flood or fear of your enemy
Trouble you at any time if you take it with you.
     Charity fears nothing.[8]
And also, God have my soul, if you will ask it,
There is neither emperor nor empress, earl nor baron,   165
Pope nor patriarch who will not for pure reason make you
Master of all those men through might of this riddle,
Not through witchcraft but through wit;* if you wish yourself
To make king and queen, and all the commons* after
Give you all that they can give—to you as best of governors;   170
And do as you decide they will do all their days after:
     The patient overcome."[9]
   "It's just a joke," said this Doctor, "a jester's story:
All the wisdom of this world and the work of strong men
Cannot produce a peace between the pope and his
     enemies,[1]
Nor can any compass a peace between two Christian kings   175
Profitable to either's people." And he pushed the table from
     him,
And took Clergy and Conscience to counsel, as it were,
That Patience must be made to part then, "for pilgrims
     often lie."
   But Conscience cried aloud and courteously said,
"Friends, farewell," and spoke fairly to Clergy,   180
"For if God will give me grace I will go with this man,
And be a pilgrim with Patience till I've experienced more."
"What!" said Clergy to Conscience, "are you covetous now
Of fees or favors, or feel inclined to solve riddles?
I shall bring you a Bible, a Book of the Old Law,   185

---

as the powerful images of transformation so prominent in the poem (for example, the Pardon).
(What a "lamp-line" is, let alone half a one, is anybody's guess.) The "Saturday" probably refers
to the Saturday of Easter week, from which the movable dates of the Church calendar are counted
(or perhaps to the fact that Saturday was the first full day of life for Adam). The "Wednesday"
is probably the Wednesday after Easter, whose Mass relates the resurrection of Christ to the
Second Coming and the Last Judgment, and may also be associated with the birth and concep-
tion of the Virgin Mary. The "middle of the moon"—i.e., the full moon—is probably the paschal
moon, which sets the dates of Passover and Easter.
8. Cf. 1 John 4.18, 1 Cor. 13.7–8.
9. Repeats XIII.135a.
1. At this date there were two competing popes (the "Great Schism"), the one supported by
France being under French "protection" at Avignon (a situation those who did not approve
referred to as the "Babylonian captivity"). Which of the two the Doctor takes for granted is
"the" Pope is not clear, nor does it matter.

And if you like I'll help you learn the least point in it
That Patience the pilgrim never perfectly knew."
"No, by Christ," said Conscience to Clergy, "God requite
    you;
For all that Patience has to proffer me my pride is but small.
But the will of that one, and the will of people here   190
Have moved my mind to mourn for my sins.
No currency could ever fully buy a creature's good will,
For no treasure's value is equal to it—to a true will.
Did not Mary Magdalene get more for a box of salve
Than Zacchaeus for saying, '*Dimidium bonorum meorum do
    pauperibus,*'[2]   195
And the poor widow profit more from a pair of half-farthings*
Than all those that made offerings into *Gazophylacium?*"[3]
First Conscience said farewell to the friar most courteously,
And second he spoke softly in Clergy's ear:
"I would liefer, by our Lord, if my life lasts,   200
Have patience perfectly than half your pack of books."
Clergy would not consent to bid Conscience farewell,
But said most soberly, "You shall see the time
When you're worn out from walking, you'll wish for my
    advice."
"That is so," said Conscience, "so God help me,   205
If Patience were our partner and imparted his thoughts to
    us both,
There is no woe in this world that we could not amend;
And cause kings to want peace, and all kinds of lands,
Saracens and Syria, and so forth all the Jews,
Turn them to the true faith and to one creed."   210
"That is so," said Clergy. "I see what you mean.
I shall dwell here as I do, doing my duty,
And inform young folks or folks with learning,
Till Patience has proved you and brought you to perfectness."
  Then Conscience departed with Patience, like a pair of
    pilgrims.   215
Then Patience had, as pilgrims do, packed food in his bag:
Sobriety and sincere speech and steadfast belief,
To comfort himself and Conscience if they should come to
    places
Where unkindness or covetousness is, hungry countries both.
And as they went on their way discussing Do-Well together,   220

2. "The half of my goods I give to the poor": Luke 19.8. On Mary Magdalene's salve, see
Luke 7.36–50.
3. "The treasury": Luke 21.1–4.

They met with a minstrel as it seemed to me then.
Patience approached him and prayed him to tell
Conscience what craft he practiced, and to what country he
    was bound.
   "I am a minstrel," said that man, "my name is *Activa Vita*.[4]
I hate everything idle, for from 'active' is my name.   225
A wafer-seller,[5] if you want to know, and I work for many
    lords,
But I've few robes as my fee from them, or fur-lined gowns.
If I could lie to make men laugh, then I might look to get
Either mantle or money among lords' minstrels.
But because I can neither play a tabor[6] nor a trumpet nor
    tell any stories   230
Nor fart nor fiddle at feasts, nor play the harp,
Joke nor juggle nor gently pipe,
Nor dance nor strum the psaltery,[7] nor sing to the guitar,
I have no good gifts from these great lords,
For any bread I bring forth, except a blessing on Sundays   235
When the priest prays the people to say their Paternoster*
For Piers the Plowman and those who promote his profit.
And that is I, Active, who hate idleness.
For all true toilers and tillers of the earth
From Michaelmas to Michaelmas[8] I feed them with wafers.   240
Beggars and beadsmen* crave bread from me,
Fakers and friars and folk with shaven heads.
I supply food to the pope and provender to his palfrey,
And I never had from him, God have my word,
Neither prebend[9] nor parsonage yet from the pope's gift,   245
Except a pardon with a piece of lead and a pair of heads in
    the middle.[1]
If I had a clerk* that could write I'd compose a letter to him

---

4. "Active Life," life engaged with the ongoing affairs of the world, as opposed to the "contemplative life," dedicated to prayer.
5. "Wafer" has a range of meanings pertinent to the ensuing action: (1) a kind of delicate crisp cake; (2) the thin rounds of unleavened bread made for use in the celebration of Mass; (3) the tiny disks made for use as a base for seals on letters and documents. As a baker, *Activa Vita* is (like Piers) part of the chain of food supply, but, unlike him, also a purveyor of luxuries. As a Host maker, he is part of the way in which literal food is the basis for a sacramental order; as a seal maker, part of the validation of human oaths and integrity. In addition, he is an entertainer or artist. "Waferer" is probably also a pun with "wayfarer," wanderer or pilgrim; a central term for generic man in Latin at this period was *viator*, "traveler."
6. Small drum.
7. Stringed instrument.
8. The feast of St. Michael, September 29, associated with the coming of fall and the end of the growing year.
9. Stipend paid to a canon, a priest attached to a cathedral.
1. The seal on a papal pardon was made of lead, stamped with the heads of St. Peter and St. Paul.

That he should send me under his seal a salve for the
    pestilence,
And that his blessing and his bulls might bring an end to
    boils:[2]

> *In my name shall they cast out demons, and they shall lay*
> *hands on the sick, and they shall be well.*[3]

And then I'd be quick to prepare pastries for the people,   250
And be bustling and busy about bread and drink
For him and for all his men, if I found that his pardon
Might cure a man as it seems to me it should.
For since he has the power that Peter had, he has the pot
    with the salve:

> *Silver and gold have I none, but what I have I give to thee;*
> *In the name of the Lord, rise and walk.*[4]

But if the power to perform miracles fails him it's because
    people are not worthy   255
To have the grace of God, and no guilt of the pope.
For no blessing may benefit us unless we better our lives,
Nor any man's Mass make peace among Christian people
Till pride is utterly cast out, and that through absence of
    bread.
For before I have made bread from meal I must often sweat,   260
And before the commons* have corn enough, many a cold
    morning.
So before my wafers are made I suffer much woe.
All London, I believe, like my wafers well,
And lour when they lack them; it is not long since
There was a commons full of care when no cart came to
    town   265
With baked bread from Stratford;[5] then beggars wept
And workmen were a bit aghast; this will be long
    remembered:
In the date *Anno Domini*, in a dry April,
A thousand and three hundred twice thirty and ten,
My wafers were wanting when Chichester was mayor."[6]   270
    I took close heed, by Christ, and Conscience did too,
Of Hawkin the Active Man and how he was dressed.
He had a coat of Christendom, as Holy Kirk* believes,

---

2. Boils in the armpit or groin were the most dramatic symptom of the plague, or Black Death.
3. Mark 16.17–18.
4. Acts 3.6. "The pot with the salve": the pope's power to absolve sins is portrayed as a pot
of medicine he can dole out. The "salve" refers to his power of sacramental anointing in various
religious rites.
5. The town of Stratford-atte-Bowe was a major supplier of bread to London.
6. There actually was a scarcity of food in 1370 when John de Chichestre was mayor. *"Anno
domini"*: in the year of our Lord.

But it was soiled with many spots in sundry places,
Here a spot of insolent speech, and there a spot of pride,   275
Of scorning and of scoffing and unsuitable behavior;
As in apparel and deportment proud among the people;
Presenting himself as something more than he seems or is;
Wishing all men would think him what he is not,
And so he boasts and brags with many bold oaths;   280
And impatient of reproof from any person living;
And himself so singular as to seem to the people
As if there were none such as himself, nor none so pope-
         holy;[7]
In the habit of a hermit, an order by himself,
A religious* *sans*[8] rule or reasonable obedience;   285
Belittling lettered men and unlettered both;
Pretending to like lawful life and a liar in soul;
With inwit and with outwit[9] to imagine and study,
As it would be best for his body, to be thought a bold man;
And interfere everywhere where he has no business;   290
Wishing every one to be assured his intellect was the best,
Or that he was most clever at his craft, or a clerk of greatest
         wisdom,
Or strongest on steed, or stiffest below the belt,
And loveliest to look at and most lawful of deeds,
And none so holy as he, nor any cleaner of life,   295
Or fairest of features in form and in shape,
And most splendid at song, or most skillful of hands,
And glad to give generously, to get praise thereby,
And if he gives to poor people, proclaims what he's giving;
Poor of possession in purse and in coffer;   300
And like a lion to look at, and lordly of speech;
Boldest of beggars; a boaster who has nothing,
In town and in taverns telling his tales,
And speaking of something he never saw and swearing it
         true;
Of deeds that he never did discoursing and boasting;   305
And for works that he did well he calls witnesses and says,
"Look, if you don't believe me or think I'm lying to you,
Ask him or him, and he can tell you
What I suffered and saw and some times had,
And what I knew or could calculate, and what kindred I
         came from."   310

7. Sanctimonious, hypocritical.
8. "Without."
9. The ability to perceive and observe, the exterior equivalent of inwit (Gloss).

He wished that men were aware of all his words and deeds
That might please the people and bring praise to himself.
> *If I pleased men, I should not be the servant of Christ; And*
> *elsewhere, no man can serve two masters.*[1]

"By Christ!" said Conscience then, "your best coat,
      Hawkin,
Has many spots and stains; it should be washed."
"Yes, if any one took heed," said Hawkin, "behind and in
      front,   315
What on the back, what over the belly, and on both sides,
He would find many filthy places and many foul spots."
And when he turned himself at that time I took note
That it was far filthier than at first it seemed.
It was splattered with spleen and stubborn will,   320
With envy and evil speech, asking for fights,
Lying and libeling, a tongue that loved to scold;
Spread abroad any bad thing anybody told him,
And blame men behind their backs and wish them bad luck;
And what he learned from Will would tell it to Wat,   325
And what he learned from Wat, Will would soon know it,
And made foes of friends with a false tongue.
"Either with what my mouth could manage or with man's
      strength
Avenge myself many times, or munch my insides;
Cursed my fellow-Christians like sharp shears cutting wool: 330
> *Whose mouth is full of cursing and of bitterness; under his*
> *tongue is travail and grief; And elsewhere, The sons*
> *of men, their teeth are arms and arrows and their*
> *tongue is a sharp sword.*[2]

No one living loves me lasting any while;
For the tales that I tell no one trusts me.
And when I can't make myself master, melancholy overcomes
      me,
So that I catch a stomach-cramp, or occasionally heartburn,
Or an ague in so great an anger, or at other times a fever   335
That takes hold on me a whole twelvemonth, until I despise
The treatment our Lord tenders and put my trust in a
      witch,
And say no clerk — nor Christ, I believe — can cure me so
      well

---

1. Gal. 1.10; Matt. 6.24.
2. Ps. 9B.7; Ps. 56.5.

As the shoemaker of Southwark or the Shoreditch woman,
    Dame Emma.[3]
For neither God's word nor his grace ever gave me help,   340
But through a charm my cure occurred, and I recovered
    my health."
    I watched it more warily and then saw it was soiled
With lecherous leanings and looks from the eye.
For every maid that he met he made her a gesture
Suggesting sin, and some he would savor   345
About the mouth, or beneath begin to grope,
Till their wills grow keen together and they get to work,
As well on fasting days as Fridays and forbidden nights
And as lief in Lent as out of Lent, all times alike;[4]
Such works with them were never out of season   350
Till they might do no more, and then told merry tales
And at how lechers make love laugh and joke,
And in their old age tell of their whoring and wenching.
    Then Patience perceived other spots on his coat,
Dirt caused by covetousness and craving unnaturally.   355
The man had his mind more on money than on God,
And he imagined how he might have it
By falsifying weights and measures, or by false witness;
Lent money for love of the collateral, and loath to deal
    honestly;
And watched for ways by which his wits might cheat men;   360
And mixed his merchandise around and made it look good:
"The worst pieces were placed underneath—that seemed a
    proper trick.
And if my neighbor had a hired hand or else a beast of
    some sort
More profitable than mine, I made many plans—
How I might have it was all I thought about,   365
And unless I got hold of it some other way, in the end I
    stole it,
Or emptied his purse privily, picked his locks.
Both by night and by day I'd always be busy
Getting through guile the goods that I own.
And if I went to the plow, I pinched so close   370
That I'd infringe by a foot or a furrow on the land

---

3. These must be people the original readers would have recognized, probably (on the basis of the next few lines) purveyors of charms against illness. Southwark and Shoreditch were disreputable parts of London.
4. Sexual intercourse was forbidden on many days of the year, for example, on fast days during Lent and Advent and on the nights before religious feasts, as well as during pregnancy and menstruation.

Of my nearest neighbor—nab a bit of his field.
And if I reaped, I'd overreach, or tell my reapers to,
And have them seize with their sickles some grain I'd never
    sown.
And anybody who borrowed from me bought the favor
    dearly   375
With private presents, or payments on account;
So no matter what might happen to him, I always made
    money.
And both to kith and to kin I was unkind with what I had;
And whoever purchased my produce, I'd complain to him
Unless he proffered to pay a penny* or two   380
More than it was worth, and yet I would swear
That it cost me much more—swore many oaths.
On holy days in Holy Church when I heard Mass
No desire swayed me, God knows, to beseech sincerely
Mercy for my misdeeds, but I mourned more   385
For my goods gone astray, believe me, than for guilts of
    my body.
And if I'd done any deadly sin, I'd not dread that so sorely
As when I'd made a loan and believed it lost—or it was
    long before repayment.
And if I performed any friendly act to help my fellow-
    Christians
Upon a cruel covetousness my conscience hung.   390
And if I sent my servants overseas to Bruges,
Or my apprentice to Prussia to profit my affairs,[5]
To buy merchandise with my money and make exchange
    for it here,
Nothing might comfort me in the meantime,
Neither Mass nor matins, nor anything I might see;   395
Nor ever performed a penance or said my Paternoster*
When my mind was not more on my goods in jeopardy
Than on the grace of God and his great helps."
     Where your treasure is, there is your heart also.[6]
    Yet the glutton's garment was soiled with great oaths,
And sloppily beslobbered, as with speaking falsely,   400
Where no need was taking God's name in vain;
Used it constantly in cursing and so sweat-covered his coat;
And ate and drank more at meals than nature might digest,
"And sometimes suffered sickness for surfeiting myself

---

5. Prussia (northern Germany) was a major distributor of English cloth to eastern Europe.
"Bruges": the center of the cloth industry in Flanders.
6. Matt. 6.21.

And then I dreaded to die in deadly sin,"   405
So that supposing he could not be saved he sank into
     wanhope,*
And that is sloth* so sluggish that no skills can help it,
Nor any mercy amend the man who dies in it.
But what are the ways by which one comes to wanhope?
When a man does not mourn for his misdeeds or make
     sorrow for them;   410
But performs poorly the penance the priest enjoins;
Does no almsdeeds; dreads no sin;
Lives contrary to the Creed and cares for no law.
Every day is a holiday with him, or a high feast,
And if he will hear anything it is a ribald's tongue.   415
When men discuss Christ or cleanness of spirit,
He is angry and will hear only words of mirth.
Penance and poor men and the passion of saints,
He hates to hear of, and all that tell about them.
These are the ways, beware, by which one comes to
     wanhope.   420
   You lords and ladies and legates of Holy Church
Who feed fool-sages,[7] flatterers and liars,
And like to listen to them in hope to laugh at them—
    Woe unto you that laugh, etc. —[8]
And give them fees and favors, and refuse poor men,
In your death-dying, I dread sorely   425
Lest those three sorts of men thrust you into great sorrow.
    Those who consent and those who do [it] will be punished
      with the same penalty.[9]
Patriarchs and prophets, preachers of God's words,
Save with their sermons men's souls from hell;
Just so flatterers and fools are the Fiend's disciples
To entice men with their tales to sin and ribaldry.   430
But clerks well-read in Holy Writ should report to lords
What David says of such men, as the Psalter tells:
    He who worketh pride and speaketh iniquities shall not
      dwell within my house.[1]
A lewd man should not have audience in hall nor in chamber
Where wise men are, God's words witness,
Nor any light-minded man be allowed among lords.   435

---

7. I.e., keep as retainers jesters who have license to speak the truth in a comic form.
8. Luke 6.25: the verse continues "now, for ye shall mourn and weep."
9. The Latin line is a legal maxim.
1. Ps. 100.7.

Clerks and knights welcome king's minstrels,
And for love of their lord listen to them at feasts;
Much more, it seems to me, rich men should
Have beggars before them, who shall be God's minstrels
As he says himself; Saint John bears witness: 440
    He who despiseth you despiseth me.[2]
Therefore I remind you rich men, when you make your
    revels,
To solace your souls have such minstrels:
A poor person for a fool-sage placed at your table,
And a learned man from whom to learn what our Lord
    suffered
To save your soul from Satan your enemy,   445
And without flattering fiddle for you Good Friday's story,
And a blind man for a banterer, or a bedridden woman
To ask alms for you before our Lord, to exhibit your good
    fame.
A man is made to laugh by minstrels like these three,
And in his death-dying they do him great comfort   450
Who in his lifetime listened to them and loved to hear them.
These solace his soul until he himself has fallen
In a wellhope,[3] since he did so well, among worthy saints,
While flatterers and fools through their foul words
Lead those that listen to them to Lucifer's feast   455
With *Turpiloquio*,[4] a lay of sorrow, and Lucifer's fiddle.
    Thus Hawkin the Active Man had soiled his coat
Till Conscience questioned him, in a courteous manner,
Why he had not washed it or whisked it with a brush.

Passus XIV

    "I have only one whole outfit," said Hawkin. "I am the
    less to blame
Though it is soiled and seldom clean: I sleep in it at night;
And also I have a housewife, hired help, and children—
    I have taken a wife and therefore I cannot come[1]—
Who will often spill on it and spoil it despite anything I do.
It's been laundered in Lent and out of Lent as well   5

2. Luke 10.16.
3. The opposite of "wanhope."*
4. "Filthy language."
1. Luke 14.20.

With the soap of sickness that searches very deep,
And lathered with the loss of property till I was loath at
       heart
To aggrieve God or good man in any way I knew,
And so was shriven by the priest, who for my sins assigned
       me
Patience as my penance, and to feed poor men,   10
All to take care of my Christendom, to keep it in cleanliness.
And I could never, by Christ, keep it clean an hour,
That I didn't soil it with sight or with some idle speech,
Or by work or by word or by will of my heart—
That I don't make it all messy from morning till evening."   15
     "And I shall teach you," Conscience told him, "how
            Contrition may be used
To scrape your coat clean of all kinds of filth:
            Contrition of heart, etc.
Do-Well will wash it and wring it with a wise confessor:
            Confession of mouth, etc.
Do-Better will scrub it and scour it till no scarlet could be
       brighter,
And dye it with God's-Grace-To-Amend-Yourself and with
       good will,   20
And then send you to Satisfaction, to let the sun bleach it:
            Satisfaction.[2]
Do-Best will keep it clean from unkind deeds.
Then no filth shall defile it nor any moth devour it,
Nor either fiend or false man befoul it in your lifetime.
No herald nor harper will have a fairer garment   25
Than Hawkin the Active Man, if you act according to my
       teaching,
Nor any minstrel be held more worthy among poor and rich
Than will Hawkin the waferer, who is *Active Vita.*"[3]
     "And I'll provide you with dough," said Patience, "though
            no plow tills,
And flour to feed folk with as may be best for the soul;   30
Though grain never grew, nor grape upon vine,
I'd allot livelihood to all that live and move,
And that enough; none shall lack what's necessary to them:
            Have no care, etc.; God feedeth the fowls of the air, etc.; the
            patient overcome, etc."[4]

2. Contrition, confession, and satisfaction are the three parts of the sacrament of penance;
satisfaction refers to the penance of prayers or works the sinner is enjoined to perform by the
priest in confession.
3. "Active Life." "Waferer": wafer-maker.
4. Matt. 6.25–26; Ps. 41.4; proverbial, but cf. Matt. 10.22.

Then Hawkin laughed a little and swore a light oath:
"Whoever believes you, by our Lord, I don't believe he's
      blessed." 35
"No?" said Patience patiently, and pulled out of his bag
Victuals of great virtue for all kinds of beasts
And said, "Lo, here's livelihood enough, if what we believe
      is true.
For none was ever lent life unless livelihood was arranged
Whereof and wherefore and whereby to live. 40
First the wild worm under wet earth,
Fish to live in the flood, and in the fire the cricket,
The curlew whose kind is to live on air—his flesh the cleanest
      among birds,
And beasts on grass and on grain and on green roots,
Meaning that all men might likewise 45
Live through loyal belief as our Lord witnesses:
> *Whatsoever ye shall ask from the Father in my name, etc.;*
> *And elsewhere, Man doth not live by bread alone but*
> *by every word that proceedeth from the mouth of*
> *God."* [5]
But I listened and looked to see what livelihood it was
That Patience so praised, and he pulled from his bag
A piece of the Paternoster* and proffered it to us all.
And so it was *fiat voluntas tua* [6] that would feed us all. 50
"Have some, Hawkin," said Patience, "and eat it when
      you're hungry,
Or when your teeth chatter for chill, or you chew your
      cheek for thirst.
Shall never handcuffs harm you, nor anger of great lords,
Prison or pain, for *patientes vincunt.* [7]
So long as you're restrained in speech and in looking, 55
In inhaling odors and in handling things, in all your five
      senses,
You need never care for corn [8] nor for clothes or drink,
Nor dread death nor Devil, but die as God pleases
Either through hunger or through heat, at his will be it;
For if you live by his lore, the shorter life the better: 60
> *If any one loves Christ he does not love this world.* [9]

---

5. John 14.13; Matt. 4.4.
6. "Thy will be done": Matt. 6.10 (the Lord's Prayer); see also Matt. 26.39, Christ in the Garden of Gethsemane.
7. "The patient overcome."
8. Wheat, i.e., food.
9. Proverbial.

For by his breath beasts grew and walked abroad:
> *He spoke, and they were made, etc.*[1]

Therefore by his breath both men and beasts live,
As Holy Writ's words witness when men say their graces:
> *Thou openest thine hand and fillest every living being with blessing.*[2]

It is found that forty winters folk lived without plowing,
And out of the flint sprang the flood that folk and beasts
> drank.[3]   65

And in Elijah's era Heaven was closed
So that no rain rained — thus men read in books
That men lived for many winters without minding the plow.
Seven slept, as the Book says, seven hundred winters
And lived without livelihood, and at the last they woke.[4]   70

And if men lived as moderation would there should nevermore
> be shortages

Among Christian creatures, if Christ's words are true.
But unkindness makes *caristiam*[5] among Christian people,
Or plenty makes pride among poor and rich.
But moderation is worth so much that it may not cost too
> dear.   75

For the mischance and misery among men of Sodom
Came about through abundance of bread and because of
> pure sloth.

> *Idleness and abundance of bread nourished the basest sin.*[6]

Since men were immoderate in their meat and drink,
Did deadly sin that the Devil found pleasing,
Vengeance fell on them for their vile sins;   80
So they sank into hell, those cities each one.
Therefore let us live with moderation, and let's make faith
> our defense,

And through faith comes contrition, Conscience knows well,
Which drives away deadly sin and reduces it to venial.[7]
And though a man might not speak, contrition might save
> him   85

1. Ps. 148.5.
2. Ps. 144.16, commonly used in saying grace before meals.
3. Num. 20.11.
4. For the Hebrew prophet Elijah (line 66), 1 Kings 17.1, Jas. 5.17. The Seven Sleepers of Ephesus were Christians walled up in a cave during the persecutions of the Emperor Decius and miraculously wakened under the Emperor Theodosius (448 A.D.) — that should be two hundred years, but various versions give different totals. Linking the Hebrew prophet Elijah with the legendary Sleepers was common in medieval biblical paraphrases.
5. "Dearth, scarcity."
6. A common observation correlating with the description of Sodom in Ezek. 16.49; for the destruction of Sodom and Gomorrah, see Gen. 18.20–19.25.
7. "Venial" sin, a slight or unwitting offense, does not damn the sinner; "deadly" sin, if not confessed and forgiven, does.

And bring his soul to bliss, so long as faith bears witness
That while he lived he believed in the lore of Holy Church.
*Ergo** contrition, faith, and conscience naturally comprise
  Do-Well,
And they're surgeons for deadly sins when shrift of mouth
  is lacking.
But shrift of mouth is worth more if a man is truly contrite, 90
For shrift of mouth slays sin, be it never so deadly—
Per confessionem to a priest *peccata occiduntur*[8]—
While contrition does nothing but drive it down into a venial
  sin,
As David says in the Psalter:* *Et quorum tecta sunt peccata.*[9]
But satisfaction searches out the root and both slays and
  purges, 95
And as if it had never been about, brings deadly sin to
  naught
So that it's never again seen or sore, but seems a wound
  healed."
  "Where does Charity dwell?" asked Hawkin. "I don't
  remember in my life
Any one that spoke with him, as widely as I've traveled."
  "Where perfect truth and poor heart are, and patience of
  tongue, 100
There Charity chiefly lives, chamberlain for God himself."
  "Is Patient Poverty," Hawkin asked, "more pleasing to
  our Lord
Than riches earned righteously and reasonably spent?"
  "Yes? *quis est ille?*" Patience exclaimed, "quick, *laudabimus
  eum!*[1]
Though men read about riches right to the world's end, 105
I never knew any one who was rich that when he had to
  make his reckoning,
When he drew to his death-day, his dread was not great,
And that at the reckoning he fell into arrears rather than
  out of debt,
Where a poor man dares plead—and prove by pure reason—
To have a lenience of his lord: he has a legal claim to it. 110
From a righteous judge he asks for joy who has been joyless
  always,
And says, 'Lo, birds and beasts that are barred from bliss
And wild worms in woods, through winters you grieve them

8. "Through confession," "sins are slain."
9. "And whose sins are covered": Ps. 31.1.
1. "Who is that man?" "We shall praise him!"

And make them almost meek and mild for hunger,
And afterward you send them summer, which is their
      sovereign joy   115
And bliss to all who have being, both wild and tame.'
Then may beggars like beasts look for better treatment
Who have lived all their lives languishing and hungry;
Unless God sent them sometime some kind of joy,
Either here or elsewhere, Kind* would never wish it.   120
For he was born to bitter fate for whom no bliss was shaped.
Angels who are now in hell once had joy,
And Dives lived in delight and *douce vie*.[2]
Just so Reason* judges that those gentlemen who were
      lords—
And their ladies as well—lived their lives in mirth.   125
But God has a curious custom, according to Kind Wit,*
Of giving many men their remuneration before they've
      earned it.
Just so God deals with some rich men: it seems to me a
      pity,
Since they have their hire here and Heaven as it were,
And great delight in living without labor of their bodies,   130
And when they die they are disallowed, as David says in
      the Psalter.*
> *They have slept and found nothing. And elsewhere, As the*
> *dream of them that awake, O Lord, in thy city even*
> *to nothing wilt thou reduce, etc.*[3]
Alas, that riches shall rob and ravish man's soul
From the love of their Lord in their last hour!
Hired hands that are paid ahead are evermore needy.
And seldom does he die out of debt who dines before he
      deserves to,   135
And until[4] he's done his duty and his day's work.
For when a workman has done his work, then one can see
      truly
What his work was worth, and what he has deserved,
And not to fetch pay in advance for fear of rejection.
So I say about you rich, it doesn't seem you ought   140
To have Heaven in your home here and Heaven hereafter
Just as a servant who gets his salary in advance and later
      insists on more
Like one who had none and has hire at last.

2. "An easy, pleasurable life." On Dives, see Luke 16.19–24.
3. Ps. 75.6; Ps. 72.20.
4. I.e., "before," but the switching of perspective in mid-sentence is in the text and characteristic of Langland's style; similar switches in sentence structure occur in lines 139 and 142.

It may not be, you rich men, or Matthew lies of God:
    It is difficult to cross from delights to delights.[5]
And if you rich people have pity and keep the poor well fed, 145
And live just as law enjoins, doing justice to them all,
Christ of his courtesy will comfort you in the end
And reward with double wealth all whose hearts well with
    pity.
And as a hired hand that had his hire before he began work,
And when he has done his duty well men do him other
    kindness, 150
Give him a coat beyond the contract, just so Christ gives
    Heaven
Both to the prosperous and the not prosperous who show
    pity in their lives;
And all who do their duty well have double pay for their
    labors,
Here on earth forgiveness of their sins and Heaven's bliss
    hereafter.
   But it is but seldom seen in holy saints' books 155
That God rewarded double rest to any rich man.
For there is much mirth among the rich, what with their
    meals and clothing,
And much mirth is in May among wild beasts;
And so forth while summer lasts their solace continues.
But beggars about midsummer have breadless suppers, 160
And yet winter is worse for them, for they walk wetshod,
Faint from thirst and from hunger and foully abused
And berated by rich men that it's heart-rending to hear.
Now, Lord, send them some summer and some kind of joy,
Heaven after they go hence who are here in much need. 165
For thou mightest have made all men so that none was
    more needy than another
And all alike witty and wise, if that had well pleased thee.
And have mercy on these rich men that don't maintain thy
    prisoners;
For the good thou hast given them *ingrati*[6] are many.
But God of thy goodness give them grace to amend. 170
For may no dearth do them harm, drought nor wet,
Nor either heat or hail if they have their health;
Of what they wish for and would have they are wanting
    nothing here.

---

5. Cf. Matt 19.23–24, probably as transmitted through the Epistles of St. Jerome.*
6. "Ungrateful"; cf. Luke 6.35.

But poor people, thy prisoners, Lord, in the pit of misery,
Comfort those creatures whom many cares afflict,   175
Dearth and drought, all their days here.
Woe in winter times for want of clothing,
And in summertime seldom sup till they're full.
Comfort thy care-worn, Christ, in thy kingdom,
For how thou comfortest all creatures clerks bear witness: 180
    Ye will be turned to me and ye will be saved.[7]
Thus *in genere*[8] of his gentle* kind* Jesus Christ said
To pillagers, to plunderers, to rich and to poor,
To whores, to whoremongers, to all kinds of people.
Thou taughtest them in the Trinity to take baptism[9]
And through christening be clean of all kinds of sin.   185
And if through our folly it befell us to fall into sin afterward,
Confession and acknowledging and craving thy mercy
Should amend us as many times as any man would desire.
And if the Devil should debate against this and disturb us
    in our consciences,
We should quickly take the acquittance and accost the Fiend
    with it: 190
    Let it be known, etc.: Through the passion of the Lord.[1]
And so repel our Opponent, and prove ourselves under
    protection.
But the parchment for these letters patent must be made of
    poverty,
And of pure patience and perfect belief.
When made of pomp and of pride the parchment crumbles,
And in practice for all people unless they're poor of heart.   195
Otherwise all is in vain, all that we ever did,
Paternoster and penance and pilgrimage to Rome,
Unless our expenses and dispensing spring of a true well,
Otherwise is all our labor lost—lo, how men write
On windows they provide the friars with[2]—if the foundation
    is false.   200
Therefore Christians should be rich in common, none
    covetous for himself.

---

7. Isa. 45.22.
8. "In a way [characteristic]."
9. Since the second person of the Trinity, Christ, underwent baptism, the Trinity itself demonstrates the necessity of this sacrament.
1. The opening phrase imitates a public letter or document from the king putting on record a contract or right (called "letters patent" in line 192). In this case the "acquittance" of line 190 (the "receipt," as it were), showing that Christ has paid sinners' debt to the Devil, is the release demonstrating the Devil has lost his claim to them.
2. Such donations, like Lady Meed's (III.43–72a), were a common misuse of the relationship between money, charity, and salvation.

For there are seven sins[3] that are always assailing us;
The Fiend follows them all and tries to foster them,
But with riches those ribalds most readily beguile men,
For where riches reign acts of reverence follow,   205
And that is pleasing to pride in poor and in rich.
But the rich is given reverence by reason of his riches,
Where the poor is pushed back, and perhaps has more
Of wit and of wisdom that are far away better
Than riches or royalty, and heard more readily in Heaven.   210
For the rich has much to reckon with, and walks right softly;
The highway toward Heaven is often blocked by riches:
　　　Thus it is impossible for a rich man, etc.[4]
While the poor presses ahead with a pack on his back:
　　　For their works follow them,[5]
Blatantly, as beggars do, and boldly he craves
For his poverty and patience a perpetual bliss: 215
　　　Blessed are the poor for theirs is the kingdom of Heaven.[6]
　　But pride reigns in riches rather than in poverty;
Either in the master or in his man he maintains some
　　　　lodging.
But in poverty where patience lives pride has no might,
And none of the seven sins may sit there for long,
Or have power in poverty, if patience accompany it.   220
For the poor is always prepared to please the rich
And is obedient to his bidding for the breadcrumbs he gives,
And obedience and boastfulness must be evermore at war,
And each hates the other in all sorts of acts.

　　If Wrath wrestles with the poor he derives the less from it, 225
For if they put in a complaint at law the poor is the weaker;
And if he chides or chafes he achieves the less,
For he looks lowly and his language is pleasant
Who must ask other men for his meals or money.

　　And if Gluttony grieves Poverty he gains the less by it,   230
For his revenue will not reach far enough to buy rich foods;
And though his gluttony be for good ale, he goes to a cold
　　　　bed,

---

3. Pride, lechery, envy, avarice, wrath, gluttony, and sloth.
4. Cf. Matt. 19.23-24.
5. Rev. 14.13.
6. Cf. the familiar Beatitude in Matt. 5.3, but Luke 6.20 is closer. (Matt. has "poor *in spirit.*")
Patience's point of view here is actually a synthesis of the two. Notice also that throughout
Patience's discussion he shifts back and forth between meaning by "poverty" the condition itself
and the person who is afflicted with it, in a manner typical of Langland's treatment of alle-
gorical entities. An additional irony of the passage is that the poor are praised for developing
the qualities that are the opposite of those attributed to the poor in social satire of the period,
where poverty and hardship were assumed to bring out the worst, except in those who had
chosen poverty voluntarily.

With his head exposed, inadequately covered
For when he stretches to his full extent, the straw is his
      sheets.
So for his gluttony and great sloth he has a grievous
      penance,   235
Which is a world of woe when he wakes and weeps for cold,
And sometimes for his sins; so he is never merry
Without mourning mixed in, and misery as well.
   And if Covetousness catch the poor, they may not come
      together,
And notably by the neck may neither grasp the other;   240
For it's common knowledge that Covetousness has a keen
      will
And has hands and arms of a great length,
And Poverty's just a puny thing, appears not up to his
      navel,
And there was never satisfactory sport between the short
      and the long.[7]
And though Avarice would anger the poor, he has but little
      power,   245
For Poverty has only packs to put his goods in,
While Avarice has huge chests and iron-bound coffers.
And which is easier to break open? Less uproar is made
By a beggar's bag than an iron-bound coffer.
   Lechery loves him not, for he has little silver to spend   250
And sits not down to dine delicately nor drinks wine often.
A straw for the stews![8] they'd not be standing, I think,
If their only patrons were poor men; there'd be no roofs
      upon their houses.
And though Sloth pursues Poverty, and serves not God's
      pleasure,
Misery is always an intermediary and makes him think   255
That God is his greatest help, and after God no one,
And he is his servant, as he says, and of the same
      household.
And whether he serves him or serves him not, he bears the
      sign of poverty
And in that livery our Lord delivered all mankind.
Therefore any poor man who is patient may claim by pure
      right,   260
After his ending here, Heaven-kingdom's bliss.

---

7. The struggle of Covetousness to catch the poor man is pictured as a wrestling match between ludicrously mismatched opponents.
8. Houses of prostitution (literally, baths).

Much more confidently may he claim it that could have his
    will here
In land and in lordship and delights of the body
And leaves it all for God's love and lives like a beggar.
And as a maid forsakes her mother for a man's love,   265
Her father and all her friends, and follows her mate—
Much is that maid to be loved by the man who weds her,
More than a maiden is who is married through brokerage
As by assent of sundry parties, and silver thrown in,
More for the sake of money than the mutual love of the
    pair—   270
So it proves with every person who forsakes possession
And applies himself to be patient, and weds Poverty,
Who is sib[9] to God himself—so close is Poverty."
    "May God have my troth," said Hawkin, "I hear you
        praise Poverty much.
What is Poverty, Patience," said he, "properly defined?"   275
"Poverty," said Patience, *"is a hateful good, a removal from cares,*
    a possession without impropriety, a gift of God, mother of
    health, a narrow path without anxiety, nurse of wisdom, a
    business without loss, an uncertain fortune, felicity without
    care."[1]
    "I can't construe this," Hawkin told him, "you must
        translate it into English."
    "All this in English," said Patience, "is very hard to
        expound,
But I shall explain some of it, so you may understand.
Poverty is the principal point that Pride hates most.   280
Then it's good for a good reason, whatever grieves Pride.
Just as contrition is a comforting thing, Conscience well
    knows,
And a sorrow in itself and a solace to the soul,
So Poverty is properly penance to the body
And a joy to patient poor, pure spiritual health,   285
And contrition is comfort and *cura animarum*;[2]
Therefore poverty is a hateful good.
Seldom does Poverty sit to decide the truth,
Or is assigned the job of justice to make judgments on men,
Nor made mayor over men, or a minister under kings;   290
Seldom is any poor man compelled to punish any people.

9. Kindred.
1. The Latin lines in the original text come from a collection of classical maxims repeated in
the Middle Ages. Phrases in this definition recur like refrains in lines 287–320a.
2. "The healing of souls."

Therefore Poverty and poor men perform the commandment
Do not judge any one:[3]
> *A removal from cares.*

Seldom does a poor man become really rich save by rightful
    inheritance.

He wins nothing with false weights nor with unlicensed
    measures,   295

He borrows nothing from his neighbors but what he knows
    he can repay:
> *A possession without impropriety.*

The fourth is a fortune from which the soul flourishes
With sobriety from all sin and also still more;
It diverts the flesh from manifold follies,
A collateral comfort, Christ's own gift: 300
> *A gift of God.*

The fifth is mother of might and of man's health,
A physician for foul ills, a friend in all temptations,
And for an unlearned man ever alike a lover wholly clean:
> *Mother of health.*

The sixth is a path of peace; yes, through the pass of
    Alton[4]

Poverty might pass without peril from robbers.   305
For where Poverty passes peace follows after,
And ever the less his load is, the lighter he is of heart:
> *Poverty will sing on his journey in the face of the thief,*[5]
And a man hardy of heart among a heap of thieves.
Therefore Seneca says *Poverty is a narrow path without anxiety.*[6]
The seventh is a well of wisdom, with few words to speak   310
For lords make little allowance for him nor listen to his
    opinion;
He tempers his tongue toward the truth who covets no
    treasure:
> *Nurse of wisdom.*

The eighth is a lawful labor and loath to take more
Than he may surely deserve, in summer or in winter;
And though he negotiates he regrets no loss if he can gain
    charity: 315
> *A business without loss.*

The ninth is sweet to the soul, no sugar sweeter,

---

3. Matt. 7.1.
4. This piece of road on the Hampshire-Surrey border was famous for the robbers who used
it to prey on prosperous travelers to and from Winchester.
5. From the Roman satirist Juvenal: Satire X.22.
6. The line repeats part of line 276; while Seneca expresses similar views, a specific source
for this line has not been identified in his work.

For Patience comprises bread for Poverty himself,
And sobriety is sweet drink and a good physician in sickness.
Thus for our Lord's love Saint Augustine,* a lettered man,
    taught me:[7]
A blessed life without busy cares for body and for soul: 320
    Felicity without care.
Now God who gives all good grant his soul rest
Who first composed this to explain to men what Poverty
    meant."
  "Alas," said Hawkin the Active Man then, "that after my
    christening
I hadn't died and been buried deep for Do-Well's sake!
So hard it is," said Hawkin, "to live and to do sin.   325
Sin pursues us always," said he, and began to grow sorrowful,
And wept water with his eyes, and bewailed the time
That ever he'd done deed that displeased dear God;
Swooned and sobbed and sighed full often
That he'd ever had land or lordship, less or more,   330
Or been master over any man more than of himself.
"I would not be worthy, God knows," said Hawkin, "to
    wear any clothes,
Neither shirt nor shoes, except for shame alone
To cover my cadaver," said he, and cried fast for mercy
And wept and wailed, and therewith I awoke.   335

Passus XV

  But after my waking it was wondrous long
Before I'd enough natural knowledge* to understand what
    Do-Well was,
And so my wits waxed and waned till I went out of my
    mind.
And some scorned my life — few would sanction it —
And looked on me as a lazy loafer, one loath to do honor   5
To lords or ladies or any other living person,
Such as people in fur-pieces with pendants of silver;
To sergeants* and to such I said not once,
"God look you, lords,"[1] nor would lowly bow,
So that folk held me a fool; and in that folly I raved   10

7. Probably a general reference to similar sentiments in Augustine rather than an allusion to
any specific passage.
1. Common polite greeting ("look": "look out for, look after").

Till Reason had ruth[2] on me and rocked me asleep,
Till I saw, as if it were sorcery, a subtle[3] thing withal,
One without tongue or teeth told me where I should go,
And where I came from and of what kind.* I conjured him
     at the last
If he were Christ's creature, for Christ's love to tell me.   15
    "I am Christ's creature," he said, "and a kinsman of his
     household,
Known well in Christ's court and to Christians in many a
     place.
Neither Peter the Porter nor Paul with his falchion[4]
Refuses to admit me at the door—no matter how late I
     knock,
At midnight, at midday, my voice is so well known   20
That every creature in his court welcomes me fairly."
    "What are you called in that court," said I, "among Christ's
     people?"
    "While I breathe breath in the body," said he, "I am called
     Anima;[5]
And when I will and wish, *Animus* is my name.
And because I'm capable of knowing, I am called *Mens*;   25
And when I make moan to God, *Memoria* is my name.
When I arbitrate issues and act as Truth teaches,
Then *Ratio* is my right name, Reason* in English.
And when I feel what folk tell, my first name is *Sensus*,
And that is wit* and wisdom, the well of all skills.   30
And when I challenge or don't challenge, choose or reject,
Then I'm called Conscience, God's clerk and his notary;
And when I love loyally our Lord and all others,
Then is loyal love my name, and in Latin *Amor*.
And when I flee from the flesh and forsake the body,   35
Then I'm a spirit speechless: then *Spiritus* is my name.
Augustine* and Isidore,[6] each of the two,
Named me with these names; now you might choose

---

2. Pity.
3. The Middle English word primarily implies something immaterial rather than something
not obvious.
4. St. Peter is the "porter" of Heaven because he holds the keys (Matt. 16.19); St. Paul was
represented with a sword, i.e., a falchion, perhaps because he was executed with one, or perhaps
to symbolize the "sword of the spirit" (Eph. 6.17).
5. The names of *Anima* ("Soul") indicate the soul's various functions: as *Anima*, "Principle of Life
or Being"; as *Animus*, "Will"; as *Mens*, "Mind"; as *Memoria*, "Memory" (but also see "Imaginative"*);
as *Ratio*, "Reason";* as *Sensus*, "Sense," or "Perception"; as *Conscientia*, "Conscience";* as *Amor*,
"Love"; as *Spiritus*, "Spirit." The ensuing passage makes the nature of the functions much clearer,
but precisely what the terms mean and how they should be translated is a matter of debate;
see Gloss discussion of those marked with an asterisk.
6. Isidore of Seville (c. 560–636), Bishop of Seville and author of a massive encyclopedic work
called the *Etymologies*.

By which you'd care to call me, now you're acquainted with
    them all."

> *Anima is distinguished by various names according to its*
> *various actions: When it vivifies the body it is Life;*
> *when it wills it is Soul; when it knows it is Mind;*
> *when it recollects it is Memory; when it judges it is*
> *Reason; when it feels it is Sense; when it denies or*
> *consents it is Conscience; when it loves it is Love;*
> *when it expires it is Spirit.*[7]

"You remind me of a bishop," said I, making a joke,   40
"For those blessed as bishops bear many names,
Praesul and *Pontifex* and *Metropolitanus*,
And a whole heap of others, *Episcopus* and *Pastor*."[8]
    "That is so," he said, "now I see your will:
You would like to learn everything that lies behind their
    names,   45
And behind mine, if you might, it seems to me from your
    words."
    "Yes, sir," I said, "so long as no one takes offense,
All the sciences under the sun and all the subtle arts,
I'd like to know them naturally, natively, in my heart."
    "Then you are imperfect," said he, "and are one of Pride's
    knights.   50
For a wish and a longing like this Lucifer fell from Heaven.

> *I shall place my foot in the north and I shall be like the*
> *most high.*[9]

It would go against Kind,"* he said, "and against all kinds
    of reason
That any creature's knowledge should include everything
    but Christ's alone.[1]
Solomon speaks against such and despises their wits,
And says, *Just as, if some one eats much honey, it is not good for*
    him, so he who is an examiner of majesty is overwhelmed by
    its glory.[2]   55
This is to mean to English men who may speak and hear,
The man who eats much honey, his maw is cloyed,

---

7. From Isidore, whose definitions were widely consulted in the Middle Ages. In this definition, the "soul" that wills refers to the center of spiritual life — to the most essential, defining function of *Anima*.

8. Medieval titles for a bishop or archbishop reflecting various pagan, governmental, and biblical functions that contributed historically to the defining of the office. *Praesul*: the leader of sacred dances and ritual; *Pontifex*: literally, "bridge-builder," one of the Roman titles for a high priest; *Metropolitanus*: head of a province, based in its central or "mother" city; *Episcopus*: overseer; *Pastor*: shepherd.

9. Cf. Isa. 14.13–14.

1. I.e., any creature's knowledge but Christ's.

2. Prov. 25.27.

And the more good matter that a man hears,
It does him double harm unless he does what it says.
'*Beatus est*,' says Saint Bernard,* '*qui Scripturas legit,*   60
Et verba vertit in opera[3] fully to his power.'
Desire to understand and be skilled in sciences
Put Adam and Eve out of Paradise.

>   *The appetite for knowledge despoiled man of the glory of*
>   *immortality.*[4]

And just as honey is hard to digest and overloads the
    stomach,
Right so any one who with his reason would derive the root   65
Of God and of his great powers will find his graces
    diminished.
For pride inheres in his interest, and an appetite of the
    body,
Against Christ's counsel and all clerks'* teaching,
Which is *Know no more than you need to know.*[5]

  Friars and many other Masters* who give ignorant men
    sermons,   70
You argue incomprehensible issues when you talk of the
    Trinity,
That the faith of unlearned folk is frequently tinged with
    doubt.
For many Doctors* it would be better to leave behind such
    teaching,
And tell men of the Ten Commandments and touch on the
    seven sins,[6]
And of the branches that burgeon from them and bring
    men to hell,   75
And how folk on follies misspend their five senses,
As well friars as other folk foolishly spend
On housing, on habiliments, on showing off high learning
More for pomp than for pure charity; the people know the
    truth.
And that I'm not lying, look, for it's lords you please,   80
And you reverence the rich more readily for their money:

>   *Confounded be all they that worship graven images; And*
>   *elsewhere, So why do you love vanity and seek after*
>   *mendacity?*[7]

---

3. "Blessed is he . . . who reads the Scriptures and turns their words into works."
4. Also from St. Bernard.
5. Rom. 12.3.
6. Pride, lechery, envy, avarice, wrath, gluttony, and sloth.
7. Ps. 96.7; Ps. 4.3.

Go to the gloss[8] on that verse, you great clerks,
And if I lie about you in my lack of learning, lead me to
          be burned!
For I feel that you refuse to take alms from no one,
Not from usurers or whores or avaricious merchants,   85
And you bow low to these lords that may allot you nobles
Against your rule and religion: I find recorded of Jesus
That he said to his disciples, '*Ne sitis personarum acceptores.*'[9]
Of this matter I might make a whole Bible,
But of curators of Christian people, as clerks bear witness,   90
I shall tell it for truth's sake; take heed whoever wishes.
As holiness and honesty spring out of Holy Church
Through lawful-living men that teach the law of God,
Just so out of Holy Church all evils spread
Where there is imperfect priesthood, preachers and teachers.   95
And for an example see how on trees in summer time
There are some boughs that bear leaves and some bear
          none.
There is some sickness in the root of such sorts of trees;
Just so parsons and priests and preachers of Holy Church
Are the root of the right faith to rule the people;   100
But where the root is rotten, Reason knows the truth,
Shall never flower nor fruit grow nor fair leaf be green.
Therefore if you lettered men would leave your lechery for
          clothing,
And, as befitted clerks, be kind and courteous with Christ's
          goods,
True of your tongue and of your tail too,   105
And hate to hear indecency, or ever to accept
Tithes[1] of things untruly gotten by tillage or barter,
Then unlearned men would not be loath to learn from your
          teaching
And would amend what they do amiss more for your
          examples
Than if you fail to practice what you preach—that seems
          hypocrisy.   110
For in a Latin text hypocrisy is likened to a loathsome
          dunghill
Spread over with snow outside, and snakes inside it,
Or to a wall that's been white-washed and is foul
          underneath.[2]

8. The *Glossa Ordinaria*, the traditional medieval commentary on the Bible, interprets the "graven images" as lies and as transitory objects of desire.
9. "Be not unjust regarders of persons": Jas. 2.1; Deut. 1.17.
1. Taxes due the Church.
2. Cf. Matt. 23.27, where the comparison is to a "whited sepulchre" with bones and stench inside.

Just so priests, preachers, and many prelates too,
You appear bleached with *belles paroles* and with *belles*
    clothes,[3]   115
But your works and your words are most wolf-like
    underneath.
    John Chrysostomus comments on clerks and priests:
Just as from the temple all good emanates, so from the temple all
    evil emanates. If the priesthood has been unspotted, the whole
    church flourishes; if, however, it has been corrupted, every
    one's faith is withered. If the priesthood has been involved in
    sin, the whole population is turned toward sinning. Just as
    when you see a tree faded and withered, you know it has a
    defect in its root, so when you see a people undisciplined and
    irreligious, without doubt the priesthood is not healthy.[4]
If unlearned men were aware what this Latin means,
And what man was my authority, it would seem to me
    much wonder   120
Unless many priests began to forbear their brooches and
    shortswords
And bore beads in their hands and a book under their arms.
Sir John and Sir Geoffrey have a silver girdle,
A shortsword or a snickersnee with splendid gilt buttons,
But a prayerbook that should be his plow to repeat *Placebo* — [5]   125
He's never saved silver to buy one because of spending on
    ale;
He sings the service without a book, says it with idle mind.
Alas, you unlearned men, you lose much on priests!
But whatever is wickedly won and with false tricks,
Would never the wisdom of wise God but wicked men
    should have it,   130
Such as imperfect priests and those who preach for money,
Executors and subdeans, summoners* and their mistresses,
What was gotten with guile is ungraciously expended.
Thus whoremongers and whores are helped with such goods
But God's folk are enfeebled and founder for lack of them.[6]   135

---

3. "Lofty, fine words," "beautiful clothes."
4. St. John Chrysostom (c. 345–407) was one of the greatest of the Fathers of the Eastern (Greek) Church — hence his great "authority" (line 120). But the passage is actually not his but from an unknown Latin author often mistaken for him; cf. Isa. 24.2.
5. "I will please [the Lord]": Ps. 114.9, part of the liturgy or of the personal devotions intended for lay people. Sir John and Sir Geoffrey (line 123) are worldly priests. (Priests as well as knights were called "sir.") A "snickersnee" is a large knife.
6. This convoluted sentence says *both* that God would rather dirty money went to dirty people instead of contaminating those who are (or should be) virtuous *and* that the fact it does go to the dirty leaves the virtuous impoverished. The two ideas are sandwiched together in characteristic Langlandian fashion. "Subdeans": parish priests chosen to assist the bishop in administering discipline in specific parts of the diocese.

Curators of Holy Kirk such as clerks that are avaricious,
What they leave behind low-living men lightly spend,
Or else they end intestate, and then—enter the bishop![7]
And he makes merry with it and his henchmen do too;
And they name him a niggard that spared no goods   140
For friend or for foreigner—'The Fiend have his soul!
For he held a wretched household all his lifetime,
And what he saved and stored away, let's spend it in mirth!'
With learned, with unlearned, who are loath to spend,
That's how their goods go when their spirit's gone hence.   145
But for good men, God knows, men greatly mourn,
And lament good meat-givers, and keep them in
        remembrance
In prayers and in penances, and in perfect charity."
    "What is charity?" I asked then. "A childish thing," he
        said.
        *Unless ye become as little children ye shall not enter into the
            kingdom of Heaven.*[8]
"Without a child's fantasy or folly, a free liberal will."   150
    "Where should one find such a friend with so free a heart?
I have lived in land," said I, "my name is Long Will,[9]
And I never found full charity, before nor behind.
Men are merciful to mendicants and to poor men,
And will lend money when they believe they can rely on
        repayment.   155
But charity that Paul praises best, and most pleasing to our
        Savior—
Is not puffed up, is not ambitious, seeketh not her own[1]—
I saw never such a man, so God help me,
Who would not ask for what is his, and at other times covet
A thing he had no need for, and nab it if he could.   160
Clerks proclaim to me that Christ is in all places,
But I never saw him surely except as myself in a mirror.
        Here darkly, then face to face.[2]
And so I trust truly, from what men tell about it,
Charity is neither what champions fight for nor exchangeable
        for cash."

---

7. I.e., people who have stored up wealth and not been generous with it: in particular, wealthy
priests (which is why the bishop—line 138—gets the estate if there is no will).
8. Matt. 18.3.
9. In this passage, "lived in land" and "Long Will" play on the name of the (supposed) author,
William Langland: see Introduction, p. viii; for his tallness, see the so-called autobiographical
passage from the C-version of the poem in the Appendix. The name "Will," however, associates
the Dreamer even more directly with the human will.
1. 1 Cor. 13.4–5.
2. 1 Cor. 13.12.

"Charity," said he, "neither makes exchanges nor
    challenges, nor does it crave.   165
As pleased with a penny* as with a pound of gold,
And as glad for a gown of a gray russet
As for a jacket cut from Tarsia cloth or from costly scarlet.[3]
He's glad with all who're glad, and good to all wicked
And loves and lends help to all that our Lord made.   170
He curses no creature and he can harbor no anger,
And has no liking to lie or laugh men to scorn.
All that men say, he assumes it's true and accepts without
    question,
And all sorts of distress he suffers with mildness.
He covets no earthly good, but Heaven's bliss."   175
    "Has he any income or assets or any rich friends?"
    "In income and assets he has no interest,
For a friend provides for him who never failed him at need:
Fiat voluntas tua[4] provides for him always,
And if he sups he eats but a snack of *Spera-in-Deo*.[5]   180
He can portray well the Paternoster* and paint it with *Aves*[6]
And he is accustomed occasionally to come as a pilgrim
To where poor men and prisoners lie, to ask pardon from
    them;
Though[7] he bears them no bread, he bears them sweeter
    sustenance;
He loves them as our Lord bids and looks after their
    welfare.   185
And when he's weary of that work then he will sometimes
Labor in a laundry the length of a mile-walk,[8]
And burst into youth's bailiwick and briskly seek out
Pride with all its appurtenances, and pack them together,
And bang them against his breast and beat them clean,   190
And lay on long with *Laboravi in gemitu meo*,[9]
And with warm water from his eyes wash them after.
Then he sings when he does so, and sometimes weeping,
A contrite and humbled heart, God, thou wilt not despise."[1]

---

3. Tarsia cloth and scarlet are costly fabrics; russet cloth is a poor one.
4. "Thy will be done": Matt. 6.10 (the Lord's Prayer). Note this is the "livelihood" Patience had in his poke, XIV.50.
5. "Hope-in-God": Ps. 41.6.
6. Prayers beginning "Hail [*Ave*] Mary": cf. Luke 1.28.
7. I.e., even if.
8. I.e., the length of time it takes to walk a mile. (People in a largely clockless society measure duration by the time it takes to perform familiar tasks.) The "laundry" is symbolic of self-examination and penance, as the next lines show; washing in pre-modern conditions was heavy labor, mostly involving beating the clothes in water.
9. "I have labored in groaning": Ps. 6.7.
1. Ps. 50.19.

"By Christ! I wish he were my acquaintance," said I, "no
    creature sooner."   195
"Without help of Piers Plowman," said he, "you'll not see
    his person ever."
"Do clerks that keep Holy Kirk know him?" I asked.
"Except by works and words," said he, "clerks have no
    way of knowing.
But Piers the Plowman perceives more deeply
What is the will and wherefore that many a one suffers: 200
    And God saw their thoughts.[2]
For there are purely proud-hearted men patient of tongue
And bland in their behavior to burgesses* and lords,
And for poor people have pepper in their nose,[3]
And look like a lion when men belittle their deeds.
For there are beggars and prayer-bidders, beadsmen[4] as it
    were,   205
Who look like lambs and seem life-holy,
But it's more to get their meals in a manner so easy
Than for penance or perfectness, the poverty they adopt.
Therefore by color[5] nor by clergy you'll never come to know
    him,
Neither through words nor works, but through will alone,   210
And no clerk knows that, nor creature on earth
But Piers the Plowman, *Petrus id est Christus.*[6]
For he does not live in lollers or land-leaping hermits,
Nor with anchorites* where a box[7] hangs; all such are
    frauds.
Fie on fakers and *in fautores suos*![8]   215
    For charity is God's champion and as a good child
    courteous,
And the merriest of mouth at meals where he sits.
The love that lies in his heart makes him lively of speech,

---

2. Luke 11.17 reads, "He [Jesus] saw their thoughts."
3. Proverbial expression meaning "treat with contempt," i.e., respond as if they were an irritant.
4. Paid prayer-sayers.
5. I.e., appearance.
6. "Peter, that is, Christ." This brief line brings together crucial images, including these: 1 Cor. 10.4 calls Christ "the rock (*petra*)" from which we drink spiritually as the Israelites in the desert drank from a spring Moses brought forth by striking a rock (Num. 20.1–13); in Matt. 16.18, Christ gives Simon the name Peter and calls him the "rock" on which the Church will be built; "Piers" is a form of the name *Petrus*, or Peter.
7. I.e., alms-box (anchorites, who were solitaries, were not supposed to go out begging). "Lollers": lazy freeloaders, a term of contempt later (but not at this date) applied to the heretical proto-Protestant followers of John Wycliffe (1320?–1384). "Land-leaping hermits": hermits who don't stay put in their wilderness hermitages.
8. "On their protectors."

And he is companionable and comforting as Christ bids
    himself:
    Be not sad as the hypocrites.[9]
For I have seen him in silk and sometimes in russet,[1]   220
Both in gray cloth and gay fur and in gilt harness,
And he'd hand it over happily to any one who needed it.
Edmund and Edward each was a king[2]
And they're established as saints, charity pursued them so
    steadily.
I have also seen charity sing and read,   225
Ride and run in ragged clothes,
But behaving like a beggar I never beheld him.
But in rich robes he most readily walks,
With skullcap and curled hair and his crown shaven.[3]
And in a friar's frock he was found once,   230
But it was many years far, far gone, in Francis'* time.
In that sect since he's been too seldom known.
He has regard for rich men and takes robes from them,
Those who without wiles lead well their lives.
    Blessed is the rich man who, etc.[4]
He comes often to the king's court[5] where the council is
    true,   235
But if Covetousness is in the council he will not come there.
Among the commons in court he comes only rarely
Because of brawling and backbiting and bearing of false
    witness.
In the consistory* before the commissary[6] he comes not
    very often,
For their lawsuits last overlong unless they get silver,   240
And for money they make marriage, and unmake it too,
And what Conscience* and Christ have knit fast together
They disrespectfully undo it, those doctors of law.
Among archbishops and bishops, for beggars' sake,
It was once his wont to dwell with them   245
And apportion to the poor Christ's patrimony;
But Avarice has the keys now and keeps it for his kinsmen,

9. Matt. 6.16.
1. See line 167 above.
2. Edmund the Martyr was King of East Anglia (died 870). "Edward": Edward the Confessor
(died 1066).
3. I.e., he is most appropriately made an abbot or bishop; lines 244–48 remark how rarely
he is seen in a position of ecclesiastical authority.
4. Ecclus. 31.8: the verse continues, "is found without stain."
5. I.e., the king's court of law (as opposed to the "common court" in line 237), not the king's
residence.
6. The bishop's official representative in part of his diocese, who can act for him in his absence
and who presides over the bishop's court.

And for his executors and his servants, and some for their
    children.
But I belittle no living person, but Lord amend us all,
And give us grace, good God, to follow charity.   250
For whoever might meet with him, his manners are such
That he neither blames nor berates, boasts nor praises,
Libels nor lauds, nor looks up sternly,
Craves nor covets nor cries for more:
    In peace in the selfsame I shall sleep, etc.[7]
The largest livelihood that he lives on is love in God's
    passion;   255
He neither begs nor beseeches nor borrows at interest.
He mistreats no man, nor lets his mouth grieve him.
  Among Christian men this mildness should endure
In all kinds of ills, have this at heart
That though they suffered all this, God suffered for us more 260
In example that we should do the same, and take no
    vengeance
On our foes who do us falseness; that is our Father's will.
For every one may know well that if God had willed
    himself,
Should never Judas nor Jew have put Jesus on the Cross,
Nor have martyred Peter or Paul, nor held them prisoners.   265
But he suffered in example that we should suffer also,
And said to such as were willing sufferers,
'*Patientes vincunt verbi gratia,*'[8] and advanced many examples.
  Lo, in *Legenda Sanctorum*,[9] the life of holy saints,
What penance and poverty and passion they suffered,   270
In hunger, in heat, in all sorts of vexations.
Antony and Egidius[1] and other holy fathers
Had their homes in the wilderness among wild animals,
Monks and mendicants, men by themselves,
In crevices and caves, conversed seldom together.   275
But neither Antony nor Egidius nor any hermit then
From lions or leopards would accept livelihood,
But from fowls that fly: thus men find in books.
Except that Egidius had a hind[2] he'd call for,

---

7. Ps. 4.9: the verse continues, "and I shall find rest."
8. "The patient overcome through grace of the word."
9. *Saints' Lives.*
1. The stories of these (and the other famous hermits mentioned in the next lines) appear in
the *Legenda Aurea, The Golden Legend,* a collection of saints' lives. St. Anthony, an early hermit
in the desert (died 356), was believed to be the founder of monasticism; Egidius (St. Giles)
was a Greek who became a hermit in southern France (died 700).
2. A female deer.

And through the milk of that mild beast the man was
    sustained;   280
But he did not have her every day to assuage his hunger,
But seldom and at scattered times, as the book says and
    teaches.
Every day Antony about high noon
Had a bird that brought him bread that he lived on,
And though[3] the good man had a guest God provided for
    them both.   285
Paul *primus heremita*[4] had penned himself up
So that no man might see him for moss and for leaves.
Fowls fed him all his food for many a winter,
Till he founded friars of Austin's* order — or else friars lie.
After his preaching Paul practiced basket-making,[5]   290
And earned with his hands what his stomach had need of.
Peter fished for his food, like his fellow Andrew;[6]
They sold some and stewed some and so they both lived.
And also Mary Magdalene[7] lived on meals of roots and
    dews,
But mostly through meditation, with her mind on God
    almighty.   295
In seven days I'd not succeed in speaking of them all
Who lived thus for our Lord's love many long years.
But there was no lion or leopard that lived in the woods,
Neither bear nor boar nor wild beast of other kind,
That didn't fall to their feet and fawn with their tails;   300
And if they could have communicated, by Christ, as I think,
They would have fed that folk before wild fowls did.
For all the courtesy that animals have they often showed
    those people,
By licking, by lowing, where they walked along through the
    woods.
But God sent them food by fowls and not by fierce beasts   305
Meaning that the meek should maintain the mild.
Right so righteous men should maintain religious* orders,
And lawful men bring livelihood to life-holy men;

---

3. I.e., even when.
4. "The first hermit": St. Paul of Thebes (died 342), who is also supposed to have supported
himself by making baskets. The Austin Friars claimed him (not without controversy) as their
founder.
5. This Paul is St. Paul the Apostle — he, however, made tents, not baskets (Acts 18.3); Lang-
land, like other medieval writers, may be confusing the two Pauls.
6. The Apostles Peter and Andrew, his brother, were fishermen when Jesus called them
(Matt. 4.18).
7. The repentant sinner and follower of Jesus in the New Testament. According to legend she
lived in solitude for thirty years in the wilderness of southern France.

And then lords and ladies would be loath to transgress,
And to take from their tenants more than Truth would
    allow,   310
If they found that friars would refuse their alms,
And bid them bring it back to where it had been borrowed.
For by God's will we are waiting always
Till birds bring us wherewithal by which to live.
For if you had pottage and a piece of bread and penny-ale[8]
    to drink   315
And a single serving of some sort of food,
You would have right enough, you religious,* and so your
    rule told me:
*Says Job, Will the wild ass bray when he hath grass or the ox low
    when he standeth before a full manger? The nature of brute
    animals condemns you, since common food suffices with
    them; from fat your iniquity proceeds.*[9]
If unlearned men knew this Latin they'd look hard at whom
    they give to,
And reflect beforehand five or six days   320
Before they resigned their revenues to religious men and
    women.
Alas, lords and ladies, there's little wisdom in your counsel,
To alienate from your heirs what your ancestors left you,
And employ it to get prayers from people who are rich,
And who are founded and funded to pray for others.   325
Who performs the prophecy of people now living,
He hath dispersed, he hath given to the poor?[1]
If any people perform that text it is these poor friars,
For what they get by begging about they use for building
    expenses,
And spend some on themselves and on such as are their
    laborers;   330
And they take from them that have and give to them that
    have not.
But commoners who've acquired money and rich clerks and
    knights,
Many of you are apt to act as if I had a forest
That was full of fair trees, and I devised a plan
How I might plant more among those that were there.   335
Right so, you rich, you give robes to those who're rich

---

8. The thinnest, or poorest, ale.
9. The first sentence is from Job 6.5. The second, which could be Langland's own, comments
on the biblical text.
1. Ps. 111.9.

And help whoever helps you and give to them who have no
    need,
Like some one who filled a cask full from a fresh river
And went forth with that water to wet down the Thames.[2]
Right so, you rich, you give robes and food   340
To those who have as you have — it is they whom you ease.
But religious who are rich should rather feast beggars
Than burgesses* that live in abundance, as the Book
    teaches:

> *Since it is sacrilege not to give to the poor what is theirs.*
> > *Likewise, to give to sinners is to sacrifice to devils.*
> > *Likewise, monk, if you are in need and receive, you*
> > *give rather than receive; if, however, you are not in*
> > *need and receive, you are stealing. Further, the monk*
> > *lacks nothing who has what suffices to nature.*[3]

Therefore I counsel all Christians to conform themselves to
    Charity,
For without challenging the debt Charity discharges the
    soul of it,   345
And through his prayers many a prisoner is freed from
    purgatory.
  But there is a deficiency in the folk who supervise the
    faith,[4]
By which lay folk become the feebler and not firm of belief.
As in Luxemburgs[5] is a base alloy, and yet they look like
    sterling.
The mark of that money is good, but the metal is inferior;   350
And so it fares with some folk now; they have a fair speech,
Shaven crown and christening, the King of Heaven's mark,
But the metal, that is man's soul, is much alloyed with sin.
Both learned and unlearned are alloyed now with sin
So that no living creature loves another, nor our Lord, as it
    seems,   355
For through war and wicked works and unseasonable
    weather
Weather-wise shipmen and witty* clerks as well
Can no longer rely on the sky aloft or on the lodestar.
Every day astronomers prove unable in their craft
Which used once to warn before what should happen later.   360

2. The main river on which London is built.
3. Statements deriving from St. Jerome,* whose scholarship was associated with asceticism
in the Middle Ages. First a hermit, Jerome later founded a monastery. Cf. 1 Tim. 6.8.
4. From here on Anima's discourse on Charity becomes generalized to include various subjects
whose connection with his original theme must be inferred by the reader.
5. Substandard coins made in Luxemburg whose importation to England was forbidden.

Shipmen and shepherds who set out to earn their wages
Saw by the sky what should befall;
About weather and winds they warned people often.
Tillers who tilled the earth could tell their masters,
From the seed that they sowed, what they might sell at
    market,   365
And what to let be and what to live on, the land was so
    true.
Now the land fails folk, and the flood does too,
Shepherds and shipmen, and so with these plowmen.
They can't interpret or distinguish one tendency from
    another.
Astronomers also are at the end of their wits;   370
What they've calculated about the element, the contrary
    occurs.
Grammar, the ground of all, now beguiles children
For there's not one of these new clerks, if you note carefully,
That can versify fairly or formally compose,
Nor one out of a hundred who can understand an author,   375
Or read a letter in any language but Latin or English.
Go now to any degree,[6] and unless Guile is the master,*
And, as an usher[7] under him to discipline us all,
Flatterer his fellow, I'd find it a wonder.
Doctors of decretals[8] and masters of divinity,   380
Who should be cognizant and competent in all kinds of
    learning,
And answer to arguments, and handle a *Quodlibet*[9] —
I dare not say it for shame — if such were examined
They should fail in their philosophy and in physics both.
    Therefore I am afraid for folk of Holy Church,   385
Lest, like some others, they leap over their offices and
    hours.*
But if they overleap[1] — as I hope they don't — our faith
    suffices,
As clerks in the Feast of Corpus Christi sing and read
That *sola fides sufficit*[2] to save ignorant people with.

---

6. I.e., look at the program of study leading to a degree at any level of the educational system.
7. The "usher" in an English school is the underteacher or assistant.
8. Authorities on papal decrees.
9. "Suppose [that]": the opening formula in a scholarly debate or exercise.
1. "Skip over parts of." "Offices": periods of liturgical prayer.
2. "Faith alone suffices": from a hymn sung on Corpus Christi. The point at issue is whether a service conducted by a priest who skips segments of it is invalid; Anima argues that what makes the difference is not the quality of the priest but the intention of the participant. "*Corpus Christi*": "The Body of Christ," a holy day in the Roman Catholic Church.

And so may Saracens be saved, Scribes and Greeks.[3]   390
Alas, then, but[4] those we learn from live the way they
    teach us,
And for[5] their living that unlearned men be the loather to
    offend God.
For the Saracens' creed is somewhat similar to ours,
For they love and believe in one Lord almighty,
And we learned and unlearned believe in one God;   395
Christians and unchristians all believe in one God.
But one Mohammed, a man, into misbelief
Brought Saracens of Syria, and see in what way.
This Mohammed was a Christian man, and because he
    might not be pope,
He set off for Syria, and with his subtle wits   400
Tamed a turtledove, and fed her all times of day and night.
The corn that she cropped he cast it in his ear,
And if he preached among the people or in places he came
    to,
Then the culver[6] would come to the clerk's ear
Intent on taking food; thus Mohammed enticed her,   405
And made folk fall on their knees, for he swore in his
    sermons
That the culver that came so came from God in Heaven
As a messenger to Mohammed, that he might teach men.[7]
And thus through wiles of his wit and through a white
    dove,
Mohammed brought into misbelief men and women,   410
So that learned there and unlearned still believe in his laws.
And since our Savior allowed Saracens to be so beguiled
By a Christian clerk accursed in his soul—
But for dread of the death I dare not speak the truth,
How English clerks feed a culver that is called Covetousness,   415
And have manners like Mohammed's so that no man honors
    truth.
    Anchorites* and hermits* and monks and friars
Are peers with the Apostles for their perfect living.
Would never the Father of Faith wish to find his ministers

---

3. Pagans generally, Moslems in particular; "Scribes": Scribes and Pharisees are linked in the
New Testament (incorrectly) as literalists of the Old Law. "Greeks": non-Christians whose tra-
dition is Greek paganism and philosophy rather than the monotheism of the Hebrew Scriptures.
4. I.e., "unless."
5. I.e., "on account of."
6. Dove.
7. The legend that Mohammed was a lapsed Christian who faked appearances of the Holy
Ghost as a dove was widespread in the Middle Ages.

Taking alms from tyrants that harass true men,   420
But doing as Antony[8] did, Dominic* and Francis,*
Both Benedict* and Bernard,* who taught them first
To live on little and in low houses by lawful men's alms.
Grace should grow and be green through their good lives,
And folk should feel, who suffer various sicknesses,   425
Both in body and in soul the better for their prayers.
Their prayers and their penances should bring peace among
All those who are at odds, if only beadsmen* were true.
  Seek and you shall receive, etc.[9]
'Salt saves cattle,' say these wives:
  Ye are the salt of the earth, etc.
The heads of Holy Church, if they were holy,   430
Christ calls them salt for Christian souls.
  And if the salt have lost its savor, wherewith shall it be
   salted?[1]
But fresh flesh or fish, when they lack salt,
Are unsavory, to be sure, whether stewed or baked;
So is man's soul, indeed, that sees no good example
Of those of Holy Church who should teach the high way   435
And be guides and go before like a good standard-bearer,
And hearten those behind and offer clear examples for
  them.
Eleven holy men converted all the world[2]
Into the right religion; the more readily, I think,
Should all manner of men be converted, we have so many
  masters,   440
Priests and preachers, and a pope on top,
That should be God's salt to save man's soul.
 At one time all was heathenness, England and Wales,
Till Gregory* caused clerks to come here and preach.
Augustine[3] christened the King at Canterbury,   445
And through miracles, as men may read, made all that
  region turn
To Christ and Christendom, and to hold the Cross in honor,
And busily baptized people and brought them to the faith
More through miracles than through much preaching;
As well with his works as with his holy words   450

8. For Antony, see line 272 above; St. Dominic, St. Francis' contemporary, was the founder of the Dominican Friars.
9. Cf. Matt. 7.7.
1. This line and 429a above: Matt. 5.13.
2. Jesus' eleven faithful Apostles. The twelfth Apostle, Judas, betrayed Jesus and then hanged himself.
3. Not St. Augustine of Hippo* but the Augustine sent to convert the English in 597; the King he converted was Ethelbert of Kent.

Taught them what baptism betokened and told them of the
    faith.
Cloth that comes from weaving is not comely to wear
Till it's fulled under foot or in fulling-frames,
Washed well with water and carded with teasels,
Stretched on tenters, and tinted, and placed in tailor's
    hand.[4]   455
And so it must be with a baby that is born of a womb:
Till it's christened in Christ's name and confirmed by the
    bishop
It is heathen as regards Heaven, and helpless of soul.
Heathen has its meaning from heath and untilled earth,
As wild beasts wax in the wilderness   460
Rude and unreasonable, running without keepers.
    You remember well how Matthew tells of a man who
    made a feast.
He fed them with no venison nor pheasants he'd had baked,
But with fowls that would not go from him, but followed
    his whistling:
    Behold my fatlings and all things are ready.[5]
And with calves' flesh he fed the folk that he loved.   465
The calf betokens cleanness in those that keep the laws,
For as the cow through kindly milk nourishes the calf into
    an ox,
So love and lewte* sustain lawful men,
And maidens and mild men desire mercy
Just as the cow's calf covets sweet milk;   470
So righteous men's minds move toward mercy and truth.
And by the hand-fed fowls those folk are betokened
Who are loath to love without learning from examples.
Just as capons in a courtyard come to men's whistling,
Intent on finding food follow men that whistle,   475
Right so rude men whose reasoning power is small
Learn to love and believe through lettered men's doings,
And on what they profess and perform they found their
    own beliefs;
And as those fowls hope to find food after the whistling,
So they hope to have Heaven on hearing their whistling.   480
And by the man that made the feast the Majesty is signified,

---

4. Cloth after weaving went through a process ("fulling") of scouring, cleansing, and thickening
by being treaded or put through a mill. Then it was dried in a stretching frame on tenterhooks
to make sure it came out even and square (line 455) and had the nap rubbed up with combs
called teasels (line 454).
5. The parable of the wedding feast is in Matt. 22.1–14, but the tame birds are not in the
biblical story.

That is God of his grace who gives all men bliss.

With weathers and wonders he warns us with a whistler

Where it is his will to work honor for us,

And feed us and feast us for evermore in one body.   485

    But who are they that excuse themselves that are parsons
        and priests,

Who are the heads of Holy Church, who have their pleasure
        here,

Without travail the tenth part of what true men produce by
        working?

They will be wrathful because I write thus, but I have
        ready witness,

Both Matthew and Mark and *Memento-Domine* David:[6]   490

    Behold, we have heard of it in Ephratah, etc.

What pope or prelate now performs what Christ bade,

    Go ye into the whole world and preach, etc.?[7]

Alas that for so long men should believe in Mohammed,

When the pope makes so many prelates to preach about—

Of Nazareth, of Nineveh, of Nephthali and Damascus,[8]

Let them travel there, as Christ teaches, since they've taken
        the name,   495

In order to be pastors and preach the passion of Jesus,

And as himself said, so to live and die:

    The good shepherd layeth down his life, etc.[9]

And said it in salvation of Saracens and others;

For Christians and unchristians Christ said to preachers,

Go ye into my vineyard, etc.[1]   500

And since these Saracens, Scribes and Greeks,

Have a clause of our Creed,[2] the quicker I think

They'd turn to it if someone troubled to teach them of the
        Trinity.

    Seek, and ye shall find, etc.[3]

For all pagans pray and have a perfect belief

In one great God whose grace they ask for,   505

---

6. "Remember-Lord": Ps. 131.1; line 490a is verse 6.

7. Mark 16.15. Cf. Matt. 28.19.

8. The pope sometimes created bishops *in partibus infidelium* ("in pagan territory"), that is, as heads of imaginary dioceses in non-Christian lands, such as the places named here. While these bishoprics should have been focuses of missionary activity, they were commonly just fictitious jobs with real incomes, intended as a reward for other activities. Such bishops are mentioned again in lines 509–10.

9. John 10.11.

1. Matt. 20.4.

2. Moslems, Jews, and such Greek philosophers as Aristotle* believe in one God, and so already share the central doctrine of Christianity; Moslems, Jews, and Christians also have much biblical tradition in common. Line 505 shows Langland was not envisaging any pagans who were genuine polytheists.

3. Matt. 7.7.

And they make their moan to Mohammed to show their
    message to him.
Thus that folk believe in a faith and in a false mediary,
And that is ruth for righteous men who reside in the
    kingdom,
And a peril to the pope and the prelates he makes
Who bear bishops' names of Bethlehem and Babylon.   510
   When the high King of Heaven sent his son to earth
He made many miracles to turn men to him,
In example that men should see that by sober reason
Men might not be saved but through mercy and grace,
And through penance and passion and perfect belief.   515
And he became man of a maid and *Metropolitanus*,[4]
And baptized and made brilliant with the blood of his heart
All who wished and would with inwit* believe it.
Many a saint since has suffered to die
All to found the faith; in various countries died,   520
In India, in Alexandria, in Armenia and Spain,
With doleful death died for their faith.
In salvation of man's soul Saint Thomas was martyred;[5]
Among unkind Christians for Christ's love he died,
And for the right of all this realm and all the realms of
    Christendom.   525
Holy Church is honored highly by his dying;
He sets an example to all bishops, serving as a bright
    mirror,
And especially to such whose name says they're of Syria,
That they should not hop about England as altar-consecrators,
Creeping in among curates to hear confessions illegally: 530
    Put not thy sickle unto another's grain.[6]
Many a man for Christ's love was martyred among the
    Romans
Before Christendom was countenanced there, or any Cross
    honored.
It is ruth to read how righteous men lived,
How they defouled their flesh, forsook their own desires,
Went far from kith and kin clad in poor garments,   535
Badly bedded, no book but conscience,
And no riches but the Rood* to rejoice in.
    Let it not be for us to glory except in the Cross of our Lord,
    etc.[7]

---

4. "Chief bishop" (literally, "archbishop"); see line 42 above.
5. Presumably, in view of line 528, St. Thomas of Syria.
6. Deut. 23.25. The status of bishop accorded to the bishops *in partibus infidelium* ("in pagan
territory") allowed them to interfere in the business of real dioceses.
7. Gal. 6.14.

And then there was plenty and peace among poor and rich,
And now it's ruth to read how the red[8] noble*
Is reverenced before the Rood, received as worthier   540
Than Christ's Cross that overcame death and deadly sin.
And now there's war and woe, and whoever wants to know
      why:
For covetousness for a cross:[9] the crown stands in gold!
Both rich and religious, that rood they honor
That is engraved on groats and on gold nobles.   545
For covetousness for that cross clerks of Holy Church
Shall overturn as Templars did;[1] the time approaches fast.
Don't you remember, you wise men, how those men honored
Treasure more than truth: I dare not tell what's true;
By reason and rightful judgment those religious* were
      damned.   550
Just so, you clerks, for your covetousness it can't be long
Before they shall condemn *dos ecclesiae*[2] and put you down
      for your pride.
    He hath put down the mighty from their seat, etc.[3]
If Conscience and the commons* and Kind Wit* and
      knighthood
Love together loyally, believe it well, you bishops,
Your lordship over lands you shall lose forever,   555
And live like *Levitici*[4] as our Lord teaches you:
    By first fruits and tithes, etc.[5]
  When Constantine of his courtesy granted Holy Kirk*
      endowment
Of lands and landsmen, lordships and revenues,
Men heard an angel on high cry at Rome,
'*Dos ecclesiae* this day has drunk venom   560
And those that have Peter's power are poisoned all.'
A medicine must be found for this that may amend prelates.
Those that should pray for peace, their possessions impede
      them;
Take their lands, you lords, and let them live by tithes.

---

8. Bright, as modifying "gold."
9. This and subsequent puns turn on the fact that coins had a cross stamped on one side; nobles*
and groats* (line 545) had a king's crown on the other.
1. The fabulously wealthy order of Knights Templars was suppressed in 1312 in a tremendous
scandal; the primary motive, a desire to confiscate their property, was masked by false accusa-
tions of homosexuality and various crimes and by "confessions" coerced by torture, which were
widely believed at the time.
2. "The worldly endowment of the church."
3. Luke 1.52.
4. "Levites": members of the Old Testament tribe of Levi chosen to assist the Temple priests.
5. The Latin words Langland uses occur in Deut. 12.6. This text was used to argue that priests
should be supported by the tithes and donations of the people, not by wealth of their own.

If possession is poison and makes imperfect clergy   565
It would be charity to discharge them of it for Holy Church's
    sake,
And purge them of poison before more peril arises.
If priesthood were perfect, the people should amend
Who act contrary to Christ's law and despise Christendom.
Every bishop that bears a Cross, by that he is bound   570
To pass through his province and let his people see him,
And talk to them and teach them to believe in the Trinity,
And feed them with spiritual food and provide for needy
    folk.
But Isaiah speaks of you and Hosea as well,
That no man should be a bishop but he who had both   575
Bodily food and spiritual food to confer on those who need
    it:
    In my house is neither bread nor clothing and therefore make
      me not king.[6]
Hosea says for such as are sick and weak
Bring all the tithes into my storehouse that there might be food in
    mine house.[7]
  But we Christian creatures whom the Cross inspires
Are firm in the faith—God forbid else!—   580
And have clerks to keep us in it and those who shall come
    after.
And Jews live in legitimate law; our Lord wrote it himself
In stone because it was steadfast and should stand forever.
Dilige deum et proximum[8] is perfect Jewish law.
And he entrusted it to Moses to teach men until Messiah
    should come,   585
And in that law they believe and look on it as the best.
Yet they were acquainted with Christ who taught
    Christendom,
And knew him for a perfect prophet who purged many
    persons
Of strange sicknesses: they saw it often,
Both miracles and marvels, and how he made men a feast   590
And fed with two fishes and five loaves five thousand people,
And by that marvel they might see that he seemed Messiah;
And when he lifted up Lazarus that was laid in grave

6. Isa. 3.7.
7. Not Hosea but Mal. 3.10.
8. "Love God and thy neighbor": Deut. 6.5, Lev. 19.18; cf. Matt. 22.37, 39–40.

And under stone dead and stank; with stout voice he called
    him:
    Lazarus, come forth![9]
Made him rise and rove about right before the Jews.   595
But they said and swore that he worked with sorcery,
And studied how they might destroy him, and destroyed
    themselves,
And through his patience their power was brought down to
    pure nothing:
    The patient overcome.[1]
Daniel divined their undoing and said
When the holy of holies comes your anointing shall cease.[2]   600
And yet those poor wretches suppose that he was
    pseudopropheta,[3]
And that his lore was a lie, and belittle it all,
And hope that he is to come who shall rehabilitate them all,
A second Moses or Messiah their masters foretell.
But Pharisees and Saracens, Scribes and Greeks   605
Are folk of one faith: God the Father they honor.
And since the Saracens and also the Jews
Know the first clause of our Creed, *Credo in Deum Patrem*
    omnipotentem,
Prelates of Christian provinces should experiment if they
    might
Lay on little by little *et in Jesu Christum filium,*   610
Till they could speak and spell *et in Spiritum Sanctum,*
Commit it to memory and repeat it with *remissionem peccatorum*
Carnis resurrectionem et vitam aeternam. Amen."[4]

Passus XVI

"Now fair befall you," said I then, "for your fair
    explanation!
For Hawkin the Active Man's love I shall always love you.
But I am still bewildered about what Charity means."
"To tell the truth," said he, "it is a tree of great excellence.

9. John 11.43.
1. Proverbial, but cf. Matt. 10.22.
2. Cf. Dan. 9.24, 26; i.e., when the Messiah comes, the special relationship between God and
the Jews will be superseded.
3. "A false prophet."
4. These Latin phrases and clauses are all from the Apostles' Creed: "I believe in God, the
Father Almighty"; "and in Jesus Christ, his Son"; "and in the Holy Ghost"; "the forgiveness
of sins, the resurrection of the body and life everlasting. Amen."

Mercy is the master root; the main trunk is pity;   5
The leaves are lawful words, the law of Holy Church;
The blossoms are obedient speech and benevolent looks.
Patience is the tree's plain name, and Poor-Simple-Of-Heart,
And so through God and good men grows its fruit Charity."
  "I would travel to see this tree," said I, "twenty hundred
    miles,   10
And to have my fill of that fruit forsake all other victuals.
Lord!" said I, "if any one knows whereabouts it grows?"
  "It grows in a garden," said he, "that God made himself—
In the midst of man's body the trunk's root makes its home.
Heart is what the orchard's called in which it grows,   15
And *Liberum Arbitrium*[1] has the land to farm
Under Piers Plowman, to plant it and weed it."
  "Piers the Plowman!" said I then, and all for pure joy
That I'd heard his name named anon I swooned after
And lay long in a love-dream;[2] and at the last I thought   20
That Piers the Plowman showed all the place to me,
And told me to gaze at the tree, at its top and at its root.
It was propped up with three poles; I perceived it at once.
  "Piers," said I, "I pray you, why do these poles stand
    here?"
  "Because of winds, if you will know," said he, "to ward it
    from falling: 25
    When the just man shall fall he shall not be bruised, for the
      Lord putteth his hand under him.[3]
And in blossom time they bite the blooms unless these props
    help.
The World is a wicked wind to those who want truth.
Covetousness comes from that wind and creeps in among
    the leaves
And threatens to devour the fruit through many fair shows.
Then with the first pole I pound him down, *Potentia Dei*
    Patris.[4]   30
The Flesh is a fierce wind and in flowering time,
Through lusts and delights so loud begins to blow
That it nourishes naughty sights and at another time words
And wicked works that come from them, worms of sin,
And they bite the blossoms down to the bare leaves.   35

---

1. "Free Will."
2. A second "dream within a dream" begins here and runs to line 167.
3. Ps. 36.24.
4. "The Power of God the Father."

Then I seize the second prop, *Sapientia Dei Patris*,[5]
That is the passion and the power of our Prince Jesu.
Through prayers and penances and God's passion in mind
I save it till I see it ripened and somewhat fruited.
And then the Devil endeavors to destroy my fruit   40
With all the wiles that he knows he works to shake the root
And casts clear to the top unkind neighbors,
Strife-breeding backbiters, brawlers and chiders,
And he lays a ladder to it—lies are its rungs—
And sometimes fetches away my flowers before my very
          eyes.   45
But *Liberum Arbitrium* waylays him sometimes,
Who is my lieutenant to look after it well by leave of myself:
          You may see that whoever sinneth against the Holy Spirit it
          will not be forgiven him; this is the same as whoever
          sinneth by free will doth not fight back.[6]
But when the Fiend and the Flesh reinforced by the World
Menace behind me to make off with my fruit,
Then *Liberum Arbitrium* lifts the third post   ·   50
And dashes down the Devil directly through grace
And help of the Holy Ghost, and thus I have the victory."
     "Now fair befall you, Piers," I said, "so fairly you describe
The power of these posts and their particular strengths.
But I have thoughts by the thousand about these three
          props,   55
Within what wood they grew and whence they came,
For they are all alike long, none littler than another,
And to my mind—it seems to me—they must have grown
          from one root;
And they seem of one size and of the same green hue."
     "That is so," said Piers, "and such may be the case.   60
I shall tell you at this time what the tree is called.
The ground it grows in, goodness is its name;
And I have told you what the tree is called: it betokens the
          Trinity."
And he looked at me irritably, and therefore I refrained
From asking him any more about it, and bade him very
          courteously   65
"To define the fruit that hangs so fairly on it."
     "Here now beneath," said he then, "if I had need of it,
I might pick Matrimony, a moist fruit withal.

---

5. "The Wisdom of God the Father."
6. Cf. Matt. 12.32.

Then Continence comes near the top like a Cailloux
    bastard.[7]
Then at the very crown comes its native fruit and cleanest
    of all,   70
Maidenhood, angels' pears, and earliest to be ripe
And sweet without swelling—its savor never sour."[8]
   I prayed Piers to pluck down an apple, if he would,
That I might have an opportunity to test what taste it had.
And Piers threw something to the summit, and that started
    to cry;   75
And he made Widowhood waver, and it wept then;
And when he moved Matrimony it made a foul noise.
I had pity when Piers shook it, so piteously it cried.
And ever as they dropped down the Devil was ready
And gathered them all together, both great and small,   80
Adam and Abraham, and Isaiah the prophet,
Samson and Samuel and Saint John the Baptist,
He bore them off boldly, nobody stopped him,
And made his hoard of holy men *in limbo inferni*,[9]
Where there's darkness and dread and the Devil is master.   85
And Piers for pure rage picked up that one post
And hit after him, happen how it might,
Filius by the Father's will, and favor of *Spiritus Sancti*[1]
To go rob that Ragman[2] and wrest the fruit from him.
   And then spoke *Spiritus Sanctus*[3] in Gabriel's mouth   90
To a maid named Mary, a meek thing withal,
That one Jesus a justice's son[4] must sojourn in her chamber
Till *plenitudo temporis*,[5] full time should come
That Piers's fruit flowered and befell to be ripe.
And then Jesus should joust for it by judgment of arms   95
Which one should fetch the fruit, the Fiend or himself.
Mildly the maid then submitted to the messenger
And said to him humbly, "Lo, I am his handmaiden
To work his will without any sin."

7. A grafted ("bastard") pear from Burgundy, reputed as especially sweet.
8. The image of the tree is used in multiple ways to represent, first, a fixed state with three conditions (assault by the world, the flesh, and the devil), then the Trinity and its distinct functions, and then the hierarchy of married chastity, continence or widowhood, and virginity. Finally, the tree introduces a historical sequence. We do not have different trees, but rather one image used to illustrate several ways of factoring out a problem, some illustrating cumulative sequences and some fixed patterns.
9. "In the border region of hell." Limbo was thought to be the abode after death of the righteous who lived before the Christian Redemption, e.g., the biblical figures in lines 81–82 above.
1. "The Son"; "the Holy Ghost."
2. A name for the Devil.
3. "The Holy Ghost."
4. Justice is one aspect of God the Father.
5. "The fullness of time": Gal. 4.4.

Behold the handmaid of the Lord; let it be done to me
according to thy word.[6]

And in the womb of that wench[7] was he forty weeks   100
Till he was born a boy from her body and grew bold to
    fight,
And would have fought with the Fiend before the time had
    fully come.
And Piers the Plowman perceived the proper time
And made him skilled in medicine that he might save his life
So that, though he was hurt by his enemy, he might heal
    himself;   105
And he had him assay his surgery on such as were sick
Till he was a perfect practitioner if any peril should arise.
And he hunted out the ill and healed blind and maimed,
And converted common women and cleansed them of sin,
And so steered toward the good sick and sinful both: 110
    They that are healthy do not need a physician, but they that
    are sick.[8]
Both leper-men and mutes, and men with bloody bowels,
Often he healed such — he held it no great feat,
Save when he gave life to Lazarus that had lain in his grave
Quatriduanus[9] cold, caused him to walk alive.
But before he performed the feat *maestus coepit esse*[1]   115
And wept water with his eyes; many there saw it.
Some that saw the sight said at that time
That he was healer of life's hurts and lord of high heaven.
Jews who judged laws jangled against him
And said he worked with witchcraft and with the Devil's
    power: 120
    Thou hast a devil, etc.[2]
"Then you are churls," Jesus chided them, "and your children
    too,
And Satan your savior; your own selves now bear witness.
For I have saved yourselves and your sons as well,
Your bodies, your beasts, and given blind men help,
And fed you with two fishes and with five loaves,   125
And left baskets of broken meat for him to bear away who
    wished."[3]

6. Luke 1.38.
7. The word is Langland's and had much the same connotations in his time as it has in ours:
his use of it is characteristic of his tendency to be irreverent toward even the most august of
his allegorical or biblical figures.
8. Matt. 9.12.
9. "For the space of four days": John 11.39.
1. "He began to be sorrowful"; cf. John 11.35: "Jesus wept."
2. John 10.20, which reads "he hath," rather than "thou hast."
3. Matt. 14.16–20.

And he rebuked the Jews boldly, and threatened to beat
    them,
And lashed them with a length of rope and leveled the stalls
Of those who made of church a market, or changed money
    there;[4]
And said it in sight of all, so that all heard it: 130
"I shall overturn this temple and tear it down,
And in three days after have it built anew,[5]
And build it every bit as big, or bigger, in all ways
As it ever was, and as wide; wherefore I bid you
To pronounce this a place of prayers and of perfectness."   135
     My house shall be called the house of prayer.[6]
  Envy and wicked will welled up in the Jews.
They took counsel and conspired to kill him when they
    might;
From this day to that day they waited their time
Till it befell on a Friday, a little before Passover.
The Thursday before that, there where he made his repast, 140
Sitting at supper, he said these words:
"I am sold by a certain one of you: he shall rue the time
That ever he sold his Savior for silver or goods."
Judas objected to this, but Jesus told him,
It was surely himself, and said, *"Tu dicis."*[7]   145
Then that wicked man went forth and met with the Jews,
And settled on a signal by which to single out Jesus,
And to this day that trick is too much used —
That is kissing and friendly countenance, and unkind will.
And this was Judas' way when he betrayed Jesus: 150
"Ave, Rabbi,"[8] said that reprobate, and walked right to him,
And kissed him so he might be caught and killed by the
    Jews.
Then Jesus spoke to Judas and to the Jews as well:
"Falsehood I find in your fair speech
And guile in your glad cheer, and gall is in your laughter. 155
You shall be a mirror to many for men's deception,
But to the world's end your wickedness shall work upon
    yourself:
     For it must needs be that scandals come; but woe to that
      man by whom the scandal cometh.[9]

4. Matt. 21.12.
5. John 2.19.
6. Matt. 21.13.
7. "Thou sayest it": Matt. 26.25; on lines 142–43, see Matt. 26.21–24.
8. "Hail, Rabbi [i.e., Master]": Matt. 26.49.
9. Matt. 18.7.

Though I am taken by treason, so you Jews may attain
     your wish,
Permit my Apostles to pass in peace where they will."
On a Thursday in a thickening light thus was Jesus
     captured—   160
Through Judas and Jews Jesus was taken
Who on the Friday following, for mankind's sake,
Jousted in Jerusalem, a joy to us all.
On Cross upon Calvary Christ took the battle
Against Death and the Devil; destroyed the power of both,   165
Died and destroyed Death, and made day of night.
   And I awaked with that and wiped my eyes,
And after Piers the Plowman I peered and stared,
Eastward and westward, I never once stopped looking,
And so set forth like an idiot, searching through the country 170
For Piers the Plowman—in many a place I sought him.
And then I met with a man on a mid-Lenten Sunday,
As hoar as a hawthorn, and Abraham was his name.
I asked him first whence he came
And of what land he was, and where he was heading.   175
   "I am Faith," said that fellow, "it's not fitting to lie,
And a herald of arms of Abraham's house.
I'm seeking for a certain man that I saw once,
A very bold bachelor;* by his blazon[1] I knew him."
   "What blazon does that warrior wear," said I then, "so
     well betide you?"   180
   "Three beings in one body, none bigger than the others,
Of one size and strength, the same in girth and length.
What one does, all do, and each does by himself.
The first has might and majesty, maker of all things;
Pater is his proper name, one person by himself.   185
The second is from that sire, Soothfastness, *Filius*,[2]
Warden of all that have wits; he was always without
     beginning.
The third goes by the name of the Holy Ghost; again, one
     person by himself,
The light of all that have life on land and on water,
Comforter of creatures; all bliss comes of him.   190
So three things belong to a lord that lays claim to lordship:
Might* and a means to make his own might known
(That is, of himself and his servant) and what accedes to
     them both.

---

1. A heraldic shield identifying a warrior.
2. "Son." "*Pater*": Father.

So God, who never had beginning but when it seemed
    good to him,
Sent forth his son as a servant at that time   195
To occupy himself here till issue had sprung,
That is, children of Charity, and Holy Church the mother.
Patriarchs and prophets and apostles were the children,
And Christ and Christendom and Christians, Holy Church,
In meaning that man must believe in one God,   200
And where it pleased him, if love prompted him, he
    appeared in three persons.
And that it may be seen as certain is showed by manhood:
What is called wedlock and widowhood along with virginity,
To betoken the Trinity, were taken out of one man,
Adam, father of us all. Eve came from his body,   205
And the issue that they had, it came from them both,
And either is the other's joy in three separate persons,
And in heaven and here have only one single name.
And thus mankind and manhood have sprung from
    matrimony,
And betoken the Trinity and true belief.   210
There is might in matrimony that multiplies the earth,
And it betokens truly, if I dared tell it here,
Him who first formed all, the Father of Heaven.
The Son, if I dared say it, much resembles the widow:
    My God, my God, why hast thou forsaken me?[3]
That is, creator became creature so he could know what
    both were.   215
As a widow without wedlock was never yet seen,
No more might God be man unless a mother bore him.
So widow without wedlock may not well be,
Nor matrimony without children is not much to be praised.
    Cursed is the man who has not left his seed in Israel.[4]
Thus manhood separate, as a thing by itself, subsists in
    three persons,   220
That is man and his mate and from marriage their children,
And it is nothing but one kind and its kindred before Jesus
    Christ in Heaven:
So the Son comes forth from the Father, and Free Will
    from both,
    The Spirit proceeding from the Father and the Son,[5]

---

3. Matt. 27.46: Christ's words on the Cross; cf. Ps. 21.2.
4. From the apocryphal Gospel of the Nativity of Mary, chap. 2.
5. From the Athanasian Creed. A number of theologians influential in medieval thought, including Sts. Augustine,* Bernard,* and Bonaventure (1221–1274), associate the human faculty of will with the Holy Ghost, or Holy Spirit.

Which is the Holy Ghost of all of them, and all are but one
    God.
    Thus in a summertime I saw him as I sat on my porch;   225
I rose up and reverenced him and greeted him right fairly.
Three men, to my sight, I made well at ease,
Washed their feet and wiped them, and afterwards they ate
Calf's flesh and cake-bread, and could see what I thought.
There are most trustworthy tokens between us, to tell of
    when I please.[6]   230
First he tested me to find whether I, Faith, loved better
Him or Isaac my heir, whom he bade me kill.[7]
Through him he learned what my will was—he will allow it
    to me.
I'm fully certain in my soul of this, and my son as well.
I circumcised my son for his sake later,   235
Myself and my servants; and all such as were male
Bled blood for that Lord's love, and hope to bless the time.
I feel full confidence and faith in this belief
For he himself promised me—and my issue too—
Land and lordship and life without end.   240
And yet he granted me more, and my issue as well,
Mercy for our misdeeds as many times as we ask it:
    As thou hast formerly promised to Abraham and to his seed.[8]
And then he sent to me to say that I should do sacrifice
And worship him with bread and with wine both,
And called me foot of his faith, to bring his folk to safety   245
And defend them from the Fiend, folk who leaned on me.
Thus I have been his herald both here and in hell,
And comforted many care-worn who count on his coming,
And so I seek him," he said, "for I heard it said lately
By somebody who baptized him—John the Baptist was his
    name—   250
Who to patriarchs and prophets and other people in darkness
Said that he saw one here who should save us all:
    Behold the Lamb of God, etc."[9]
    Then I wondered at his words and at his wide clothes,
For in his bosom he bore a thing that he blessed constantly.
And I looked in his lap;[1] a leper lay therein   255
Among patriarchs and prophets playing together.

---

6. Gen. 18.1–16. The three angels entertained by Abraham, who brought him God's promise
of the birth of Isaac, were interpreted in the Middle Ages as a representation of the Trinity.
7. Gen. 22.1–19.
8. Cf. Luke 1.55.
9. John 1.29.
1. The fold of a robe over the chest to form a pouch; therefore, the bosom. Cf. Luke 16.22–23.

"What are you eyeing so eagerly," he asked, "and what do
        you hope to have?"
"I'd like to learn," said I then, "what's lying in your lap."
"Look," he said, and let me see. "Lord, mercy!" I cried.
"This is a present of great price; what prince shall receive
        it?"   260
"It is a precious present, but the Fiend has placed a lien on
        it,
And on me as well," said that man. "No pledge may release
        us
And nobody can go bail for us, or bring us from his sway—
No bailsman can fetch us free out of the Devil's pound—
Till he comes whom I'm describing: Christ is his name   265
Who shall some day deliver us out of the Devil's power
And pay a better price for us than we people are all worth,
That is life for life; or else lie thus forever
Lolling in my lap till such a lord fetch us."
    "Alas," said I, "that sin shall so long obstruct   270
The might of God's mercy that might amend us all."
I wept for his words; with that I saw another man
Running rapidly along the same road we were taking.
I asked him first from whence he came,
Who he was, and whither he went, and at once he told me.   275

Passus XVII

"I am *Spes*, a spy,"[1] said he, "and seek tidings of a knight
Who gave me a commandment upon the Mount of Sinai[2]
To rule all realms with: I have the writ right here."
"Is it sealed?" I said. "May one see your letters?"
"No," he said, "I seek him who has the seal in keeping,   5
And that is Cross and Christendom, and Christ to hang on
        it;
And when it is sealed therewith, I know well the truth,
That Lucifer's lordship shall last no longer.[3]
And that's my letter's meaning; you may know it all."
"Let's see your letters," said I, "it may be a law we know." 10

---

1. Scout. "*Spes*": hope.
2. Where God gave the Ten Commandments to Moses (Exod. 19-20), who here represents
Hope, as Abraham represents Faith.
3. A writ is not operative until it has the seal, or stamped imprint, of the issuing authority.
Christ hanging on the Cross is the "seal" of the Ten Commandments because he came "not
to destroy, but to fulfill," the Law (Matt. 5.17), thus ending the Devil's domination over mankind.

He pulled out a diploma, a piece of a hard rock[4]
Whereon were written two words with this gloss as well:
Love God and thy neighbor,[5]
This was the text truly—I took careful heed.
The gloss was gloriously written with a gilt pen: 15
On these two commandments hang all the law and the prophets.
   "Are these all your lord's laws?" said I. "Yes, believe me,"
      he said.
"If one works by this writing I will guarantee
No devil will do him harm, nor death grieve him in his
      soul;
For though I say so myself, I have saved with this charm   20
Both of men and of women many score thousands."
   "He tells the truth," said this herald.[6] "I have tested it
      often.
Look, here in my lap are some who believed in that charm,
Joshua and Judith and Judas Maccabeus,[7]
Yes, and sixty thousand more than these who are not seen
      here."   25
   "Your words are wonderful," said I. "Which of you is
      truest
And best to believe for body and soul?
Abraham says that he saw all of the Trinity,
Its components three persons, each partable from the other,
And all three only one God; thus Abraham taught me;   30
And he has saved those that so believed and were sorry for
      their sins,
He cannot state the sum, and some are in his lap.[8]
What need was there now to bring on a new law
Since the first is sufficient for salvation and bliss?
And now *Spes* speaks up—who has spied out the law—   35
And tells nothing of the Trinity's entrusting him with his
      letters,
To believe in and love one Lord almighty
And then, just as I should myself, so love all people.
One who steps with one staff seems in better health
Than he who steps with two staves, it seems to all our eyes.   40

4. Moses' "letters" turn out to be a rock because the Ten Commandments were given to Moses engraved on stone. Piers's name, in Latin, *Petrus*, also means "rock."
5. This summary of Jewish law, which had become a traditional formula in Judaic thought, was endorsed as such by Christ in the "gloss" quoted in line 16 (Matt. 22.37–39).
6. I.e., Abraham.
7. Heroes of the Old Testament Book of Joshua and the Apocryphal books of Judith and Maccabees.
8. Cf. Luke 16.22–23 on the lap, or bosom, of Abraham.

Since that's the case, by the Cross, Reason declares to me
It is easier for ignorant men to understand one lesson
Than to teach them two — and the least too hard to learn.
It's very hard for any man to believe what Abraham says
And it's even harder to love an evil person.   45
It's less hard to believe in three lovely persons
Than to love and lend help to both lawless and just.
Go your way!" said I to *Spes*, "so God help me,
Those that learn your law will not long follow it."
  And as we went thus on our way, talking with one
      another,   50
Then we saw a Samaritan,[9] sitting on a mule,
Riding very rapidly the road we were taking,
Coming from a country that men call Jericho;
To a jousting in Jerusalem he jogged along fast.
Both the herald and Hope and he met together   55
Where a man was wounded and waylaid by thieves.
He might neither step nor stand nor stir foot or hand,
Nor help himself at all, for he seemed half-alive,
And as naked as a needle, and no help about.
Faith had first sight of him, but he fled aside   60
And would not come as near to him as nine fields' length.
Hope came hopping after, he who had boasted so
How he with Moses' commandment had helped many men,
But when he saw the sight of that man, he sheered aside,
As full of dread, by this day, as a duck that sees a falcon.   65
But as soon as the Samaritan caught sight of this man
He alighted from Lyard[1] and led him by hand,
And came close to the man to take account of his wounds,
And perceived by his pulse that he was in peril of death
And unless he had succor soon, he should never arise.   70
And he stepped swiftly to his bottles and unstopped them
      both;
He washed his wounds with wine and with oil,
Put balm on his head, and a bandage, and bore him in his
      arms,
And brought him, lying on Lyard, to *Lex Christi*,[2] a farm

9. For the parable of the good Samaritan, told by Jesus to identify the "neighbor" whom we
are to love as ourselves, see Luke 10.30-36. In this parable, a man wounded by thieves and
lying by the roadside is ignored by two fellow Jews but rescued by a Samaritan, a man from
a neighboring country despised by Israel. Langland elaborates this story and gives it a point
that fits his larger historical allegory: the Samaritan is going *to* Jerusalem, not away from it,
and the "priest" and "Levite" of Luke become equated with Abraham and Moses. Some of these
elements come from traditional medieval commentary and sermons explicating this parable.
1. Common name for a horse.
2. "The law of Christ"; see Gal. 6.2: "Bear ye one another's burdens, and so fulfill the law of
Christ."

Some six miles or seven beside the New Market;[3]   75
Put him up at an inn and called the inn-keeper:
"Keep this man," said he, "in your care till I come from the
        jousts.
And look, here's silver," he said, "for salve for his wounds."
And he paid him two pennies,* expenses for his living,
And said, "What more he spends for medicine I'll make
        good later,   80
For I cannot stay," said that man and he bestrode Lyard
And rode hastily the road right to Jerusalem.
    Faith followed after fast and did his very best to catch
        him,
And *Spes* sped smartly to see if he might
Overtake him and talk with him before the trail came to
        town.   85
And when I saw this I did not stay but bestirred myself
And pursued that Samaritan that was so full of pity,
And offered him to be his man. "Many thanks," he said,
"But your friend and your fellow you will find me at need."
And I thanked him then, and thereupon I told him   90
How Faith fled away, and his fellow *Spes* too,
At the sight of that sorrowful man that was set upon by
        thieves.
"They can be excused," said he; "they could not help much.
No medicine under the moon can restore the man to health,
Neither Faith nor fine hope, so festered are his wounds,   95
Without the blood of a babe born of a maid.
If he is bathed in that blood, baptized as it were,
And then given plasters of penance and passion of that baby,
He should stand and step, but full strength will not return
Till he has eaten all the babe and drunk of his blood.   100
For no one in the world ever went through that wilderness
Who was not rifled or robbed, whether riding or walking,
Save Faith and myself and *Spes* his companion,
And yourself now and such as shall follow our works.
For an outlaw is in the wood, lurking under the hillside,   105
And may see each man, and mark with care
Who is behind and who in front and who are on horse;
For he who is on horse acts braver than any one on foot.
Because he saw me that am Samaritan pursue Faith and
        his fellow

---

3. I.e., isolated some miles away from a market town; whether the name of a particular town
is meant is not clear.

On my mount that is called *Caro*[4] — I acquired it from
    mankind —   110
He was faint-hearted, that outlaw, and hid *in inferno*.[5]
But before three days from this day I dare guarantee
That he will be fettered, that felon, fast with chains,
And never again grieve any one who goes along this road:
    O death, I will be thy death, etc.[6]
And then shall Faith walk these wooded fields and serve as
    forester here   115
And teach those who come into this country but cannot
    discover
Which is the way that I went, and whither to Jerusalem.
And Hope shall be inn-keeper where the man lies recovering;
And all who are feeble and faint, whom Faith may not
    teach,
Hope shall lead them along with love, as his letter tells him,   120
And put them up at his inn and heal them through belief
    in Holy Church
Till I have salve for all sick; and then I shall return
And come again through this country and comfort all the
    sick
Who crave it or covet it and cry after it.
For the babe was born in Bethlehem who will save with his
    blood   125
All that live in Faith and follow his fellow's teaching."
    "Ah, sweet sir," I said then, "which shall I believe? —
(For Faith and his fellow have informed me both) —
In three perpetual persons who are partable from each other,
Yet all three only one God? thus Abraham taught me.   130
And afterward Hope, he bade me to love
One God with all my might, and all men after
Love them like myself, but our Lord above all."
    "After Abraham," said he, "that herald of arms,
Set fast your faith and firm belief;   135
And just as Hope enjoined you, I enjoin you to love
Your fellow-Christian men evermore, as much as yourself.
And if Conscience complain about this, or Kind Wit either,
Or heretics with arguments, show your hand to them.
For God is as a hand; now hear this and know it.   140
The Father was first like a fist with one finger folded

---

4. "The Flesh": this is the horse called Lyard earlier; calling him *Flesh* relates the Samaritan
to the incarnated Christ.
5. "In hell."
6. Hos. 13.14.

Till he felt it was fitting to unfold his finger,
And he put it forth as with a palm to whatever place it
    should go.
The palm is the vital part of the hand, and puts forth the
    fingers
To administer and to make what the hand's might conceives
    of.   145
And it betokens truly, tell it if you like,
The Holy Ghost of Heaven: he is like the palm.
The fingers that are free to fold and to serve
Betoken surely the Son that was sent to earth,
Who touched and tasted, at teaching of the palm,   150
Saint Mary, a maid, and took mankind upon him:
    Who was conceived of the Holy Ghost, etc.[7]
Then is the Father like a fist with a finger to touch—
    I will draw all things to myself, etc.[8]—
All that the palm perceives is profitable to feel.
Thus are they all only one, as if it were a hand,
And three separate things seen in a single apparition,   155
The palm because he puts the fingers forth and makes the
    fist too.
Right so, Reason readily shows this
How he who is the Holy Ghost fulfills both Sire and Son.
And as the hand holds hard and fast to all things
Through four fingers and a thumb put forth by the palm,   160
Just so the Father and the Son and Holy Spirit the third
Hold the whole wide world within the three of them,
Both welkin[9] and the wind, water and earth,
Heaven and hell and all that is therein.
Thus it is—no man need now believe anything different—   165
That three things belong in our Father of Heaven
And are each separate by themselves; sundered were they
    never;
No more may a hand move without fingers.
And as my fist is a full hand folded together,
So is the Father a full God, former and creator.   170
    Thou maker of all things, etc.[1]
The whole force is from him for the forging of things.
The fingers form a full hand to portray or paint;
Carving and sketching are the craft of the fingers.
Just so is the Son the skill of the Father

---

7. From the Apostles' Creed.
8. John 12.32.
9. I.e., the sky.
1. From the medieval Latin hymn "Jesus, Savior of Mankind" ("*Jesu salvator saeculi*").

And full God as the Father is, no feebler and no better.   175
The palm is perfectly the hand, has power by itself
Aside from the folded fist or the functioning of the fingers.
For the palm has power to push out the knuckles
And to unfold the fist, for his function it is,
And to receive what the fingers reach for or to refuse it   180
When he feels the fist's and the fingers' will;
So is the Holy Ghost God, neither greater nor less
Than the Sire is or the Son and of the same power,
And all three only one God, like my hand and my fingers.
Whether folded or unfolded, my fist and my palm   185
Are all only one hand, however I turn it.
But whoever is hurt in the hand, in its very middle,
He may clasp nothing securely; Reason declares it.
For the fingers that should fold and form the fist,
From pain in the palm, the power fails them   190
To clutch or to claw, to clasp or to hold.
If the middle of my hand were maimed or pierced
I could wield no whit of what I might reach;
But though my thumb and my fingers were both thick-
    swollen,
And the middle of my hand was maimed in no way,   195
There are many means by which I might help myself,
Both move and make amends, though all my fingers ached.
By this example," he said, "I see an indication
That whoso sins against the Holy Spirit shall not have
    absolution,
Either here or elsewhere, as I have heard tell: 200
    Who sinneth against the Holy Spirit, etc.
For he pricks God as in the palm, *qui peccat in Spiritum
    Sanctum.*[2]
For God the Father is like a fist; the Son is like a finger;
The Holy Ghost of Heaven, he is like the palm.
For whoso sins against the Holy Spirit, it seems that he
    hurts
God in what he grasps things with, and thus his grace is
    quenched.[3]
                                                            205

2. The Latin clause repeats line 200a, both already translated in line 199. Langland follows
Mark 3.29, which, however, has "shall blaspheme" (*blasphemaverit*) for "sinneth" (*peccat*). The
meaning of this verse, which makes offending the Holy Ghost more serious than any other
offense, was a long-standing subject of discussion, as it still is. Much of the rest of the *Passus*
is concerned with solving this problem.
3. Analogies attempting to explain the Trinity, one of the most difficult concepts in Christian
theology, were common in medieval religious writings. The fist analogy (like the candle and
sun analogies that follow) may be Langland's own; it may have been suggested by the line
"holding the world in his fist," from a sixth-century hymn about God as creator, actually quoted
in the C-text.

For to a torch or a taper the Trinity is likened,
As if wax and a wick were twined together,
And then a fire flaming forth from both.
And as wax and wick and warm fire together
Foster forth a flame and a fair blaze   210
That gives light to these laborers when they labor at night,
So do the Sire and the Son and also *Spiritus Sanctus*[4]
Foster forth among the folk faith and belief
Which makes all kinds of Christians clean of their sins.
And as sometimes you see suddenly a torch,   215
When its blaze has been blown out, the wick still burns—
Without flame or flare fire lingers in the wick—
So is the Holy Ghost God and grace without mercy
To all unkind creatures that covet to destroy
Loyal love or life that our Lord created.   220
And as glowing gleeds[5] don't gladden these workmen
Who work and wake on winter nights
As a torch does or a taper that's taken fire and blazes,
No more do Sire and Son and Holy Spirit together
Grant any grace or forgiveness of sins   225
Till the Holy Ghost begins to glow and to blaze,
So that the Holy Ghost glows only like a gleed without
        flame
Till loyal love lies on him and blows.
And then he flames like fire on Father and on *Filius*[6]
And melts their might into mercy, as men may see in winter 230
Icicles on eaves through heat of the sun
Melt in a minute's time to mist and to water.
So grace of the Holy Ghost melts the great might of the
        Trinity
Into mercy for merciful men—and melts it for no others.
And as wax on a warm gleed without more fuel   235
Will burn and blaze if they blend together,
And bring solace to those sitting in darkness, seeing nothing,
So will the Father forgive folk of mild hearts
Who ruefully repent and make restitution,
Inasmuch as they may make amends and repayments;   240
And if assets are insufficient for one who dies in such a
        will,
The mercy that his meekness earns will make good the
        remnant.

---

4. "The Holy Spirit."
5. I.e., coals.
6. "Son."

And as the wick and fire will make a warm flame
To make men glad who must sit in the dark,
So will Christ of his courtesy, if men cry mercy of him,   245
Both forgive and forget, and further pray for us
From the Father of Heaven to have forgiveness.
But strike fire from a flint four hundred winters,
Unless you have tow to take fire from it, tinder or taper,
All your labor is lost, and all your long slaving;   250
For no fire may burst into flame if it lacks kindling.
So is the Holy Ghost God and grace without mercy
To all unkind creatures: Christ himself bears witness:
> *Verily I say unto you, I know you not, etc.*[7]
Be unkind to your fellow-Christians and any prayers you
    can make,
Hand out alms and do acts of penance forever, day and
    night,   255
And purchase all the pardon of Pamplona[8] and of Rome,
And indulgences enough, and be *ingratus*[9] to your kind,*
The Holy Ghost will not hear you or help you—and with
    reason.
For unkindness quenches him so that he cannot shine
Or burn or blaze bright, for the blowing of unkindness.   260
Paul the Apostle proves I'm not lying:
> *If I speak with the tongues of men, etc.*[1]
Therefore beware, you wise men, who deal with worldly
    matters;
You that are rich and can reason well, rule your souls well;
Be not unkind, I counsel you, to your fellow-Christians.
For many of you rich men, by my soul, men tell,   265
You burn but you blaze not; that is a blind beacon:
> *Not every one that saith Lord, Lord, shall enter, etc.*[2]
Don't you remember, you rich men, in what misadventure
Dives[3] died, damned for his unkindness
In denying meat* and money to men that had need of them?
I urge every rich man to take heed of him   270
And give your good to that God from whom grace arises.

---

7. Matt. 25.12: Christ's words at the Last Judgment, rejecting the sinners at his left hand.
8. The bishop of Pamplona in Spain was famous for issuing batches of indulgences used by the abbey of Roncesvalles to raise money in England through its daughter-house in London (Chaucer's Pardoner claimed to be collecting for "Rounceval").
9. "Unkind, ungrateful." "Indulgences": formal remissions of the temporal or purgatorial punishment for sin.
1. 1 Cor. 13.1: the verse continues, "and of angels, but have not charity, I am become as sounding brass or a tinkling cymbal."
2. Matt. 7.21.
3. See Luke 16.19–24.

For those that are unkind to his,[4] I have no other hope
But that they'll dwell where Dives is days without end.
Thus is unkindness the contrary quality that quenches, as it
    were,
The grace of the Holy Ghost, God's own kind.   275
For what Kind* creates unkind kills, like those cursed
    thieves,
Unkind Christian men, for covetousness and envy
Murder a man for his possessions, by word of mouth or
    with hands.
For what the Holy Ghost has in his keeping, these evil ones
    destroy,
And that is life and love, the firelight of man's body.   280
For every manner of good man may well be likened
To a torch or a taper to reverence the Trinity,
And whoever murders a good man, my inwit* seems to tell
    me,
He puts out the precious light that our Lord loves most
    dearly.
But yet in more manners men offend the Holy Ghost;   285
But this is the worst way that any one might
Sin against the Holy Ghost, assent to destroy
For covetousness of any kind of thing what Christ bought
    dear.
How might he ask mercy, or any mercy help him,
Who would wickedly and wilfully do away with mercy?   290
Innocence is nearest God and night and day it cries
'Vengeance, vengeance! forgiven be it never
To those who sullied us and shed our blood—as it seemed,
    unmade us:
    Revenge the blood of the just!'[5]
Thus 'Vengeance, vengeance!' full charity demands.
And since this is a point of prime importance to Holy
    Church and Charity,   295
I do not believe that our Lord will ever at the last moment
Love that life that is lacking in charity,
Nor have pity for any prayer that his plaints may make."
    "Suppose I had sinned so and was soon to die,
And now regret my guilty act against the Holy Spirit,   300
Confess myself and cry for grace from Christ who made all,
And mildly ask his mercy, might I not be saved?"

4. I.e., to God's people.
5. Cf. Rev. 6.9–10.

"Yes," said the Samaritan, "you might so repent
That righteousness might turn to ruth because of repentance.
But it is seldom seen, where truth serves as witness,   305
That any creature convicted before a king's justice
Is ransomed for his repentance where all reason damns him.
For where the injured party prosecutes, so ponderous is the
     charge,
That the king may grant no mercy till both men accord
And each has equity, as Holy Writ tells: 310
     The sin is never remitted, etc.[6]
Thus it fares with such folk who follow all their will,
Live evilly and don't leave off till life forsakes them.
Dread rising from despair then drives away grace
So that mercy may not come to their minds at that time;
Good hope that should help alters to wanhope* —   315
Not from any impotence of God, as if he had not the power
To amend all that is amiss and his mercy greater
Than all our wicked works, as Holy Writ witnesses:
     His mercy is above all his works[7] —
But before his righteousness turns to ruth some restitution
     is needed;
His sorrow is satisfaction for such a one as may not pay.   320
   There are three things that make a man by force
To flee from his own house, as Holy Writ shows.
The first one is a shrewish wife who will not be chastised;
Her mate flees her for fear of her tongue.
And if his house's roof has holes in it and it rains on his
     bed   325
He looks and looks till he can lie down dry.
And when his eyes smart from smoke from a smoldering
     fire,
It's even worse than his wife or his wet bed;
For smoke and smut smart in his eyes
Till he's blear-eyed or blind, and a burr in his throat;   330
He coughs and curses and asks Christ to give him sorrow
That should have brought in better wood or blown it till it
     blazed.
These three that I speak of are thus understood:
The wife is our wicked flesh that will not be chastised
Because nature cleaves to it to contravene the soul;   335

---

6. St. Augustine, Epistle 153, section 20. The point is that a king, as justice, cannot allow
mercy toward the repentant until a base line of equity has been reestablished by making good
to the injured party the damage suffered.
7. Ps. 144.9.

And though it falls it finds excuses that 'Frailty caused it,'
And 'That is fast forgotten and forgiven too
To a man who asks for mercy and means to amend.'
The rain that rains where we should rest in bed
Consists of sickness and sorrows that we should suffer,   340
As Paul the Apostle put it to the people:
            Virtue is perfected in sickness.[8]
And though men make much complaint in their anger
And take their tribulations impatiently, true reason
            recognizes
That they have cause to act contrariwise on account of their
            sickness;
And at their lives' end our Lord has little trouble   345
In having mercy on such men whom such misery afflicts.
But the smoke and the smolder that our eyes smart from,
That is covetousness and unkindness that quench God's
            mercy;
For unkindness is the contrary of every kind of reason.
For no one is so sick or so much a wretch   350
That he may not love if he likes and deliver from his heart
Good will, good words too, wish and will
To all manner of men mercy and forgiveness,
And love them like himself, and lead a better life.[9]
I may delay no longer," said he, and spurred Lyard hard   355
And went away like wind, and I awoke with that.

Passus XVIII

Wool-chafed[1] and wet-shoed I went forth after
Like a careless creature unconscious of woe,
And trudged forth like a tramp, all the time of my life,
Till I grew weary of the world and wished to sleep again,
And lay down till Lent, and slept a long time,   5

---

8. 2 Cor. 12.9.
9. In other words, the excuses offered by the flesh (the shrewish wife) and by impatience at
the suffering encountered in life (the rain), while only excuses, are at least responses to real
forces exterior to the self that encourage its rebelliousness; hence these sins are relatively for-
givable. But the greed and irascibility that come from within the self (the smoke) are intrinsic
to it; such gratuitous sins of the will, unlike those of the flesh or of lack of fortitude, are sins
both against one's neighbor and against the Holy Ghost. The first two types of sin, however
wrong, are "natural," the latter "unnatural" (against "kind"*).
1. Scratchy wool was worn next to the body as an act of penance.

Rested there, snoring roundly, till *Ramis-Palmarum*.[2]

I dreamed chiefly of children and cheers of *"Gloria, laus!"*[3]

And how old folk to an organ sang *"Hosanna!"*

And of Christ's passion and pain for the people he had
  reached for.

One resembling the Samaritan and somewhat Piers the
  Plowman   10

Barefoot on an ass's back bootless came riding

Without spurs or spear: sprightly was his look,

As is the nature of a knight that draws near to be dubbed,

To get himself gilt spurs and engraved jousting shoes.

Then was Faith watching from a window and cried, *"A, fili
  David!"*   15

As does a herald of arms when armed men come to joust.

Old Jews of Jerusalem joyfully sang,

  "Blessed is he who cometh in the name of the Lord."[4]

And I asked Faith to reveal what all this affair meant,

And who was to joust in Jerusalem. "Jesus," he said,

"And fetch what the Fiend claims, the fruit of Piers the
  Plowman."   20

"Is Piers in this place?" said I; and he pierced me with his
  look:

"This Jesus for his gentleness* will joust in Piers's arms,

In his helmet and in his hauberk, *humana natura*,[5]

So that Christ be not disclosed here as *consummatus Deus*.[6]

In the plate armor of Piers the Plowman this jouster will
  ride,   25

For no dint will do him injury as *in deitate Patris*.[7]

"Who shall joust with Jesus," said I, "Jews or Scribes?"[8]

"No," said Faith, "but the Fiend and False-Doom*-To-Die.

Death says he will undo and drag down low

All that live or look upon land or water.   30

Life says that he lies, and lays his life in pledge

That for all that Death can do, within three days he'll walk

---

2. Palm Sunday (literally, "branches of palms"): this part of the poem reflects the biblical account of Christ's entry into Jerusalem.
3. "Glory, praise [and honor]": the first words of an anthem sung by children in medieval religious processions on Palm Sunday.
4. Matt. 21.9: on the first Palm Sunday, crowds greeted Christ crying "Hosanna [line 8] to the son of David [line 15]" and the present line.
5. "Human nature," which Christ assumed in order to redeem humanity. "Hauberk": coat of mail.
6. The perfect (three-personed) God.
7. "In the godhead of the Father": as God Christ could not suffer, but as man he could. "Dint": blow.
8. "Scribes" were persons who made a very strict, literal interpretation of the Old Law and hence rejected Christ's teaching of the New.

And fetch from the Fiend the fruit of Piers the Plowman,
And place it where he pleases, and put Lucifer in bonds,
And beat and bring down burning death forever.   35
     O death, I will be thy death."[9]
    Then Pilate came with many people, *sedens pro tribunali,*[1]
To see how doughtily Death should do, and judge the
       rights of both.
The Jews and the justice were joined against Jesus,
And all the court cried upon him, "*Crucifige!*"[2] loud.
Then a plaintiff appeared before Pilate and said,   40
"This Jesus made jokes about Jerusalem's temple,
To have it down in one day and in three days after
Put it up again all new—here he stands who said it—
And yet build it every bit as big in all dimensions,
As long and as broad both, above and below."   45
"*Crucifige!*" said a sergeant, "he knows sorcerer's tricks."
"*Tolle! tolle!*"[3] said another, and took sharp thorns
And began to make a garland out of green thorn,
And set it sorely on his head and spoke in hatred,
"*Ave, Rabbi,*" said that wretch, and shot reeds[4] at him;   50
They nailed him with three nails naked on a Cross,
And with a pole put a potion up to his lips
And bade him drink to delay his death and lengthen his
      days,
And said, "If you're subtle, let's see you help yourself.
If you are Christ and a king's son, come down from the
      Cross!   55
Then we'll believe that Life loves you and will not let you
      die."
    "*Consummatum est,*"[5] said Christ and started to swoon,
Piteously and pale like a prisoner dying.
The Lord of Life and of Light then laid his eyelids
      together.
The day withdrew for dread and darkness covered the sun;   60
The wall wavered and split and the whole world quaked.
Dead men for that din came out of deep graves
And spoke of why that storm lasted so long:
"For a bitter battle," the dead body said;

9. Hos. 13.14.
1. "Sitting as a judge": Matt. 27.19.
2. "Crucify!": John 19.6.
3. "Away with him, away with him!": John 19.15.
4. Arrows, probably small ones intended to hurt rather than to kill. "*Ave, Rabbi*": "Hail, Rabbi
[i.e., Master]": Matt. 26.49; these are actually the words Judas spoke when he kissed Christ
in order to identify him to the arresting officers.
5. "It is finished": John 19.30.

"Life and Death in this darkness, one destroys the other.   65
No one will surely know which shall have the victory
Before Sunday about sunrise"; and sank with that to earth.
Some said that he was God's son that died so fairly:
    Truly this was the Son of God.[6]
And some said he was a sorcerer: "We should see first
Whether he's dead or not dead before we dare take him
    down."   70
Two thieves were there that suffered death that time
Upon crosses beside Christ; such was the common law.
A constable came forth and cracked both their legs
And the arms afterward of each of those thieves.
But no bastard was so bold as to touch God's body there;   75
Because he was a knight and a king's son, Nature decreed
    that time
That no knave should have the hardiness to lay hand on
    him.
  But a knight with a sharp spear was sent forth there
Named Longeus[7] as the legend tells, who had long since
    lost his sight;
Before Pilate and the other people in that place he waited
    on his horse.   80
For all that he might demur, he was made that time
To joust with Jesus, that blind Jew Longeus.
For all who watched there were unwilling, whether
    mounted or afoot,
To touch him or tamper with him or take him down from
    the cross,
Except this blind bachelor* that bore him through the
    heart.   85
The blood sprang down the spear and unsparred[8] his eyes.
The knight knelt down on his knees and begged Jesus for
    mercy.
"It was against my will, Lord, to wound you so sorely."
He sighed and said, "Sorely I repent it.
For what I here have done, I ask only your grace.   90
Have mercy on me, rightful Jesu!" and thus lamenting
    wept.
  Then Faith began fiercely to scorn the false Jews,[9]
Called them cowards, accursed forever.

---

6. Matt. 27.54.
7. Longeus (usually Longinus) appears in the apocryphal Gospel of Nicodemus, which provided
Langland with the material for much of his account of Christ's despoiling of hell.
8. Opened; in the original there is a play on words with "spear."
9. Another instance of the anti-Semitism characteristic of the late Middle Ages. In some earlier
passages, Langland spoke favorably of Jews.

"For this foul villainy, may vengeance fall on you!
To make the blind beat the dead, it was a bully's thought.   95
Cursed cowards, no kind of knighthood was it
To beat a dead body with any bright weapon.
Yet he's won the victory in the fight for all his vast wound,
For your champion jouster, the chief knight of you all,
Weeping admits himself worsted and at the will of Jesus.   100
For when this darkness is done, Death will be vanquished,
And you louts have lost, for Life shall have the victory;
And your unfettered freedom has fallen into servitude;
And you churls and your children shall achieve no
        prosperity,
Nor have lordship over land or have land to till,   105
But be all barren and live by usury,
Which is a life that every law of our Lord curses.
Now your good days are done as Daniel prophesied;
When Christ came their kingdom's crown should be lost:
        When the Holy of Holies comes your anointing shall cease.[1]
    What for fear of this adventure and of the false Jews   110
I withdrew in that darkness to *Descendit-ad-Inferna*[2]
And there I saw surely *Secundum Scripturas*[3]
Where out of the west a wench,[4] as I thought,
Came walking on the way—she looked toward hell.
Mercy was that maid's name, a meek thing withal,   115
A most gracious girl, and goodly of speech.
Her sister as it seemed came softly walking
Out of the east, opposite, and she looked westward,
A comely creature and cleanly: Truth was her name.
Because of the virtue that followed her, she was afraid of
        nothing.   120
When these maidens met, Mercy and Truth,
Each of them asked the other about this great wonder,
And of the din and of the darkness, and how the day
        lowered,
And what a gleam and a glint glowed before hell.
    "I marvel at this matter, by my faith," said Truth,   125
"And am coming to discover what this queer affair means."
    "Do not marvel," said Mercy, "it means only mirth.
A maiden named Mary, and mother without touching
By any kind of creature, conceived through speech

---

1. Cf. Dan. 9.24, probably via the liturgy for Advent.
2. "He descended into hell": from the Apostles' Creed.
3. "According to the Scriptures."
4. The word is again Langland's, carrying much the same meaning in his time as in ours.

And grace of the Holy Ghost; grew great with child;   130
With no blemish to her woman's body brought him into
    this world.
And that my tale is true, I take God to witness,
Since this baby was born it has been thirty winters,
Who died and suffered death this day about midday.
And that is the cause of this eclipse that is closing off the
    sun,   135
In meaning that man shall be removed from darkness
While this gleam and this glow go to blind Lucifer.
For patriarchs and prophets have preached of this often
That man shall save man through a maiden's help,
And what a tree took away a tree shall restore,[5]   140
And what Death brought down a death shall raise up."
   "What you're telling," said Truth, "is just a tale of
    nonsense.
For Adam and Eve and Abraham and the rest,
Patriarchs and prophets imprisoned in pain,
Never believe that yonder light will lift them up,   145
Or have them out of hell—hold your tongue, Mercy!
Your talk is mere trifling. I, Truth, know the truth,
For whatever is once in hell, it comes out never.
Job the perfect patriarch disproves what you say:
    Since in hell there is no redemption."[6]
   Then Mercy most mildly uttered these words: 150
"From observation," she said, "I suppose they shall be
    saved,
Because venom destroys venom, and in that I find evidence
That Adam and Eve shall have relief.
For of all venoms the foulest is the scorpion's:
No medicine may amend the place where it stings   155
Till it's dead and placed upon it—the poison is destroyed,
The first effect of the venom, through the virtue it
    possesses.
So shall this death destroy—I dare bet my life—
All that Death did first through the Devil's tempting.
And just as the beguiler with guile beguiled man first,   160
So shall grace that began everything make a good end
And beguile the beguiler—and that's a good trick:
    A trick by which to trick trickery."[7]

---

5. The first tree bore the fruit that Adam and Eve ate, thereby damaging mankind; the second tree is the Cross on which Christ was crucified, thereby redeeming mankind.
6. Cf. Job 7.9.
7. From a medieval Latin hymn.

"Now let's be silent," said Truth. "It seems to me I see
Out of the nip[8] of the north, not far from here,
Righteousness come running—let's wait right here,   165
For she knows far more than we—she was here before us
        both."
    "That is so," said Mercy, "and I see here to the south
Where Peace clothed in patience[9] comes sportively this
        way.
Love has desired her long: I believe surely
That Love has sent her some letter, what this light means   170
That hangs over hell thus: she will tell us what it means."
When Peace clothed in patience approached near them both,
Righteousness did her reverence for her rich clothing
And prayed Peace to tell her to what place she was going,
And whom she was going to greet in her gay garments.   175
    "My wish is to take my way," said she, "and welcome
        them all
Whom many a day I might not see for murk of sin.
Adam and Eve and the many others in hell,
Moses and many more will merrily sing,
And I shall dance to their song: sister, do the same.   180
Because Jesus jousted well, joy begins to dawn.
        *Weeping may endure for a night, but joy cometh in the
            morning.*[1]
Love who is my lover sent letters to tell me
That my sister Mercy and I shall save mankind,
And that God has forgiven and granted me, Peace, and
        Mercy
To make bail for mankind for evermore after.   185
Look, here's the patent," said Peace: "*In pace in idipsum*:
And that this deed shall endure, *dormiam et requiescam.*"[2]
    "What? You're raving," said Righteousness. "You must be
        really drunk.
Do you believe that yonder light might unlock hell
And save man's soul? Sister, don't suppose it.   190
At the beginning God gave the judgment himself
That Adam and Eve and all that followed them

8. The word is Langland's, and the sense obscure: it probably meant "coldness" to him, though
an Old English word similar to "nip" meant "gloom."
9. What Langland envisioned clothes of patience to look like—aside from their "richness" (line
173)—it is impossible to say: to him any abstraction could become a concrete allegory without
visual identification.
1. Ps. 29.6.
2. The "patent" or "deed" is a document conferring authority; this one consists of phrases from
Ps. 4.9: "In peace in the selfsame"; "I will sleep and find rest."

Should die downright and dwell in torment after
If they touched a tree and ate the tree's fruit.
Adam afterwards against his forbidding   195
Fed on that fruit and forsook as it were
The love of our Lord and his lore too,
And followed what the Fiend taught and his flesh's will
Against Reason. I, Righteousness, record this with Truth,
That their pain should be perpetual and no prayer should
    help them,   200
Therefore let them chew as they chose, and let us not
    chide, sisters,
For it's misery without amendment, the morsel they ate."
  "And I shall prove," said Peace, "that their pain must
    end,
And in time trouble must turn into well-being;
For had they known no woe, they'd not have known
    well-being;   205
For no one knows what well-being is who was never in
    woe,
Nor what is hot hunger who has never lacked food.
If there were no night, no man, I believe,
Could be really well aware of what day means.
Never should a really rich man who lives in rest and ease   210
Know what woe is if it weren't for natural death.
So God, who began everything, of his good will
Became man by a maid for mankind's salvation
And allowed himself to be sold to see the sorrow of dying.
And that cures all care and is the first cause of rest,   215
For until we meet *modicum*,[3] I may well avow it,
No man knows, I suppose, what 'enough' means.
Therefore God of his goodness gave the first man Adam
A place of supreme ease and of perfect joy,
And then he suffered him to sin so that he might know
    sorrow,   220
And thus know what well-being is—to be aware of it
    naturally.
And afterward God offered himself, and took Adam's
    nature,
To see what he had suffered in three separate places,
Both in Heaven and on earth, and now he heads for hell,
To learn what all woe is like who has learned of all joy.   225
So it shall fare with these folk: their folly and their sin

---

3. A small quantity.

Shall show them what sickness is—and succor from all pain.
No one knows what war is where peace prevails,
Nor what is true well-being till 'Woe, alas!' teaches him."
   Then was there a wight[4] with two broad eyes: 230
Book was that beaupere's[5] name, a bold man of speech.
"By God's body," said this Book, "I will bear witness
That when this baby was born there blazed a star
So that all the wise men in the world agreed with one
     opinion
That such a baby was born in Bethlehem city   235
Who should save man's soul and destroy sin.
And all the elements," said the Book, "hereof bore witness.
The sky first revealed that he was God who formed all
     things:
The hosts in Heaven took *stella comata*[6]
And tended her like a torch to reverence his birth.   240
The light followed the Lord into the low earth.
The water witnessed that he was God for he walked on it;
Peter the Apostle perceived his walking
And as he went on the water knew him well and said,
     'Bid me come unto thee on the water.'[7]
And lo, how the sun locked her light in herself   245
When she saw him suffer that made sun and sea.
The earth for heavy heart because he would suffer
Quaked like a quick thing, and the rock cracked all to
     pieces.
Lo, hell might not hold, but opened when God suffered,
And let out Simeon's sons[8] to see him hang on Cross.   250
And now shall Lucifer believe it, loath though he is,
For Jesus like a giant with an engine[9] comes yonder
To break and beat down all that may be against him,
And to have out of hell every one he pleases.
And I, Book, will be burnt unless Jesus rises to life   255
In all the mights* of a man and brings his mother joy,
And comforts all his kin, and takes their cares away,
And all the joy of the Jews disjoins and disperses;

---

4. Creature, person.
5. "Fine fellow": Book's two broad eyes suggest the Old and New Testaments.
6. "Hairy star," i.e., comet.
7. Matt. 14.28.
8. Simeon, who was present at the presentation of the infant Jesus in the temple, had been told by the Holy Ghost that "he should not see death" before he had seen "the Lord's Christ" (Luke 2.26). The apocryphal Gospel of Nicodemus echoes the incident in reporting that Simeon's sons were raised from death at the time of Jesus' Crucifixion.
9. A device, probably thought of as a gigantic slingshot, though of course Christ needs nothing to break down his enemies but his own authority.

And unless they reverence his Rood* and his resurrection
And believe on a new law be lost body and soul."   260
   "Let's be silent," said Truth, "I hear and see both
A spirit speaks to hell and bids the portals be opened."
    Lift up your gates.[1]
  A voice loud in that light cried to Lucifer,
"Princes of this place, unpin and unlock,
For he comes here with crown who is King of Glory."   265
Then Satan[2] sighed and said to hell,
"Without our leave such a light fetched Lazarus away:[3]
Care and calamity have come upon us all.
If this King comes in he will carry off mankind
And lead it to where Lazarus is, and with small labor bind
    me.   270
Patriarchs and prophets have long prated of this,
That such a lord and a light should lead them all hence."
   "Listen," said Lucifer, "for this lord is one I know;
Both this lord and this light, it's long ago I knew him.
No death may do this lord harm, nor any devil's trickery,   275
And his way is where he wishes—but let him beware of the
    perils.
If he bereaves me of my right he robs me by force.
For by right and by reason the race that is here
Body and soul belongs to me, both good and evil.
For he himself said it who is Sire of Heaven,   280
If Adam ate the apple, all should die
And dwell with us devils: the Lord laid down that threat.
And since he who is Truth himself said these words,
And since I've possessed them seven thousand winters,
I don't believe law will allow him the least of them."   285
   "That is so," said Satan, "but I'm sore afraid
Because you took them by trickery and trespassed in his
    garden,
And in the semblance of a serpent sat upon the apple tree
And egged them to eat, Eve by herself,
And told her a tale with treasonous words;   290
And so you had them out, and hither at the last."

---

1. The first words of Psalm 23.9, which reads in the Latin Bible, "Lift up your gates, O princes, and be ye lifted up, ye everlasting doors, and the King of Glory shall come in."
2. Langland, following a tradition also reflected in Milton's *Paradise Lost*, pictures hell as populated by a number of devils: Satan, Lucifer (line 273ff.), who began the war in Heaven and tempted Eve; Goblin (line 293); Belial (line 321); and Ashtoreth (line 404). Lucifer the rebel angel naturally became identified with the word "Satan," which in the Old Testament had originally meant an evil adversary; many of the other devils are displaced gods of pagan religions.
3. For Christ's raising of Lazarus from the dead, cf. John 11.

"It's an ill-gotten gain where guile is at the root,
For God will not be beguiled," said Goblin, "nor tricked.
We have no true title to them, for it was by treason they
   were damned."
 "Certainly I fear," said the Fiend,[4] "lest Truth fetch them
   out.   295
These thirty winters, as I think, he's gone here and there
   and preached.
I've assailed him with sin, and sometimes asked
Whether he was God or God's son: he gave me short
   answer.
And thus he's traveled about like a true man these two and
   thirty winters.
And when I saw it was so, while she slept I went   300
To warn Pilate's wife what sort of man was Jesus,
For some hated him and have put him to death.
I would have lengthened his life, for I believed if he died
That his soul would suffer no sin in his sight.
For the body, while it walked on its bones, was busy
   always   305
To save men from sin if they themselves wished.
And now I see where a soul comes descending hitherward
With glory and with great light; God it is, I'm sure.[5]
My advice is we all flee," said the Fiend, "fast away from
   here.
For we had better not be at all than abide in his sight. 310
For your lies, Lucifer, we've lost all our prey.
Through you we fell first from Heaven so high:
Because we believed your lies we all leapt out.
And now for your latest lie we have lost Adam,
And all our lordship, I believe, on land and in hell." 315
  Now shall the prince of this world be cast out.[6]
 Again the light bade them unlock, and Lucifer answered,
  "Who is that?"[7]
What lord are you?" said Lucifer. The light at once replied,
  "The King of Glory.
The Lord of might* and of main and all manner of powers:
  The Lord of Powers.

---

4. Here and in line 309, "the Fiend" is presumably Lucifer's most articulate critic, Satan, whom Christ names as his tempter in Matt. 4.10.
5. In Matt. 27.19, Pilate's wife warns Pilate to "have nothing to do with that just man [Jesus]," for she has been troubled by a dream about him: Langland has the Fiend admit to having caused the dream in order that Pilate's wife should persuade her husband not to harm Jesus and thus keep him safe on earth and ensure that he not come to visit hell and despoil it.
6. John 12.31. "Prince of this world" is a title for the Devil.
7. This phrase and the next two translated from the Latin come directly or loosely from Ps. 23.8, following immediately on the words quoted in line 262a.

Dukes of this dim place, at once undo these gates
That Christ may come in, the Heaven-King's son."   320
And with that breath hell broke along with Belial's bars;
For any warrior or watchman the gates wide opened.
Patriarchs and prophets, *populus in tenebris*,[8]
Sang Saint John's song, *Ecce agnus Dei*.[9]
Lucifer could not look, the light so blinded him.   325
And those that the Lord loved his light caught away,
And he said to Satan, "Lo, here's my soul in payment
For all sinful souls, to save those that are worthy.
Mine they are and of me — I may the better claim them.
Although Reason records, and right of myself,   330
That if they ate the apple all should die,
I did not hold out to them hell here forever.
For the deed that they did, your deceit caused it;
You got them with guile against all reason.
For in my palace Paradise, in the person of an adder,   335
You stole by stealth something I loved.
Thus like a lizard with a lady's face[1]
Falsely you filched from me; the Old Law confirms
That guilers be beguiled, and that is good logic:
        A tooth for a tooth and an eye for an eye.[2]
*Ergo** soul shall requite soul and sin revert to sin,   340
And all that man has done amiss, I, man, will amend.
Member for member was amends in the Old Law,
And life for life also, and by that law I claim
Adam and all his issue at my will hereafter.
And what Death destroyed in them, my death shall restore 345
And both quicken[3] and requite what was quenched through
        sin.
And that grace destroy guile is what good faith requires.
So don't believe it, Lucifer, against the law I fetch them,
But by right and by reason here ransom my liegemen.
        I have not come to destroy the law but to fulfill it.[4]
You fetched mine in my place unmindful of all reason   350
Falsely and feloniously; good faith taught me
To recover them by reason and rely on nothing else.
So what you got with guile through grace is won back.

---

8. "People in darkness": Matt. 4.16, citing Isa. 9.2.
9. "Behold the Lamb of God": John 1.36.
1. In medieval art the Devil tempting Eve was sometimes represented as a snake (see the "serpent" of line 288) and sometimes as a lizard with a female human face, standing upright.
2. Matt. 5.38, citing Exod. 21.24.
3. Revitalize.
4. Matt. 5.17.

You, Lucifer, in likeness of a loathsome adder
Got by guile those whom God loved;   355
And I, in likeness of a mortal man, who am master of
    Heaven,
Have graciously requited your guile: let guile go against
    guile!
And as Adam and all died through a tree
Adam and all through a tree return to life,
And guile is beguiled and grief has come to his guile: 360
    And he is fallen into the ditch which he made.[5]
And now your guile begins to turn against you,
And my grace to grow ever greater and wider.
The bitterness that you have brewed, imbibe it yourself
Who are doctor[6] of death, the drink you made.

   For I who am Lord of Life, love is my drink   365
And for that drink today I died upon earth.
I struggled so I'm thirsty still for man's soul's sake.
No drink may moisten me or slake my thirst
Till vintage time befall in the Vale of Jehoshaphat,[7]
When I shall drink really ripe wine, *Resurrectio mortuorum.*[8]   370
And then I shall come as a king crowned with angels
And have out of hell all men's souls.
Fiends and fiendkins shall stand before me
And be at my bidding, where best it pleases me.
But to be merciful to man then, my nature requires it.   375
For we are brothers of one blood, but not in baptism all.
And all that are both in blood and in baptism my whole
    brothers
Shall not be damned to the death that endures without end.
    Against thee only have I sinned, etc.[9]
It is not the custom on earth to hang a felon
Oftener than once, even though he were a traitor.   380
And if the king of the kingdom comes at that time
When a felon should suffer death or other such
    punishment,
Law would he give him life if he looks upon him.[1]
And I who am King of Kings shall come in such a time
Where doom* to death damns all wicked,   385

---

5. Ps. 7.16.
6. The ironical use of the word carries the sense both of "physician" and of "one learned in a discipline."
7. On the evidence of Joel 3.2, 12, the site of the Last Judgment was thought to be the Vale of Jehoshaphat.
8. "The resurrection of the dead": from the Nicene Creed.
9. Ps. 50.6.
1. I.e., "Law dictates that the king pardon the felon if the king sees him."

And if law wills I look on them, it lies in my grace
Whether they die or do not die because they did evil.
And if it be any bit paid for, the boldness of their sins,
I may grant mercy through my righteousness and all my
    true words;
And though Holy Writ wills that I wreak vengeance on
    those that wrought evil,   390
    No evil unpunished, etc.[2]
They shall be cleansed and made clear and cured of their
    sins
In my prison purgatory till *Parce!*[3] says 'Stop!'
And my mercy shall be shown to many of my half-brothers,
For blood-kin may see blood-kin both hungry and cold,
But blood-kin may not see blood-kin bleed without his pity: 395
    I heard unspeakable words which it is not lawful for a man
        to utter.[4]
But my righteousness and right shall rule all hell
And mercy rule all mankind before me in Heaven.
For I'd be an unkind king unless I gave my kin help,
And particularly at such a time when help was truly
    needed.
    Enter not into judgment with thy servant.[5]
Thus by law," said our Lord, "I will lead from here   400
Those I looked on with love who believed in my coming;
And for your lie, Lucifer, that you lied to Eve,
You shall buy it back in bitterness"—and bound him with
    chains.
Ashtoreth and all the gang hid themselves in corners;
They dared not look at our Lord, the least of them all,   405
But let him lead away what he liked and leave what he
    wished.
    Many hundreds of angels harped and sang,
    Flesh sins, flesh redeems, flesh reigns as God of God.[6]
Then Peace piped a note of poetry:
    As a rule the sun is brighter after the biggest cloud; A⸍ter
        hostilities love is brighter.[7]

2. "[He is a just judge who leaves] no evil unpunished [and no good unrewarded]": not from
the Bible, but from Pope Innocent III's tract *Of Contempt for the World*; see IV.143–44.
3. "Spare!"
4. In 2 Cor. 12.4, St. Paul tells how in a vision he was snatched up to Heaven, where he heard
things that may not be repeated among men. Langland is apparently invoking a similar mystic
experience when he puts into Christ's mouth a promise to spare many of his half-brothers, the
unbaptized. The orthodox theology of the time taught that all the unbaptized were irredeemably
damned, a proposition Langland refused to accept: in his vision he has heard words to the
contrary that might not be repeated among men since they would be held heretical.
5. Ps. 142.2.
6. From a medieval Latin hymn.
7. These Latin verses are from Alain of Lisle, a late-twelfth-century poet and philosopher.

"After sharp showers," said Peace, "the sun shines
    brightest;
No weather is warmer than after watery clouds;   410
Nor any love lovelier, or more loving friends,
Than after war and woe when Love and peace are masters.
There was never war in this world nor wickedness so sharp
That Love, if he liked, might not make a laughing matter.
And peace through patience puts an end to all perils."   415
"Truce!" said Truth, "you tell the truth, by Jesus!
Let's kiss in covenant and each of us clasp other."
"And let no people," said Peace, "perceive that we argued;
For nothing is impossible to him that is almighty."
"You speak the truth," said Righteousness, and reverently
    kissed her,   420
Peace, and Peace her, *per saecula saeculorum*:[8]
    Mercy and Truth have met together; Righteousness and Peace
        have kissed each other.[9]
Truth sounded a trumpet then and sang *Te Deum*
    Laudamus,[1]
And then Love strummed a lute with a loud note:
    Behold how good and how pleasant, etc.[2]
Till the day dawned these damsels caroled.
When bells rang for the Resurrection, and right then I
    awoke   425
And called Kit my wife and Calote my daughter:
"Arise and go reverence God's resurrection,
And creep to the Cross on knees, and kiss it as a jewel,
For God's blessed body it bore for our good,
And it frightens the Fiend, for such is its power   430
That no grisly ghost may glide in its shadow."

Passus XIX

Then I roused and wrote the record of my dream,
And clothed myself carefully and came to the church
To hear the whole Mass and receive the Eucharist after.
In the middle of the Mass when men went to the Offering[1]

---

8. "Forever and ever" (the liturgical formula).
9. Ps. 84.11.
1. "We praise thee, God" (a celebrated Latin hymn, associated with religious feast days and occasions of public rejoicing).
2. Ps. 132.1: the verse continues, "[it is] for brothers to dwell in unity!"
1. The point in the Mass when the worshipers make their offerings (unlike its modern counterpart, the medieval congregation went forward in procession to do so) is also the point at which the priest places on the altar the bread and wine that will become the body and blood of Christ.

I slipped into sleep again, and straightway I dreamed   5
That Piers the Plowman was painted all bloody
And came in with a Cross before the common people,
And most like in all limbs to our Lord Jesu.[2]
And then I called to Conscience to answer my question
      truly:
"Is this Jesus the jouster," I asked, "that Jews put to death,   10
Or is it Piers the Plowman? Who painted him so red?"
   Conscience, upon his knees, replied, "These are Piers's
      arms,
His colors and his coat-armor, but he that comes so bloody
Is Christ with his Cross, conqueror of Christians."
   "Why do you call him Christ, since Jews called him
      Jesus?   15
Patriarchs and prophets prophesied before
That all kinds of creatures should incline and kneel
As soon as they heard some one speak the name of God
      Jesu.
*Ergo** there is no name like the name of Jesus,
Nor none so needful to name by night and by day.   20
For all dark devils are in dread to hear it,
And the sinful are solaced and saved by that name.
And you call him Christ; for what cause, tell me,
Is 'Christ' of more might* and a more worthy name
Than 'Jesu' or 'Jesus' whom all our joy came from?"   25
   "Surely you know," said Conscience, "if you're of sound
      mind,
That knight, king, conqueror can be one person.
To be named a knight is fair, for men shall kneel to him;
To be called a king is fairer, for he can make knights;
But to be called a conqueror, that comes by special grace,   30
And from hardiness of heart and from heart-felt courtesy,
To make lads lords of the lands he wins
And foul slaves of free men who will not follow his laws.
The Jews who were gentle* men held Jesus in scorn,
Both his lore and his law; now are they low churls.   35
As wide as the world is not one of them lives
But under tribute and taxation, like ragtag curs and churls.
And those who became Christians by counsel of the Baptist
Are franklins,[3] free men, from the baptism they received
And gentle men with Jesu, for Jesus was baptized   40
And on the Cross on Calvary crowned King of the Jews.

2. Medieval legend portrayed Pope Gregory* celebrating Mass and seeing, at the moment he
put the bread on the altar, the figure of the crucified Christ hovering over it.
3. Free landowners, as opposed to serfs; by the fourteenth century, members of the gentry.

It befits a conquering king to keep watch and to defend
His laws and his liegemen in the lands of his conquest.
And so Jesus did with the Jews: he dispensed justice and
        taught them
The law of life that shall last forever,   45
And defended them from foul ills, fevers and fluxes,
And from fiends that were in them, and from false belief.
Then he was called Jesus by the Jews, gentle prophet,
And king of their kingdom, and bore the crown of thorns.
And then he conquered on the Cross like a noble
        conqueror;   50
No death could destroy him or dash him down
So that he did not arise and reign and ravage hell.
And then he was called conqueror by the quick[4] and the
        dead.
For he gave Adam and Eve bliss, and others as well
That had before lain long as Lucifer's churls,   55
And he took Lucifer the loathsome who was lord of hell
And bound him as he is bound with bonds of iron.
Who was hardier than he? He shed his heart's blood
To make all folk free who follow his law.
And since he allots liberally to all his loyal liegemen   60
Places in Paradise at their parting hence,
He may well be called a conqueror, and that is what
        'Christ' means.[5]
But the cause of his coming thus with the Cross of his
        passion
Is to teach us by that token that when we face temptation,
To fight against it and defend ourselves from falling into
        sin,   65
And to see by his sorrow that whoso loves joy
Must apply himself to penance and to poverty, too,
And in this world must wish for much woe to suffer.
    But to discuss Christ further and how he came to that
        name,
To tell the facts faithfully, his first name was Jesus.   70
When he was born in Bethlehem, as the Book tells,
And came to take mankind, kings and angels
Reverenced him right fairly with riches of the earth.

---

4. Living.
5. Literally, "Christ" means "the anointed"; since kings were anointed, it is not clear why
Langland associated the name Jesus with king or messiah and "Christ" with conqueror; since
the latter word is Greek, a language unfamiliar to him, he may have thought that "conqueror"
was its literal meaning.

Angels out of Heaven came kneeling and sang
   Glory to God in the highest, etc.[6]
Kneeling kings came afterwards, carrying incense to him,   75
Myrrh and much gold, unmindful of reward
Or any kind of requital, but proclaimed him sovereign
Both of sand, sun, and sea, and set out after
For the kingdoms they came from, counseled by angels.
And there was that word fulfilled that you spoke of: 80
   All things heavenly and earthly should bow at this name of
     Jesu.[7]
For all the angels of Heaven kneeled at his birth,
And all the wisdom of the world was in those three kings.
Reason and righteousness and ruth were their offerings;
Wherefore and why wise men at that time,
Masters and lettered men, said that Magi was their name.   85
The first king came with reason under cover of incense.
The second king then came carrying as his offering
Reason's fellow, righteousness, under cover of red[8] gold;
Gold is likened to lawfulness that shall last forever
And incense represents reason — so right goes with truth.[9]   90
The third king kneeling then came close to Jesus
And presented him with pity, appearing as myrrh;
For myrrh means mercy and mild speech of tongue.[1]
Honest earthly things were thus offered at once
By kings of three kingdoms who came kneeling to Jesu.   95
   But for all these precious presents our Lord Prince Jesu
Was neither king nor conqueror till he commenced to grow
In the manner of a man, and one with much skill,
As it becomes a conqueror to call on many skills,
And to wield many wiles and tricks, one who will be a
     leader.   100
And Jesus did so in his days, if one dared tell it.
Sometimes he suffered, and sometimes he hid,
And sometimes he fought fiercely, and fled at other times,
And sometimes he gave goods and granted health both,
Life and limb; as he liked, he worked   105

---

6. Luke 2.14.
7. Phil. 2.10, already referred to in lines 15–17 above.
8. Rich, bright (not the color red).
9. The manuscripts are puzzling as to what this line actually says; the translation departs from the Kane-Donaldson edition, which here might be translated literally, "For it [gold] shall turn treason to right and to truth." The translation in line 90 above seems closer to A. V. C. Schmidt's and Derek Pearsall's editions of *Piers Plowman*.
1. Allegorical interpretations of the three gifts of the wise men (Matt. 2.1–12) were very common in medieval commentary. It is not clear what Langland took the word "Magi" to mean (line 85).

In the way that a conqueror works; so Jesus went about it
Till he had all them for whom he bled.
This Jesus at a Jew's feast, when he was just a boy,
Turned water into wine, as holy words relate.[2]
And there God of his grace began to Do-Well.[3]   110
For wine is likened to law and to life-holiness,
And law was lacking then, for men loved not their enemies,
And Christ counsels thus, and commands as well,
Both learned and unlearned, to love our enemies.
So first at that feast that I referred to before   115
Of his grace and goodness God began to Do-Well,
And then the custom was to call him not only Christ but
        Jesu,
Young fry full of wisdom, *Filius Mariae*.[4]
For before his mother Mary he performed that miracle,
So that she first and foremost should firmly believe   120
That he was begotten by grace and not begotten of man.
He performed that with no subtle sleight, but by speech
        alone,
According to the kin he came of; there he commenced
        Do-Well.
    And when he'd grown more mature, in his mother's
        absence,
He made lame leap about, and gave light to blind,   125
And fed with two fishes and with five loaves
Near-famished folk, more than five thousand.[5]
Then he comforted those full of care and acquired a greater
        name
Which was Do-Better, wherever he went.
For by his doing the deaf heard and the dumb spoke,   130
And he healed and helped all who asked him for grace.
And then he was called in the country by the common
        people
For the deeds that he did *Fili David Jesus*.[6]
For David was doughtiest of deeds in his time;
Then the maidens sang, '*Saul interfecit mille et David decem
        milia*,'[7]   135

2. Jesus' first miracle at the wedding at Cana, John 2.1–11.
3. Here Langland begins a highly metaphorical application of the three Do's to the life of Christ, which has been variously interpreted; it is his last systematic use of this major motif in the poem.
4. "Son of Mary." The term "fry" translates "fauntkyn," which has the same connotation as the modern "small fry."
5. See, for example, Isa. 35.6, Luke 9.10–13, John 9, and Mark 8.22–26.
6. "Jesus, son of David": Matt. 21.9.
7. "Saul hath slain his thousands and David his ten thousands": 1 Sam. 18.7.

Therefore the country Jesus came into called him *Fili
    David*,
And named him of Nazareth; and no man so worthy
To be kaiser* or king of the Kingdom of Judah,
Or justice over the Jews as they thought Jesus was.
Caiaphas[8] was envious of him, along with other Jews,   140
Who to do him to death day and night conspired.
They killed him cross-wise on Calvary on Friday,
And buried his body, and bade that men should
Keep it from night-comers, in care of armed knights,
So that no friend could fetch it; for prophets had foretold   145
That that blessed body should rise from its burying-place
And go into Galilee, and gladden his Apostles
And his mother Mary; thus men prophesied before.
The knights assigned to keep it safe conceded themselves
That angels and archangels, ere the day dawned,   150
Came kneeling to the corpse and in chorus sang
Christus Rex resurgens,[9] and it arose thereafter
Veritable man before them all, and went forth with them.
The Jews besought the knights' silence, saying that they
    should
Tell the commoners that there came a company of his
    Apostles   155
And bewitched them as they kept watch and stole away
    with it.
But Mary Magdalene met him on the road
Going toward Galilee[1] in Godhood and in manhood
And alive and alert, and loudly she cried
To every company she encountered, '*Christus resurgens!*'   160
Thus it came out that Christ overcame, recovered and
    lived:
    Ought Christ thus to suffer and to enter, etc.[2]
For what a woman knows may not well remain secret.
   Peter perceived all this and pursued after
To seek Jesus, as did James and John as well,
And Thaddeus and ten others, with Thomas of India.[3]   165

8. The high priest who condemned Jesus in the Jewish trial before he was handed over to the Romans: Matt. 26.3, 57–68.
9. "Christ the King is risen"; Rom. 6.9. For the guards and the fear that the disciples would steal the body and say that Christ was risen, see Matt. 27.62–66, but in the biblical account the guards, unlike the Marys who visit the tomb, do not see angels.
1. John 20.11–18, but she meets him at the sepulchre; in Matt. 28.1–8 she and "the other Mary" are told to say to the disciples that Jesus will meet them in Galilee.
2. Luke 24.26: the Latin verse reads, "Ought not Christ to have suffered these things and thus to enter into his glory?"
3. James, John, Thomas, and Thaddeus (Matt. 10.2–4) were Apostles; according to tradition, Thomas became the Apostle to India (*Legenda Aurea*, chap. 5).

And as all these wise ones were together
All shut up in a house whose doors were barred
Christ came in—and all were closed, both doors and
      gates—
To Peter and to his Apostles, and said, '*Pax vobis*.'[4]
And he took Thomas by the hand and taught him to probe   170
And feel with his fingers his fleshly heart.
Thomas touched it, and with his tongue he said,
      '*My Lord and my God*.
You are my Lord, I believe, God Lord Jesu,
Who died and endured death, and shall judge us all,
And are now alive in all limbs and shall last forever.'   175
Then Christ replied courteously, declaring to him,
'Thomas, because you trust in this and truly believe it,
Blessed may you be, and shall be forever.
And blessed may they be, in body and in soul,
Who shall never see the sight of me, as you see now,   180
And loyally believe all this; I love them and bless them:
      Blessed are they who have not seen and have believed.'
   And when this deed was done he put Do-Best in train,
And gave Piers pardon, and he granted power to him,
Might* to absolve all men of all manner sins,
To all manner of men mercy and forgiveness,   185
On condition that they come and confess the debt they owe
To Piers the Plowman's pardon, '*Redde quod debes*.'
Thus Piers has power, once his pardon is paid,
To bind and unbind both here and elsewhere,[5]
And absolve men of all sins, save only of debt.   190
And soon afterward on high up into Heaven
He went, where he dwells, and will come at the last
And reward him right well who *reddit quod debet*,[6]
Makes perfect payment, as pure truth wishes,
And intends to punish any people who do not pay their
      debt,   195
And judge them at Doomsday,* both the dead and the
      living,
The good to Godhead and to great joy,
And the wicked to woe, without end to dwell there."
   Thus Conscience discoursed of Christ and of the Cross
And said I should kneel to it; then came, it seemed to me,   200

4. "Peace [be] unto you": this Latin phrase and the next two (lines 172a, 181a) come from John
20.19, 28, 29.
5. For Christ's gift of authority to Peter, see Matt. 16.19. "Pay what thou owest" (line 187):
Matt. 18.28; cf. Rom. 13.7.
6. "Pays what he oweth" (see preceding note).

One *Spiritus Paraclitus*[7] to Piers and to his fellows.

In likeness of lightning he lighted on them all

And made them speak and understand all sorts of
languages.

I wondered what that was, and nudged Conscience,

And was frightened for the light, for in fire's likeness   205

Spiritus Paraclitus overspread them all.

Conscience kneeling counseled me, "This is Christ's
messenger

And he comes from the great God; Grace is his name.

Kneel now," commanded Conscience, "and if you can sing

Welcome him and worship him with *Veni Creator Spiritus*."[8]   210

Then I sang that song; so did many hundreds,

And cried with Conscience, "Help me, Christ, with Grace!"

   Then Grace began to go with Piers Plowman,

And counseled him and Conscience to call the commons*
together:

"For today I will distribute and divide up grace   215

To all kinds of creatures that claim five wits,*

Treasure to live by to their lives' end,

And weapons to fight with that will never fail.

For Antichrist[9] and his followers will grieve all the world,

And crush you, Conscience, unless Christ helps you.   220

And flocks of false prophets, flatterers and cheats,

Shall come and have the cure of souls of kings and earls;

And pride shall be Pope, Prince of Holy Church,

Covetousness and Unkindness cardinals to lead him.

Therefore," said Grace, "before I go I'll give you treasure,   225

And a weapon to fight with when Antichrist attacks you."

And he gave each man a grace to guide himself with

So that idleness would not overcome him, nor envy or
pride:

   There are divisions of graces, etc.[1]

And certain ones he gave wisdom which their words would
show,

And so to win with honesty what the world requires,   230

Such as preachers and priests and apprentices of the law:[2]

---

7. The Holy Ghost, also called "the Comforter": see John 14.26. The Dreamer, who was attending Easter Mass, now finds himself in the midst of the feast of Pentecost, which commemorates the descent of the Holy Ghost on the Apostles.

8. "Come, Creator Spirit [the Holy Ghost]": from a Latin hymn sung on Pentecost.

9. A false Christ, the great opponent of Christ at the end of time: 1 John 2.18, 22; the idea was a major element in late medieval Apocalyptic thought.

1. 1 Cor. 12.4: the verse continues, "but the same Spirit [in each]."

2. I.e., law students. In this speech, many professions about whose practice Langland usually has little or no good to say are endorsed in principle.

They to live lawfully by labor of their tongue,
And with their intelligence teach others as Grace would
    teach them.
And some he taught the skill to assess what they saw
So that they might support themselves by selling and
    buying.   235
And some learned from him to labor on land and on water,
And by that labor live a lawful life and true.
And some he taught to till, to cock hay and to thatch,
And earn their livelihood by the lore he taught them.
And some to divine and divide, to be well-versed in
    numbers;   240
And some to make sculptures or sketches, or skillfully mix
    colors;
And some to foresee and to say what should occur
Both of well-being and of woe, and beware in advance,
Such as astronomers with astronomy and wise philosophers.
And some to ride out and recover what had been
    wrongfully seized;   245
He instructed them to restore it through strength of their
    hands,
And fetch it from false men with Folville's laws.[3]
And some learned from him to live in longing to be hence,
In poverty and in patience, praying for all Christians,
And he taught them all to live by law and each craft to
    love the other,   250
That no swaggering or dissension be seen among them all.
"Though some are cleaner than some others, you see well,"
    said Grace,
"That competence in every craft comes from my gift.[4]
See that nobody blames his fellow, but like brothers love
    each other;
And he who is master of the most crafts be mildest of
    bearing.   255
And crown Conscience king, and make Craftsmanship your
    steward,
And according to Craftsmanship's counsels clothe and feed
    yourselves.
For I make Piers Plowman my proxy and my reeve,*
And registrar to receive *redde quod debes*.[5]

---

3. "Folville's law" had become a proverbial expression for taking the law into one's own hands (so called after a notorious family in the mid-fourteenth century), a practice that Langland seems to endorse when in redress of otherwise unredressable injustice.
4. Many manuscripts include here another line, "He that practices the fairest craft, to the foulest I could have put him."
5. "Pay what thou owest" (XIX.187).

My purveyor and my plowman Piers shall be on earth,   260
And in order to till Truth, a team shall he have."
   Grace gave Piers a team, four great oxen.
The first was Luke, a large beast with lowly mien,
And Mark, and Matthew the third, mighty beasts both;
And joined to them one John, most gentle* of all,   265
The prize ox of Piers's plow, surpassing all the others.[6]
And Grace of his goodness gave Pier four horses,
To harrow afterward all that his oxen plowed.
One had the name Austin,* and Ambrose* another,
Gregory* the great clerk and the good Jerome.*   270
To teach the faith these four followed Piers's team
And in an instant harrowed all Holy Scripture,
With two harrows that they had, an old and a new:
     That is, the Old Testament and the New.[7]
And Grace gave Piers seed-grain, cardinal virtues,[8]
And sowed it in man's soul and then spoke their names.   275
Spiritus prudentiae[9] was the first seed's name,
And whoever ate of that would use imagination,
Before he did any deed, discern well the end;
And he taught men to select a ladle with a long handle,
Contrived for keeling a crock to save the fat on top.   280
The second seed was called *Spiritus temperantiae.*[1]
He who ate of that seed had such a nature
That neither feast nor famine should effect a swelling of his
      maw;
Nor should any scorner disturb his even temper;
Nor should wealth of worldly riches nor winning of money   285
Nor any worthless idle word nor wicked speech move him;
Should no conspicuous cloak come upon his back,
Nor any meat* in his mouth that Master John[2] had spiced.
The third seed that Piers sowed was *Spiritus fortitudinis,*[3]
And whoever ate of that seed was always hardy   290
To suffer all that God sent, sickness and miseries.
No liar with his lies nor loss of worldly good

---

6. The oxen, the traditional animals to pull a plow, are the four Evangelists, Luke being traditionally represented as an ox.
7. I.e., all Scripture is to be interpreted by correlating every part of it with both the Old and the New Testaments, a traditional practice in medieval exegesis. No source has been identified for this Latin phrase.
8. Prudence, temperance, justice, and fortitude.
9. "The Spirit of prudence."
1. "The Spirit of temperance."
2. I.e., an expensive chef.
3. "The Spirit of fortitude."

Might make him, for any mourning, other than merry in
    soul,
And steadfast and steady to withstand slanders.
He replies to all with patience, and *Parce mihi, Domine*,[4]   295
And took cover under the counsel of Cato* the wise:
    Be of strong mind since ye are damned unjustly.[5]
The fourth seed that Piers sowed was *Spiritus justitiae*,[6]
And he that ate of that seed should be even-handed and
    true
With God, and aghast of nothing save of guile alone.
For guile goes so secretly that good faith sometimes   300
Shall not be observed by *Spiritus justitiae*.[7]
Spiritus justitiae does not spare to scourge the guilty
And to correct the king if the king is caught in guilt.
For he takes account of no king's wrath when his court is in
    session;
He never dreaded to hand down decisions of justice,   305
Not for duke or for death; so that he did not dispense law,
For present or for prayer or for any prince's letters.
He did equity to all insofar as he was able.
   Piers sowed these four seeds and then saw to their
    harrowing
With Old Law and New Law so that love might increase   310
Among the four virtues, and bring vices to destruction.
"For commonly in the country crabgrass and weeds
Harm the grain when they grow on the same ground
    together,
And so do vices virtues; therefore," said Piers,
"All that claim kind wit* harrow with the counsel of these
    doctors,*   315
And according to their teaching till the cardinal virtues."
   "Before your grain," said Grace, "begins to ripen,
Prepare yourself a house, Piers, to put your crops in."
"By God, Grace," said Piers, "you must give timber,
And arrange for that house ere you go hence."   320
And Grace gave him the Cross, with the garland of thorns,
That Christ suffered on at Calvary for mankind's sake.
And from his baptism and the blood that he bled on the
    Cross
He made a kind of mortar, and mercy was its name.

---

4. "Spare me, Lord": cf. Job 7.16.
5. From Cato's *Distichs*.
6. "The Spirit of justice."
7. I.e., can sometimes not be discerned even by Justice.

And with it Grace began to make a good foundation,   325
And wattled it and walled it with his[8] pain and his passion;
And out of all Holy Writ he made a roof afterward;
And he called that house Unity, Holy Church in English.
And when this deed was done, Grace designed a cart
That is called Christendom to carry home Piers's sheaves,   330
And let him have horses to haul his cart, Contrition and
      Confession;
And made priesthood hedge-warden while he himself went
As wide as the world is, with Piers to plow Truth
And the Land of Belief, the law of Holy Church.
    Now Piers has gone to the plow, Pride observed it   335
And gathered himself a great host to begin an attack
On Conscience and all Christians and cardinal virtues,
Blow them down and break them and bite the roots in two.
And he sent forth Presumption, his sergeant-at-arms,
And his spy Spoil-Love, one Speak-Evil-Behind.   340
These two came to Conscience and to Christian people
And told them tidings—they'd be constrained to forgo
The seeds that Sir Piers sowed, the cardinal virtues.
"And Piers's barn will be broken down; and they that abide
      in Unity
Shall come out, Conscience, and your two cart-horses,   345
Confession and Contrition, and your cart the Faith
Shall be camouflaged so cleverly and covered by our
      sophistry
So that Conscience will not be able to discriminate between
      a Christian and a heathen,
And no manner of merchant who deals with money will
      know
Whether he wins it with right, with wrong, or with
      usury."[9]   350
With such coloring and cleverness Pride comes armed
With the Lord who lives for delight of his body,
"To lay waste on welfare[1] and wicked living
All the world in a while through our wit," said Pride.

---

8. I.e., Christ's. "Wattle and daub" is the term for a method of construction in which twigs,
etc., mixed with clay, are used to fill in the spaces between posts. Piers's "barn" closely resembles
the great tithe-barns of the period, which in turn greatly resemble country churches in their
construction.
9. Serious attempts were made by theologians to set criteria for discerning the "just price" a
merchant might charge, so that buying cheap in one locale and selling high in another would
not be mere banditry; these efforts must have seemed to many people to shade imperceptibly
into the kinds of subterfuges used to disguise the taking of interest on loans described in V.241ff.
1. I.e., living well.

Said Conscience to all Christians then, "My counsel is to
    go   355
Hastily into Unity and let's hold ourselves there.
Let's pray that there be peace in Piers Plowman's barn.
For certainly, I'm sure we are not strong enough
To go against Pride unless Grace is with us."
And then Kind Wit* came to give Conscience instructions,   360
And cried out and commanded all Christian people
To dig a ditch deep around Unity
That Holy Church might stand in holiness as if it were a
    fort.
Then Conscience commanded all Christians to dig
And make a big moat that might be a defense   365
To help Holy Church and all who guard it.
Then all kinds of Christians except common women[2]
Repented and forsook sin, except only them,
And an assizer* and a summoner* who were forsworn often;
Wittingly and willfully they held with the false,   370
And were forsworn for silver—and surely knew the truth!
There was no Christian creature that had kind wit,
Except for such wicked ones as I spoke of,
Who did not to some extent help holiness to grow,
Some by saying prayers and some by pilgrimages   375
And other private penance, and some by giving pennies*
    away.
And then there welled up water for wicked deeds
Issuing harshly out of men's eyes.
Cleanness of the commons* and clerks' clean living
Made Unity, Holy Church, to stand in holiness.   380
    "I care not," said Conscience, "though Pride come now.
The Lord of lust shall be thwarted all this Lent, I hope.
Come," said Conscience, "you Christians, and dine,
You who have labored loyally all this Lenten time.
Here is blessed bread, and God's body thereunder.   385
Grace through God's word gave Piers power,
Might* to make it, so men might eat it after
To help their health once every month,
Or as often as they had need, those who had paid
To Piers the Plowman's pardon *redde quod debes*."[3]   390
    "How's that?" said all the commons. "You counsel us to
    repay
All we owe any man ere we go to Mass?"

2. I.e., prostitutes.
3. "Pay what thou owest."

"That is my counsel," said Conscience, "and cardinal
      virtues';
Or else each man forgive the other, and that's what the
      Lord's Prayer asks:
    And forgive us our debts, etc. [4]
And so to be absolved and then receive the Eucharist."   395
    "Yes? bah!" said a brewer. "I will not be ruled,
By Jesus, for all your jangling, by *Spiritus justitiae*, [5]
Nor by Conscience, by Christ, while I can sell
Both dregs and draff, [6] and draw from one hole
Thick ale and thin ale; that's the kind of man I am!   400
And I won't go hacking [7] after holiness. Hold your tongue,
      Conscience!
Of *Spiritus justitiae* you speak a lot of nonsense."
    "Scoundrel!" said Conscience. "Cursed wretch!
Unblessed are you, brewer, unless God be your help.
Unless you live by the lore of *Spiritus justitiae*,   405
The chief seed that Piers sowed, you shall never be saved.
Unless Conscience is your commons* and cardinal virtues,
Believe it well, you will be lost, both body and soul."
    "Then is many a man lost," remarked an ignorant vicar.
"I am a curator of Holy Kirk,* and there came never in
      my time   410
To me any man that could tell me about cardinal virtues,
Or that counted Conscience as worth a cock's feather.
I never knew a cardinal that did not come from the pope,
And we clerks when they come pay the cost of their
      provisions,
Of their furs and their palfreys' food, and the pillagers that
      follow them.   415
The commons *clamat cotidie*, [8] each man to other,
'The country is the curseder that cardinals come into,
And where they loll about and linger, most lechery reigns
      there.'
Therefore," said this vicar, "by very God, I wish
That no cardinal would come among the common people,   420
But in their holiness hold themselves still
In Avignon among the Jews — *Cum sancto sanctus eris, etc.* [9] —

---

4. The verse continues, "as we forgive our debtors."
5. "The Spirit of justice."
6. The refuse left after brewing.
7. I.e., riding on a worn-out horse.
8. "Cry out daily."
9. "With the holy thou wilt be holy": Ps. 17.26. Jews as moneylenders were thought to be essential to supporting the court of the pope at Avignon, during the period of the "Great Schism," when there were two popes.

Or in Rome as their rule directs, to watch over the relics;
And you, Conscience, in the King's court, and should
      never come away;
And Grace that you go crying of should be guide of all
      clerks;   425
And Piers the Plowman with his new plow and his old
Emperor of all the world, so that all men might be
      Christians.
Imperfect is that pope who should give all people help
And pays soldiers to slay such as he should save.
But long live Piers Plowman whose deeds are like God's: 430
Who raineth upon the just and the unjust at once,[1]
And sends the sun to save a cursed man's harvest
As bright as to the best man or the best woman.
Just so Piers the Plowman takes pains to plow
As well for a waster and wenches of the brothel   435
As for himself and his servants, except he is served first.
So blessed be Piers the Plowman who takes such pains to
      plow,
And tills and toils for a traitor just as hard
As for a man of true integrity all times alike.
And worshiped be he who wrought all, both good and evil,   440
And suffers the sinful till such time as they repent.
And may Piers amend the pope who pillages Holy Church
And over the king claims to be keeper of Christians,
And does not care though Christians are killed and robbed,
And pays people to fight and spill Christian blood   445
Against the Old Law and the New Law, as Luke bears
      witness:
      Thou shalt not kill; vengeance is mine, etc.[2]
It seems as if as long as he himself has his will
He takes no heed at all of any one else.
And Christ of his courtesy save the cardinals
And turn their wit into wisdom and into wealth of spirit.   450
For the commons," said this curate, "account very little
The counsel of Conscience or cardinal virtues
Unless it appears to promise a profit of some kind.
Deceit and double-dealing don't disturb them at all,
For *Spiritus prudentiae*[3] among the people is guile,   455
And all those fair virtues seem like vices to them.

1. Matt. 5.45.
2. Exod. 20.13, Luke 18.20, Deut. 32.35, Heb. 10.30.
3. "The Spirit of prudence."

Each man schemes up a stratagem to conceal sin
And makes it appear as politic or a proper mode of action."
Then a lord laughed: "By this light," he said,
"I hold it right and reasonable to receive from my reeve*   460
All that my auditor or else my steward
Counsels me to take by their accounts and my clerk's
     books.
With *Spiritus intellectus*[4] they took the reeve's records,
And with *Spiritus fortitudinis*[5] I'll fetch it, willy-nilly."
And then there came a king, and by his crown he spoke: 465
"I am king with crown to rule the commonwealth,
And to defend Holy Kirk and clergy from cursed men.
And if I lack enough to live on the law wills I take it
Where I may have it quickest, for I am head of law;
You are only members, and I am over all.   470
Since I am head of you all, I am healer of you all
And chief help for Holy Church, and chieftain of the
     commons.
And what I take of you two, I take it by instruction
Of *Spiritus justitiae*, for I am judge of you all.
So I may boldly receive communion for I'm in no man's
     debt,   475
Nor do I crave anything of my commons save what's
     required by my nature."
     "On condition," said Conscience, "that you defend the
     commonwealth
And rule your realm with reason, as right and truth
     demand,
You may have what you ask for, as your law declares.
     All things are yours for defense, but not for plunder."[6]
This vicar's home was far away, and he fairly took his
     leave,   480
And I awakened therewith and wrote what I had dreamed.

---

4. "The Spirit of understanding, the intellectual spirit"—ironically, since the practices described are misuses of the intellect.
5. "The Spirit of fortitude."
6. Apparently a legal tenet (line 479). The Latin line has an internal rhyme in the style of the jingles Langland uses in the Prologue. An alternative translation might read, "All things are yours for a defense-capacity, but not for an offense-rapacity."

Passus XX

Then as I walked on my way when I'd awakened thus,
Heavy-hearted I went, and anguished in spirit.
I didn't know where to eat nor at what place I might,
And as noon drew near Need stood before me
And accosted me discourteously, and called me a fraud.   5
   "Couldn't you excuse yourself, like the king and the
         others,
That what you got to go on living with, garments and
         sustenance,
Amounted to no more than *Spiritus temperantiae*[1]
         recommended to you,
And you nabbed nothing else but what Need told you to?
And Need has no law, and shall never fall in debt,   10
For there are three things that he takes to save his life:
That is food when men refuse him it and he finds no
         money in his purse,
And none will stand surety for him, and he can supply no
         pledge;
If in that case he cadges something, acquires it by sleight,
Surely he doesn't sin who so gets his food.   15
And though he comes thus to some clothing and can make
         no better bargain,
Need shall straightway serve as his bondsman.
And if he'd like to lap water, nature's law decrees
That he drink at every ditch before he dies of thirst.[2]
So needy in his great need may take what's necessary for
         him   20
Without counsel of Conscience or cardinal virtues,
So long as he pursue and preserve *Spiritus temperantiae*.
For there's no virtue to be preferred to *Spiritus temperantiae*,
Neither *Spiritus justitiae* nor *Spiritus fortitudinis*.[3]
For *Spiritus fortitudinis* offends very often;   25
He'll do more than moderation asks many a time and oft,
And beat this body over bitterly and that body too little,
And inflict greater grief on men than good faith wishes.
And *Spiritus justitiae* will judge, willy-nilly,

---

1. "The Spirit of temperance."
2. Although medieval ethics held that taking what you need when that need is dire enough to be life-threatening was justified, some readers argue that Need here guilefully offers excuses for an irresponsible life.
3. "Spirit of justice"; "Spirit of fortitude."

According to the king's counsel if it's the commons'*
    pleasure.   30
And *Spiritus prudentiae*[4] will fail in many a particular
Of what he supposes would happen if it weren't for his wit;
Such supposing is not wisdom nor sage prognostication:
    Man proposes and God disposes;[5]
God governs all good virtues.

But Need is next him for he soon knows meekness   35
And is lowly as a lamb for lack of what he needs;
For Need by necessity makes needy men feel humble.
Philosophers forsook wealth for they wished to be needy
And lived most wretched lives and looked for no riches.
And God's spirit would forgo all his great joy,   40
And he came and took mankind[6] and became needy.
He was so needy, as the Book says in many sundry places,
That he spoke this speech in his sorrow on the Cross:
'The fowl may fly and the fox creep to a hole
And the fish swim with his fin to find his rest;   45
While need grips me so narrowly that I must needs remain
And suffer sorrow most sour that shall turn to joy.'[7]
Therefore don't be abashed to abide and to be needy
Since he who was the world's creator was willfully needy,
And never was there any so needy, and none died poorer."   50

When Need had scolded me so I fell asleep at once
And dreamed most marvelously that in man's form
Antichrist came then and cut Truth's branches,
Quickly turned the tree upside down and tore up the roots,
And made False spring up and spread and support men's
    needs.   55
In every country where he came he cut away Truth
And got Guile to grow there as if he were a god.
Friars followed that fiend, for he gave them copes,*
And religious orders did him reverence and rang their bells,
And all the convent came to welcome a usurper   60
And all his followers as well as him, save only fools,
Which fools would prefer far more to die
Than to live any longer since Lewte* was so despised,
And a false fiend Antichrist put all folk beneath his rule.
And mild men and holy whom no misery frightened   65
Defied all falseness and folk who practiced it.

4. "Spirit of prudence."
5. Proverbial, ultimately deriving from Prov. 16.9.
6. I.e., human nature.
7. Langland is paraphrasing Matt. 8.20, words not, however, spoken from the Cross.

And what king gave comfort to the false, conscious of their
    guile,
These others cursed, and his counselors, whether clerks or
    laymen.
Antichrist thus soon had hundreds at his banner,
And Pride bore it presumptuously, displaying it about,   70
With a lord who lived for delight of his body,
Who came against Conscience, the keeper and the guide
Of Christian kindred and of cardinal virtues.
"I counsel," said Conscience then, "come with me, you
    fools,
Into Unity, Holy Church, and let's hold ourselves there,   75
And let's cry out to Kind* that he come and defend us
Fools from these Fiend's limbs for love of Piers the
    Plowman.[8]
And let's cry to all the commons* to come into Unity
And abide there and strike blows against Belial's children."[9]
Kind heard Conscience then and came out of the planets   80
And sent forth his foragers, fevers and fluxes,
Coughs and cardiac ailments, cramps and toothaches,
Rheums and running sores and rankling scurvy,
Boils and blisters and burning agues,
Frenzies and foul disorders; foragers of Kind   85
Had pricked and preyed upon people's skulls.[1]
A number large as a legion straightway lost their lives.
There were howls of "Help! here comes Kind
With Death that is dreadful to undo us all!"
The lord who lived for delight then cried aloud   90
For a knight called Comfort to come bear his banner:
"Alarm! Alarm!" said that lord, "each man look out for
    himself!"
Then these men met—before minstrels could pipe
Or heralds of arms had identified lords—
Old Age the hoary; he was in the vanguard   95
And bore the banner before Death; he claimed it by right.
Kind came after with many cutting sores
Such as poxes and pestilence, and brought many people to
    ruin.
So Kind with bodily corruptions killed very many.

8. Here, as in lines 61–63 above, Langland echoes 1 Cor. 1.22–29, especially "For the foolishness
of God is wiser than men. . . . God chose what is foolish in the world to shame the wise."
9. A major devil.
1. Nature is on Conscience's side because the nature of things is not corruptible. Sickness and,
in the next lines, Old Age and Death, fight for Kind insofar as they remind human beings
of their finitude and their need to think about ultimate truth.

Death came driving after him and dashed all to dust   100
Companies of kings and knights, kaisers and popes.
Learned or unlearned, he let no man stand
That[2] he hit squarely who ever stirred afterward.
Many a lovely lady and their lover-knights
Sank down swooning for sorrow of Death's blows.   105
Then Conscience of his courtesy craved of Kind
To cease and abstain and see whether they would
Leave Pride privily and be proper Christians.
And Kind ceased straightway, to see the people amend.
    Then Fortune began to flatter those few that were alive   110
And promised them long life, and sent Lechery out
Among all manner of men, married and unmarried,
And gathered a great host all against Conscience.
This Lechery laid on with a laughing face
And with privy[3] speech and painted words,   115
And armed himself in idleness and in arrogant bearing.
He bore a bow in his hand with many broad arrows
Which were feathered with fair promise and many a false
        betrothal.
With unseemly stories he distressed very often
Conscience and his company, Holy Kirk's teachers.   120
Then Covetousness came and considered how he might
Overcome Conscience and cardinal virtues,
And armed himself in avarice and lived hungrily.
His weapon was all-wiles, to win money and hide it;
With glozings[4] and garblings he beguiled the people.   125
Simony* pursued him to assail Conscience,
And put pressure on the pope, and they appointed prelates
As allies of Antichrist, to hold safe their temporalities.[5]
And he came to the King's Council like a keen baron
And cuffed Conscience in court before them all;   130
And made Good Faith flee, and False to abide
And boldly bore down with many a bright coin
Much of the wit and wisdom of Westminster Hall.[6]
He jogged to a justice and jousted in his ear
And overturned all his integrity with "Take this and think
        better of me."   135
And for the Arches[7] in haste he headed afterward

2. I.e., whom.
3. Private.
4. Deceptions: "glossing" or interpreting a text had come to be taken, in popular parlance, as
synonymous with covering up or distorting its meaning.
5. Their wordly possessions.
6. Where the law courts were.
7. The Archbishop of Canterbury's court in London.

And turned Civil* into Simony,* and then subverted the
    Official.[8]
For a miniver[9] mantle he made true matrimony
Divide before Death came and fashioned divorces.
  "Alas!" said Conscience and cried, "would Christ of his
    grace   140
That Covetousness were a Christian since he's so keen a
    fighter,
And stout-hearted and steadfast while his purse-strings
    hold."
And then Life laughed and let his clothing be slashed[1]
And in haste armed himself in whoreson's words,[2]
And judged Holiness a joke and Gentleness* a waster,   145
And alleged that Lewte* was a churl and Liar a gentleman.
Conscience and his counsel, he accounted them folly.
Thus for a little luck Life revived
And pricked forth with pride; he praises no virtue,
And cares not how Kind slew folk, and shall come at the
    last   150
And kill all earthly creatures save Conscience alone.
Life leapt aside and selected a mistress.
"Health and I," said he, "and Highness of Heart
Shall induce you to have no dread of either Death or Age,
And so forget sorrow, and have no sense of sin."   155
Life liked this, and his love Fortune,
And at last they begot in their gloating a graceless brat,
One who caused much care and was called Sloth.
Sloth matured with wondrous speed and was soon of age
And wedded one Wanhope,* a wench of the brothel.   160
Her sire was an assizer* who never swore truthfully,
One Tom Two-Tongue, convicted at every inquest.
This sloth grew skilled in war and made himself a sling,
And threw Dread-Of-Despair a dozen miles about.
Then Conscience in his care called upon Old Age   165
And said he should strive to fight and scare away
        Wanhope.
And Old Age took Good Hope, and hastily he stationed
    him,
And drove Wanhope away, and he fights with Life.

---

8. The presiding judge of an ecclesiatical court. The sense is that Simony's wealth subordinates
Civil Law by bribing court officers.
9. A white or light gray fur.
1. It was fashionable to have the hems and borders of clothes "slashed" or cut into elaborate
decorative shapes.
2. Indecent language.

And Life fled for fear to Physic for help
And besought succor from him, and had some of his salve,   170
And gave him gold aplenty which gladdened his heart.
And they gave him a gift in return, a glass helmet.[3]
Life believed that medicine would delay Old Age
And drive away Death with drugs and prescriptions.
And Old Age ventured against Life, and he hit at the last   175
A physician in a furred hood so that he fell in a palsy,
And there that doctor died before three days passed.
    "Now I see," said Life, "that surgery and medicine
Cannot do any good at all against Old Age."
And in hope for his health he grew hardy of heart   180
And so rode off to Revel, a rich place and a merry one—
The Company of Comfort men called it once.
    And Old Age came after him, and went over my head,
And made me both bald in front and bare on the crown;
So hard he went over my head it will always be evident.   185
    "Mister bad-mannered Age," I said, "may mischief go
        with you!
Since when was the highway over men's heads?
If you had any courtesy," I said, "you would have asked
        leave."
    "What, leave, lazy loafer?" he said, and laid on me with
        age,
And hit me under the ear; I can hardly hear.   190
He buffeted me about the mouth and beat out my molars
And fettered me with fits of gout; I'm not free to go far.
And of the woe that I was in my wife had pity
And wished most warmly that I were in Heaven.
For the limb that she loved me for and liked to feel   195
Notably at night when we were naked in bed,
I might by no means make it do her will,
So Old Age with her aid had beaten it down.
And as I sat in this sorrow I saw Kind* passing by
And Death drew near me; dread made me quake,   200
And I cried to Kind, "Can you bring me out of care?
Lo, Old Age the hoary has attended to me.
Avenge me if you see fit, for I would fain be hence."
    "If vengeance is what you want, wend your way into
        Unity,
And hold yourself there always till I send for you,   205
And see you learn a craft to carry on before you come
        thence."

3. I.e., something that purports to provide protection but doesn't.

"Counsel me, Kind," said I. "What craft is best to learn?"
"Learn to love," said Kind, "and leave all other crafts."
"How can I get my keep thus, and clothe and feed myself?"
"If you love folk faithfully you shall find you never lack   210
Worldly food or clothes to wear while your life lasts."
And by counsel of Kind I commenced to roam
Through Contrition and Confession until I came to Unity.
And there Conscience was constable[4] to save Christian
          people,
And was strongly besieged by seven great giants[5]   215
That held with Antichrist hard against Conscience.
Sloth with his sling made a savage assault.
Proud priests came with him; a pack bigger than a
          hundred,
In paltoks and peaked shoes, purses and long knives,[6]
Came against Conscience; they held with Covetousness.   220
     "By the Mary!" cried a cursed priest from a far corner of
          Ireland.[7]
"I make no more of Conscience while I amass silver
Than I do of drinking a draught of good ale,"
And so said sixty of the same country,
And shot shots in attack, many a sheaf of oaths,   225
And broad hooked arrows, "God's heart and his nails!"
And almost had Unity and Holiness down.
     Conscience cried, "Help, Clergy, or I'll fall
Because of imperfect priests and prelates of Holy Church!"
Friars heard him cry out and came to help him,   230
But because they did not know their craft well Conscience
          rejected them.
Then Need drew near and announced to Conscience
That they came for covetousness, to have cure of souls,
"And since they are poor, perhaps, having no patrimony,
To fare well they will flatter folk that are rich.   235
And since they elected to live a life of cold and hardship,
Let them chew as they chose, uncharged with cure of souls.
For he who must beg his livelihood lies more often
Than he who labors for his livelihood and lets beggars
          share it.
And forasmuch as they forsook the felicity of earth   240
Let them be like beggars and live by angel's food."

4. The governor or warden of a royal castle.
5. I.e., the Seven Deadly Sins.
6. Cloaks and fashionable pointed shoes, as well as purses and daggers, are accoutrements
appropriate to dangerous soldiers rather than to priests.
7. Considered at this date a barbaric country, full of treacherous people.

At this counsel Conscience then commenced to laugh,
And comforted them courteously and called in all friars
And said, "Sirs, you are all surely welcome
To Unity and Holy Church; but one thing I pray you: 245
Hold yourselves in Unity, and have no envy
Of learned or unlearned, but live by your rule.
And I will give you my guarantee: you shall get bread and
           clothing
And other necessities enough; you'll not lack anything
If you leave off studying logic and learn to love.   250
For love they left their lordship, both land and school,[8]
Friar Francis* and Dominic,* for love of holiness.
And if you covet cure of souls, Kind will tell you
That in moderation God made all manner of things,
And established them in a certain and settled number.   255
And named them names, and numbered the stars:
           *Who numbereth the multitude of the stars and calleth their
           names to them all.*[9]
Kings who protect the kingdom with their company of
           knights
Have officers under them, each a settled number:
And if they pay men to make war, they mark them down
           in a roster;
No paymaster will pay them wages, though they fight like
           proper soldiers,   260
Unless their names are noted among the number of the
           hired.
All others in battle are held to be thieves,
Pillagers and plunderers, in every parish cursed.
Monastic men and women, all members of religious orders,
Each order has its rule that asks a settled number   265
Of lettered and unlettered; the law desires and demands
A certain number for a certain sort, save only with friars.
Therefore," said Conscience, "by Christ, Kind Wit* tells me
It is wicked to pay your wages; you're waxing out of
           number.
Heaven has even number and hell is without number.[1]   270
Therefore I would strongly wish that you were in the
           register

---

8. I.e., both their landed property and their intellectual positions.
9. Ps. 146.4.
1. Indefinite number was perceived in the Middle Ages as imperfect and threatening; Job 10.22
describes limitless number as being orderless, and Rev. 20.8 calls the number of the evil limitless.
Matt. 10.30 and Rev. 7.4–8 describe God's providence as numbering everything precisely.

And your number under a notary's seal,[2] and neither more
    nor less."
  Envy heard this and ordered friars to go to school
And learn logic and law and also contemplation,
And preach to men about Plato, and support it by Seneca[3]   275
That all things under Heaven ought to be held in
    common.[4]
I believe that he lies, who so preaches to unlearned men,
For God made a law for men and Moses taught it:
Thou shalt not covet they neighbor's goods.[5]
But this is poorly preserved in parishes of England,   280
For parsons and parish priests who are supposed to shrive
    the people
Are called curates because they should know and cure
    them,
Assign penance to all people who are their parishioners
And make them ashamed in their shrift; but shame makes
    them go off
And flee to the friars as false folk go to Westminster[6]   285
Who borrow money and bear it there and bid
    importunately
Their friends to forgive the debt, or grant a further term.
But while he is in Westminster he will keep busy
And make himself merry with other men's goods.
And so it fares with many folk who confess themselves to
    friars,   290
Such as assizers* and executors; they will assign the friars
A portion of the estate to pray for them, and play with the
    remainder,
And leave the dead man in debt until the Day of Doom.*
Envy hereupon hated Conscience
And gave fellowships to friars to study philosophy in
    school,   295
While Covetousness and Unkindness came to attack
    Conscience.

---

2. A document made binding by a notary's endorsement.
3. A Roman philosopher, whose sayings were popular in the Middle Ages.
4. Envy here expresses views held seriously by some medieval thinkers, especially certain friars.
The founders of the mendicant orders and the more radical of their fourteenth-century followers
insisted on institutional as well as personal poverty. The rest of the Church and the secular
government attacked these views, thinking them a threat to the very notion of private property
and an incitement to social unrest. The fact that Langland attributes such views to Envy speaks
for itself.
5. Exod. 20.17: the Latin Bible has "house" (*domum*) where Langland has "thing" (*rem*)—i.e.,
translated more freely, "good(s)."
6. Where the law courts were.

In Unity, Holy Church, Conscience held himself
And appointed Peace porter to bar the gates
To all tale-tellers and tattlers of gossip.
With their help Hypocrisy made a hard assault: 300
Hypocrisy at the gate began a grim fight
And wounded most maliciously many a wise teacher
Who'd been in accord with Conscience and cardinal virtues.
Conscience called a doctor who could give good shrift:
"Go give salve to those that are sick whom sin has
          wounded."   305
Shrift composed a sharp salve and made men do penance
For the dubious deeds that they had done before,
And that Piers's pardon might be paid, *redde quod debes*.[7]
Some did not like this surgeon, and they sent letters
To see if there were a doctor in the siege that applied softer
          compresses.   310
Sir Love-To-Live-In-Lechery lay there and groaned;
From fasting on Friday he fared as he would die.
"There is a surgeon in the siege who has a soft touch,
And knows far more about physic and fashions gentler
          remedies;
One Friar Flatterer is both physician and surgeon."   315
Said Contrition to Conscience, "Have him come into Unity,
For we have here many a man hurt by Hypocrisy."
    "We have no need," said Conscience. "I know no better
          doctor
Than parson or parish priest, penitencer[8] or bishop,
Except for Piers the Plowman who has power over all   320
And may deal out indulgences unless debt prevents it.
I may well consent," said Conscience, "because you desire
          it,
That Friar Flatterer be fetched and give physic to you
          sick."
The Friar heard hereof and hurried fast
To a lord for a letter to allow him leave   325
To have a cure like a curate;[9] and he came with his letter
Boldly to the bishop and went back with his authority
To hear confession in any countries that he came into;
And he came to where Conscience was and clapped at the
          gate.

---

7. "Pay what thou owest."
8. Confessor.
9. A friar was not authorized to beg in a parish in competition with the parish priest without
permission, but permission could be obtained from the lay lord of the area.

Peace, porter of Unity, prepared to open up   330
And asked in haste what he wanted there.
"In faith," said the Friar, "for profit and health
I would converse with Contrition and therefore I came
    here."
"He is sick," said Peace, "and so are many others.
Hypocrisy has hurt them; they'll not easily recover."   335
   "I am a surgeon," said the Friar, "and skilled at mixing
    salves.
Conscience is well acquainted with me, and knows how
    competent I am."
   "I pray you," said Peace then, "before you proceed
    further,
What are you called? I request you not to conceal your
    name."
   "Certainly," said this fellow, "Sir *Penetrans domos*."[1]   340
   "Yes? Well, you can go away again," said Peace. "By
    God, for all your medicine,
Unless you're competent in some craft, you're not coming
    in here.
I knew such a one once, not eight winters ago,
Who came in thus coped to a court where I lived,
And served as surgeon for both our sire and our dame.   345
And at the last this limiter,[2] when my lord was out,
He salved our women so till some were with child."
   Courteous Speech called on Peace to cast open the gates.
"Let the Friar and his fellow in, and give them fair
    welcome.
He may see and hear here, it may happen so, .   350
That Life through his lore will leave Covetousness
And be in dread of Death, and withdraw from Pride
And become accorded with Conscience, so that they'll kiss
    each other."
Thus because of Courteous Speech the Friar was called in,
And came to Conscience, and courteously greeted him.   355
   "You are welcome," said Conscience. "Can you heal the
    sick?
Here is Contrition," said Conscience, "my cousin, wounded.
Comfort him," said Conscience, "and take care of his
    injuries.

---

1. "Sir House-Penetrator." 2 Tim. 3.6 reads, "For of these [men] are those who penetrate houses
(*penetrant domos*) and lead captive simple women burdened with sins, who are led to manifold
desires."
2. I.e., friar.

The compresses of the parson and his powders bite too
    sorely;
And he lets them lie too long, and is reluctant to change
    them.   360
From Lenten to Lenten he lets his remedies bite."
  "That's too long, I believe," said this limiter, "I'll amend
    it."
And he sets out to search Contrition's wounds and
    prescribes a remedy
Of "a privy payment and I shall pray for you
And for all that you're beholden to all my lifetime,   365
And make a *Memoria* for you at Mass and at matins,*
As friars of our fraternity, for a little silver."[3]
Thus he goes about gathering cash and glozing[4] those he
    shrives
Until Contrition had clean forgotten to cry and to weep
And wake for his wicked works as he was wont to do.   370
Because of the comfort his confessor gave he abandoned
    contrition,
Which is the sovereign salve for sins of every kind.
  Sloth saw that, and so did Pride,
And came to attack Conscience with a keen will.
Conscience cried again to Clergy to help,   375
And bade Contrition come to keep the gate.
  "He lies drowned in dream," said Peace, "and so do
    many others.
The Friar with his physic has enchanted the folk here,
And given them a drugged drink: they dread no sin."
  "By Christ," said Conscience then, "I will become a
    pilgrim,   380
And walk as wide as the world reaches
To seek Piers the Plowman, who might expunge Pride,
And see that friars had funds who flatter for need
And contradict me, Conscience; now Kind avenge me,
And send me heart and health till I have Piers the
    Plowman."   385
And Conscience cried for Grace until I became wakeful.

---

3. The Friar offers to sell Contrition the spiritual benefits that accrue to a member of his order
of friars. *"Memoria"*: remembrance; i.e., "I'll pray for you." In the Mass, the commemoration
of the dead begins, *"Memento"* ("Remember").
4. I.e., deceiving.

Appendix

The Dreamer in the C-Version

The C-text, the last of the three versions of *Piers Plowman*, contains a passage often thought to be autobiographical. The poet who made the C-version prefixed to the Confession of the Seven Deadly Sins (*Passus* V of the B-text) an apology by the Dreamer, "Long Will," who is at once long, or tall, and long on willing, or, arguably, willful. While there is no conclusive historical evidence for doing so, readers of *Piers Plowman* have generally regarded this passage as a source of information about the real author, about whom we otherwise know so little. Scholarship has determined that the way of life it describes is plausible, as well as compatible with the way the poem portrays the Dreamer and with the character of the poem itself. Throughout all the versions of the poem, the Dreamer manifests grave concern about whether a writer's way of life is justifiable in a world where there is such need for practical service and where religious tradition offers such definite answers to basic human questions. (*Passus* XI.84–106a and *Passus* XII.1–28 are crucial to these issues.) The account of the Dreamer's life in the C-text seems to be the poem's final word on the subject. (Talbot Donaldson translated the Dreamer's apology in the following passage from lines 1–104 of the C-text in Huntington Library MS HM 143.)

> Thus I awoke, as God's my witness, when I lived in
>   Cornhill,[1]
> Kit and I in a cottage, clothed like a loller,[2]
> And little beloved, believe you me,
> Among lollers of London and illiterate hermits.
> For I wrote rhymes of those men as Reason* taught me.   5
> For as I came by Conscience* I met with Reason,
> In a hot harvest time when I had my health,

---

1. An area of London associated with vagabonds, seedy clerics, and people at loose ends.
2. Idler, vagabond. The term was eventually applied to the proto-Protestant followers of John Wycliffe. It is unlikely that Langland has this meaning in mind, but many post-Reformation readers thought that he did. "Kit": B.XVIII.426 refers to "Kit my wife and Calote [i.e., Colette] my daughter." The Dreamer seems to be someone with clerical training who has received consecration into minor clerical orders (such as that of deacon) but who is not a priest. Even priests came to be required to observe celibacy only gradually, and lesser clerics could marry, although marriage blocked their further advancement in the Church.

And limbs to labor with, and loved good living,
And to do no deed but to drink and sleep.
My body sound, my mind sane, a certain one accosted me;   10
Roaming in remembrance, thus Reason upbraided me:
    "Can you serve," he said, "or sing in a church?
Or cock hay with my hay-makers, or heap it on the cart,
Mow it or stack what's mown or make binding for sheaves?
Or have a horn and be a hedge-guard and lie outdoors at
            night,   15
And keep my corn in my field from cattle and thieves?
Or cut cloth or shoe-leather, or keep sheep and cattle,
Mend hedges, or harrow, or herd pigs or geese,
Or any other kind of craft that the commons* needs,
So that you might be of benefit to your bread-providers?"   20
    "Certainly!" I said, "and so God help me,
I am too weak to work with sickle or with scythe,
And too long,³ believe me, for any low stooping,
Or laboring as a laborer to last any while."
    "Then have you lands to live by," said Reason, "or
            relations with money   25
To provide you with food? For you seem an idle man,
A spendthrift who thrives on spending, and throws time
            away.
Or else you get what food men give you going door to door,
Or beg like a fraud on Fridays⁴ and feastdays in churches.
And that's a loller's life that earns little praise   30
Where Rightfulness rewards men as they really deserve.
    *He shall reward every man according to his works.*⁵
Or are you perhaps lame in your legs or other limbs of
            your body,
Or maimed through some misadventure, so that you might
            be excused?"
    "When I was young, many years ago,
My father and my friends provided me with schooling,   35
Till I understood surely what Holy Scripture meant,
And what is best for the body as the Book tells,
And most certain for the soul, if so I may continue.
And, in faith, I never found, since my friends died,
Life that I liked save in these long clothes.⁶   40

3. I.e., tall, perhaps with a pun on willfulness. The Dreamer is called "Long Will" in *Passus*
XV.152 of the B-text.
4. Fast days, because Christ was crucified on a Friday.
5. Matt. 16.27; cf. Ps. 61.12.
6. The long dress of a cleric, not limited to actual priests.

And if I must live by labor and earn my livelihood,
The labor I should live by is the one I learned best.
>   *[Abide] in the same calling wherein you were called.*[7]
And so I live in London and upland[8] as well.
The tools that I toil with to sustain myself
Are Paternoster* and my primer, *Placebo* and *Dirige*,[9]   45
And sometimes my Psalter* and my seven Psalms.
These I say for the souls of such as help me.
And those who provide my food vouchsafe, I think,
To welcome me when I come, once a month or so,
Now with him, now with her, and in this way I beg   50
Without bag or bottle but my belly alone.

    And also, moreover, it seems to me, sir Reason,
No clerk should be constrained to do lower-class work.
For by the law of Leviticus[1] that our Lord ordained
Clerks with tonsured crowns should, by common
>   understanding,   55
Neither strain nor sweat nor swear at inquests,
Nor fight in a vanguard and defeat an enemy:
>   *Do not render evil for evil.*[2]
For they are heirs of Heaven, all that have the tonsure,
And in choir and in churches they are Christ's ministers.
>   *The Lord is the portion of my inheritance. And elsewhere,*
>   *Mercy does not constrain.*[3]
It is becoming for clerks to perform Christ's service,   60
And untonsured boys be burdened with bodily labor.
For none should acquire clerk's tonsure unless he claims
>   descent
From franklins[4] and free men and folk properly wedded.
Bondmen and bastards and beggars' children—
These belong to labor; and lords' kin should serve   65
God and good men as their degree requires,
Some to sing Masses or sit and write,
Read and receive what Reason ought to spend.

---

7. 1 Cor. 7.20, with variations.
8. North of London, in rural country.
9. "I will please [the Lord]" and "Make straight [my way]": Ps. 114.9 and Ps. 5.9. *Placebo* and *Dirige* are the first words of hymns based on two of the seven "penitential" Psalms that were part of the regular order of personal prayer. The "primer" was the basic collection of private prayers for lay people.
1. Lev. 21 sets restrictions on members of the priesthood.
2. 1 Thess. 5.15, with variations.
3. I.e., "mercy is not restricted": source unknown; the quotation above is from Ps. 15.5.
4. Free men. By this date, the term did not just mean non-serfs but designated landowners who were becoming members of the gentry class yet were not knights. The distinction Langland seems to make in this line between franklins and free men may reflect the rising status of certain families of "freedmen," the original meaning of the word "franklins."

But since bondmen's boys have been made bishops,
And bastards' boys have been archdeacons,   70
And shoemakers and their sons have through silver become
     knights,
And lords' sons their laborers whose lands are mortgaged to
     them—
And thus for the right of this realm they ride against our
     enemies
To the comfort of the commons* and to the king's honor—
And monks and nuns on whom mendicants must depend   75
Have had their kin named knights and bought knight's-fees,⁵
And popes and patrons have shunned poor gentle* blood
And taken the sons of Simon Magus⁶ to keep the sanctuary,
Life-holiness and love have gone a long way hence,
And will be so till this is all worn out or otherwise changed.   80
Therefore proffer me no reproach, Reason, I pray you,
For in my conscience I conceive what Christ wants me to
     do.
Prayers of a perfect man and appropriate penance
Are the labor that our Lord loves most of all.
   "*Non de solo*," I said, "forsooth *vivit homo*,   85
Nec in pane et in pabulo;⁷ the Paternoster witnesses
*Fiat voluntas Dei*⁸—that provides us with everything."
   Said Conscience, "By Christ, I can't see that this lies;
But it seems no serious perfectness to be a city-beggar,
Unless you're licensed to collect for prior or monastery."   90
   "That is so," I said, "and so I admit
That at times I've lost time and at times misspent it;
And yet I hope, like him who has often bargained
And always lost and lost, and at the last it happened
He bought such a bargain he was the better ever,   95
That all his loss looked paltry in the long run,
Such a winning was his through what grace decreed.
       The kingdom of Heaven is like unto treasure hidden in a
          field.
       *The woman who found the piece of silver, etc.*⁹

---

5. The estate a knight held from his overlord in return for military service was called his "fee."
6. See Gloss, under "simony."
7. "Not solely [by bread] doth man live, neither by bread nor by food"; the verse continues, "but by every word that proceedeth out of the mouth of God": Matt. 4.4, with variations; cf. Deut. 8.3.
8. "God's will be done." The Lord's Prayer (the "Paternoster") reads, "Thy will be done" (Matt. 6.10).
9. Matt. 13.44; Luke 15.9–10. Both passages come from parables that compare finding the kingdom of Heaven to risking everything you have to get the one thing that matters most.

So I hope to have of him that is almighty
A gobbet of his grace, and begin a time
That all times of my time shall turn into profit."   100
   "And I counsel you," said Reason, "quickly to begin
The life that is laudable and reliable for the soul."
    "Yes, and continue," said Conscience, and I came to the
        church.[1]

---

1. The four lines that follow this passage connect it to the beginning of the second dream (the B-text's *Passus* V): "And to the church I set off, to honor God; before the Cross, on my knees, I beat my breast, sighing for my sins, saying my Paternoster, weeping and wailing until I fell asleep."

Gloss

(The function of the Gloss is explained in the Introduction, under "Using This Edition.")

Ambrose, St. (340?–397) one of the four great Fathers of the Western Church, Bishop of Milan, a teacher of St. Augustine, and author of major commentaries and hymns.

anchorites like hermits, they were vowed to a life of solitude and meditation, but they chose to live in a populous area walled into a small dwelling, usually attached to a church. They often taught and counseled through a window to the outside world and participated in the life of the church through a second window, opening into it.

Anima the soul. Medieval thought attributed many more functions to the soul than are generally associated with the modern word. These functions are discussed in detail in IX.5–59 and XV.22–39.

Aristotle (384–322 B.C.) the Greek philosopher who had the greatest influence on the development of medieval scholastic philosophy and theology.

assizers members of the assize or inquest, which was the ancestor of the modern jury. Serving on the assize was considered a great hardship, not simply because this function, like jury duty today, was time-consuming. Instead of assessing evidence, medieval "jurors" took oaths vouching for the credibility of one of the parties to the lawsuit. This would be a demanding responsibility in the best of times, but under the problematic conditions of medieval "justice" (of which Langland is so critical) jurors were often subjected to great pressures in the form of bribes, threats, or even blackmail. It is understandable that as late as the fifteenth century it was not uncommon for an individual to have more faith in trial by ordeal or combat than in a jury.

Augustine, St. (354–430) one of the four major Fathers of the Western Church, Bishop of Hippo, most often cited by Langland in connection with his autobiography, the *Confessions*, and his treatise on the Trinity, *De Trinitate*, and often referred to in the poem as Austin or Austin the Old. He was later claimed by the Austin Friars as their founder.

Austin, Austin Friars   see **Augustine.**

bachelor   Bachelor of Divinity, but also, occasionally, novice knight, as in the case of Longeus in *Passus* XVIII.

Benedict, St. (480?–543?)   the founder of the Benedictine Order, whose Rule became the central influence on Western monasticism. In addition to binding the monk to poverty, chastity, and obedience, the Rule divided his day into thirds: one for liturgical prayer, one for study, and one for manual labor. Unlike the later orders of friars, monks were committed to living their lives in a single, enclosed community. Cf. **friars** below.

Bernard, St. (1091–1153)   Abbot of Clairvaux and one of the founders of the Cistercian Order, which attempted a return to strict observance of the original Benedictine Rule. A mystic, preacher, and religious writer, Bernard was also a major political leader, who played a central role in mobilizing the Second Crusade (1146).

bought   often means "redeemed," in the sense that Christ's sacrifice on the Cross "purchased" salvation for the human race.

bull   an official document issued by the pope and sealed with his *bulla*, or seal. Pardoners (see below) had, at least in theory, to have such a papal permit, which had also to be endorsed by the local bishop.

burgess   a town-dweller who had full rights as the citizen of a municipality. Towns, which had a status outside the feudal system of land tenure, operated under governmental and legal systems quite distinct from those of rural areas.

Cato   Dionysius Cato, supposed author of the *Distichs of Cato*, an early-fourth-century collection of Latin maxims, one of the first books studied in medieval grammar schools.

civil   civil as opposed to criminal law, especially noted for its bribery and corruption in the later Middle Ages. This corruption resulted at least partly from the fact that law, particularly as it affected ownership of property, was changing drastically; people were devising ways to own land and possessions outright, rather than simply as part of a feudal contract by which land was held in return for service.

clergy, clerks   the Middle English word *clergie* has two meanings that Langland sometimes connects and sometimes differentiates: (1) intellectual learning or book-learning; (2) clerics, those who traditionally were the only ones to have such learning (though this situation was beginning to change in the later Middle Ages). Hence the character Clergy is married to Scripture, but in some contexts the term means intellectual learning pure and simple. Theology was the culminating science in medieval university training and was based on the interpretation of Scripture. Knowledge of Scripture, in turn, as Study explains in *Passus* X, presupposed the "seven arts," which formed the basic curriculum in medieval education and which are, therefore, allegorically Scripture's "siblings." They consist of the trivium, comprising grammar, rhetoric, and logic, which teach language and rational discourse, and the quadrivium, comprising arithmetic, geometry, astronomy, and music. Clerics were under canon rather than secular law, so that proving one's power to read (usually by translating a verse from the Psalms) could remove a person from the jurisdiction of the secular law even in the case of a crime as serious as murder.

common (adjective)   in common, not peculiar to particular individuals or groups. See also **common** (noun).

common, commons (noun)   the Middle English word *commune, communes* has several distinct meanings on which Langland plays: (1) the community taken as a whole; (2) the common people or working classes as opposed to the aristocracy and clergy; (3) the food that supports the whole community. A fourth meaning, the members of the lower house of Parliament, was just coming into use but does not appear to be one that Langland uses (though the possibility has sometimes been suggested).

Compostela see **James.**

conscience   the Middle English word, like the modern one, includes as its dominant meaning "ethical integrity"; but, like its other descendant, the modern word "consciousness," it also includes a wider range of awareness. Langland's major character who bears this name develops in importance and complexity as the poem progresses, so that both aspects of the word's meaning must be borne in mind in following his role. See also the discussion of mental faculties under **wit** below.

consistory   literally, a bishop's court or the "senate" of cardinals convened by the pope to deliberate on church affairs. Langland often uses the term metaphorically, especially as a term for the Day of Doom (see **doom** below).

contra   "on the contrary!" or "I object!" — the technical term used to introduce a rebuttal in scholastic philosophical argument.

Distichs   see **Cato.**

doctor   normally, Doctor of Divinity, though Langland does occasionally mean a medical doctor by the term.

Dominic, St. (1170–1221)   contemporary of St. Francis, founder of the Dominican Order of Friars, who were primarily intellectuals and preachers (see **friars**).

doom, Doomsday   the word "doom" means "judgment" or "verdict," not necessarily in a negative sense; "Doomsday" is the Last Judgment, when Christ at his Second Coming will separate humanity into the good and the evil.

ergo   "therefore"—like *contra*, a central term in scholastic argument. *Ergo* introduces the logical conclusion of the propositions, or arguments, advanced.

evensong   vespers, the evening prayer service said just before sunset. On the seven canonical "hours" of the liturgical day, see **hours**.

farthing   a coin worth a quarter of a penny.

florin   a gold coin, so called by analogy with the gold coins of Florence, whose coinage was viewed as an international standard. It was worth about two shillings or twenty-four silver pennies.

Francis, St. (1182–1226)   founder of the Franciscan Order of Friars, originally dedicated to a life of complete poverty, not only personal but also institutional. That is, as Francis envisaged his order, a brother was not to possess a house, a horse, or money himself; more radically still, he was not to have use of such things, on the grounds that they belonged to his order, rather than to himself. Franciscans were at first dedicated to preaching to and caring for the poorest and most outcast, those least served by the regular church parish system. By the fourteenth century, however, many were major university intellectuals ("masters," that is, masters of divinity), and only a few extremists held to the ideal of institutional poverty.

friar   friars were members of a new kind of religious order that developed in the early thirteenth century. Unlike monks, they were not committed to an enclosed life in one place (cf. **Francis** and **Dominic**). They lived, in principle, entirely on donations and were therefore called mendicant or begging orders. Friars generally traveled in pairs and had license to beg in a limited geographical area and, hence, were also known as *limiters*. The four orders of friars in Langland's England were the Franciscans, Dominicans, Austin (Augustinian) Friars, and Carmelites.

gentle, gentleness the Middle English word combined the class meaning "aristocratic, chivalric, or genteel" with the moral and social meaning preserved in the modern word "gentle," a quality originally thought of as class-based. Some of Langland's uses of the term reflect contemporary discussion by the emerging middle class about what meaning the term could have for them other than mere social upward mobility.

Gregory the Great, St. (Pope 590–604) one of the four major Fathers of the Western Church, a great organizational as well as intellectual leader and author of religious works; he is most often mentioned by Langland as the author of the *Moralia*, a moral and allegorical commentary on the Book of Job.

groat a silver coin worth four pennies.

hermits vowed to a life of solitude, austerity, and meditation in the wilderness (in contrast to **anchorites**, see above).

Holy Kirk Holy Church. The term "kirk," particularly in Scotland, has acquired a Protestant aura, which the Middle English word did not, of course, have. The translation, like Langland's text, uses the terms "kirk" and "church" interchangeably for alliterative purposes.

hours clerics and monastic orders organized their day around seven canonical "hours," or periods of liturgical prayer: matins (with lauds), prime, terce, sext, none, vespers, and complin.

Imaginative not "imagination" in the modern, especially Romantic and post-Romantic sense, but the faculty of forming mental images of things in the exterior world or in the past. Imaginative thus makes it possible for the mind to work since it cannot act on the data given by experience and the senses directly but must interiorize them before it can do so. Medieval psychology did not generally associate this faculty with the creation of art, but rather with memory and with the power of the mind to make analogies and abstractions for use in reasoning. Langland's association of the figure of Imaginative in *Passus* XII with poetic composition, which seems quite normal to the modern reader, was a highly unusual, if not unique, defense of the writing of poetry in his time. See also the "autobiographical" passage from the C-text printed in the Appendix.

inwit see the discussion of various related intellectual faculties under **wit** below.

James, St. one of the original twelve Apostles, whose name is especially associated with the New Testament Epistle of St. James and with his great shrine at Compostela, in Galicia, in Spain, the goal of one of the most important medieval pilgrimage routes.

Jerome, St. (340?–420) one of the four major Fathers of the Western Church, whose translation of the Bible into Latin is termed the "Vulgate" text.

kaisers emperors, from the Latin *Caesar*.

kind nature or the nature of things in general. A crucial term in *Piers Plowman, kind* has three main meanings: (1) God conceived of primarily in his creative aspect (as distinguished from his other major aspect in the poem, as Truth — see **truth** below); (2) the nature of something, as in the modern expression "this kind of thing rather than that kind" (Langland uses the expression "the law of kynde" to cover what we would call the law of nature as well as the instinctual morality of decent human beings, insofar as the latter seems to be cross-cultural); (3) kindness in the modern sense, i.e., benevolence, but conceived of as the norm of human behavior rather than as some special sort of altruism: to be "unkind" is to be distorted and unnatural as well as cruel. *Kind love*, "natural love": a love that is an instinctive and a natural expression of a benevolent will and cannot be taught, just as "natural [*kind*] faith" is. Langland's most crucial (and perhaps most controversial) use of the word is in the term *kind knowing*, "natural knowledge": experiential knowledge — whether interiorly or exteriorly derived — as opposed to reasoning and to book-learning. The Dreamer uses the term when he responds to a character's intellectual explanation of something with the comment that he has no "natural knowledge" of it and must find another way to learn it. He is not rejecting the explanation or even finding it unintelligible; rather, he is saying he has not interiorized it in such a way that it can become a part of his life. Contrast *kind knowing* with the other intellectual faculties discussed under **wit** below, particularly *kind wit* and *inwit*.

kind love see **kind.**

kind wit see **kind** and **wit.**

kirk see **Holy Kirk.**

know naturally see **kind.**

law-sergeants   important lawyers whose badge of office was a silk coif or scarf.

lewte   the primary meaning is "justice," as distinct from "law" as such. The medieval conception of justice, however (as the fact that the modern descendant of this word is "loyalty" illustrates), is more oriented toward relationships than ours, and so the translation has opted to maintain the Middle English word.

limiter   see **friar.**

lovedays   manor courts set aside certain days to try to reconcile adversaries in a negotiated settlement; this laudable aim was too often achieved by bribery rather than by genuine resolution of the problem. Friars were also associated with the holding of such sessions of reconciliation, which, while in the spirit of the order's original function, were widely perceived as motivated by a desire for additional income, with little concern for either justice or repentance.

low, lowly, lowliness   humble, humility, without the negative connotation ("coarse or vulgar") that has become attached to the modern word.

mark   equivalent to 160 pennies, several weeks' wages.

master   Master of Divinity.

matins   the first of the seven canonical "hours," or periods of liturgical prayer into which the day was divided — "morning prayer," as distinct from Mass.

meat   food, nourishment (not just flesh).

Meed   reward, recompense, the profit motive. A major concept that develops throughout the poem, *meed* is defined by various characters in terms ranging as widely as "bribery," "heavenly reward," and "wages." It is a crucial term in the poem's analysis of the relationship between ethics and economic structure. Because of the wider range of meanings carried by *meed* than by any single modern equivalent, the translation has kept the Middle English word.

might, mighty   the Middle English term *might* simply means the strength necessary to do a particular thing, not necessarily the overwhelming force implied by the modern word.

Moralia   see **Gregory the Great.**

natural knowledge   see **kind.**

noble   a gold coin worth eighty pennies.

palmer   a virtually professional pilgrim who took advantage of the hospitality offered pilgrims everywhere to go on traveling year after year. As transients dependent on charity, palmers earned a somewhat unsavory reputation for tall tales and more general dishonesty. Strictly speaking, palmers were pilgrims who had been to Jerusalem, or who had made a lifelong commitment to pilgrimage.

pardoner   an official empowered to transmit temporal indulgence (i.e., remission of some part of the punishment due in purgatory for one's sins on earth) from the pope in return for contributions to charitable enterprises. These contributions were not considered purchases of forgiveness but gifts freely given in return for God's free gift of mercy, which the Church administered through its agents; they were part of the "satisfaction," in the sequence "contrition, confession, satisfaction," required for the forgiveness of sins. But in practice the gifts were widely perceived as financial transactions, and their receipt came to be regarded as a fundamental abuse of the power entrusted by Christ to the Church. In theory, a pardoner had to have a papal authorization (see **bull** above), which had also to be endorsed by the local bishop, and, since he was not a cleric, he was not allowed to preach as one. In practice, most of these safeguards were routinely evaded and many pardoners were con men, pure and simple. As a group they were as sharply criticized by thoughtful medieval Catholics as they were later by Protestant critics.

Paternoster   "The Lord's Prayer" ("Our Father, who art in heaven . . .").

penny   a silver coin, quite valuable in medieval England. This Gloss defines other coins in relation to it. The term was also used as shorthand for money per se.

provisors   clerics who, instead of being appointed to their offices by the local or national hierarchy, had obtained them by petitioning the pope directly, going over the heads of the intervening officials. Such "petitions" were routinely accompanied by bribes.

Psalter   the Book of Psalms, or a separate volume containing it, sometimes in conjunction with other prayers for private use. The Psalms were collectively attributed to King David and regularly interpreted, like the rest of the Hebrew Scriptures, as foreshadowing the events recorded in the New Testament.

reason   the process, considered by medieval thinkers to be the unique and distinctive capacity of human beings, as opposed to animals, of reaching truth by discursive logic or rational argument. See **wit** below.

reeve   the superintendent of a large manor or farming estate. The reeve was a member of the manor community, that is, a peasant or even a serf, and elected by them, though paid by the lord of the manor, to organize and account for the work. As a result, he generally understood his social superiors' finances better than they did, and frequently profited at their expense.

religion, religious   the translation almost never uses this word in the usual modern sense, but in a now less common one — the members of religious orders or their way of life, as opposed to other kinds of clerics, such as parish priests. E.g., "you religious" means "you monks and nuns"; "run into religion" means "join a religious order."

Rood   a crucifix, i.e., a Cross with a figure of the crucified Christ on it, though the term is sometimes applied to a large cross without a figure.

St. James   see **James.**

Sapience   four "Wisdom Books" are attributed to King Solomon; two, The Book of Wisdom and Ecclesiasticus, are considered part of the Bible by Catholics but not by Protestants, while the other two, Proverbs and Ecclesiastes, are accepted by both groups.

Scripture   the term often means the canonical Bible strictly defined, but can also include sacred writings more generally.

sergeants   see **law-sergeants.**

simony   buying and selling the functions, spiritual powers, or offices of the Church for money. The word derives from the name of Simon Magus, a magician who tried to persuade the early Apostles to sell him their power to perform miracles through the Holy Spirit (Acts 8).

sloth   not merely, as in modern English, laziness, but a more fundamental irresponsibility or parasitic way of living (defined by Dante as "love deficient"). *Wanhope*, "despair," was considered its ultimate form.

soothness, sooth; soothfast   truth or reality; truthful or honest. Middle English had two words for "truth": see **truth** below.

summoner an official who served summonses to the ecclesiastical courts, which dealt with many issues we now regard as part of private morality rather than the concern of judicial action, whether clerical or secular. Summoners, who were not clerics themselves, were among the most feared and hated of church officials because of their power to blackmail and to demand bribes.

truth the Middle English term *trouthe* has three meanings on which Langland plays: (1) fidelity, integrity (as in modern "troth"); (2) reality, actuality, or a statement in conformity with what is; (3) the ultimate reality, God, who appears directly in the poem under the figure of two allegorical characters, of which Truth is one (Kind — see above — is the other).

unkindness see **kind.**

Walsingham an English town, site of a famous shrine to the Virgin Mary and often referred to by Langland as the destination of pilgrimages of dubious motivation.

wanhope see **sloth.**

Westminster area (now part of London) famous for its courts of justice.

wit mental capacity, intellectual ability. Wit is the dimension of the mind that permits human beings to perform their distinctive function, reasoning (see **reason** above). The translation never uses the term in its later meaning of "witticism, humor." Wit is a quality that, like learning itself, can be put to bad use as well as to good. The allegorical character Wit is scolded by his wife Study for trying to explain intellectual matters to a morally unqualified person, and Warren Witty and his fellow Wisdom are among the hangers-on who stand ready to profit from the trial of Lady Meed. Langland differentiates wit from *conscience*, a more intuitive faculty (see above), and from two others: one is *inwit*, which seems to mean consciousness of the kind that permits a person to use mental faculties and which was believed to be absent in drunks, the insane, the immature, and those especially vulnerable to exploitation. The other is *kind wit*, which sometimes clearly means "common sense" or "practical thought," as opposed to formal or abstract reasoning or book-learning, but is also related to the term "natural knowledge," *kind knowing* (see **kind** above).

wits, the five   the five senses — sight, hearing, touch, taste, and smell. Langland sometimes speaks as if they can have normative or moral value as well, as when he makes them the five sons of "Sir Inwit" (see **wit**), whose function is to guard Lady Anima, the soul, in the "castle" of the body in which Kind — God — has placed her.